Ringers & Rascals

Ringers & Rascals

The True Story of Racing's Greatest Con Artists

DAVID ASHFORTH

ECLIPSE PRESS
Lexington, Kentucky

Library of Congress Control Number: 2003114575

ISBN 1-58150-106-4

Printed in the United States
First Edition: May 2004

Distributed to the trade by
National Book Network
4720-A Boston Way
Lanham, MD 20706
1.800.462.6420

ECLIPSE PRESS

a division of
Blood-Horse Publications
PUBLISHERS SINCE 1916

Contents

To Anon., who got away with it.

The Beginning

One morning in September 1992, the telephone rang. The caller did not say who he was. "Would you like to meet Ken Richardson?" "Yes." "Someone will ring you later today." Then he put the phone down.

Later that day another man rang. He introduced himself as Paul Dumbleton, Richardson's solicitor. We arranged to meet at the Selfridge Hotel, near Oxford Street, in London.

We sat on leather armchairs and sipped coffee. Dumbleton peered at me through round spectacles, and opened and closed his briefcase. A little later, at a house near Glastonbury, Dumbleton brought me a thick, red, bound volume, *A Petition to Her Majesty's Secretary of State for Home Affairs, The Rt Hon. K. Baker. Regina v Richardson, Mathison and Boddy. The Flockton Grey Case.*

As I read the petition, my interest grew. I wanted to find out what had really happened.

It was over ten years since Flockton Grey's curious victory at Leicester racecourse; eight years since the trial, at York Crown Court. Documents had been lost, destroyed, locked away. Witnesses had died, disappeared, forgotten, wanted to forget.

Even the trial's traces had faded. The official shorthand notes had been destroyed and contemporary newspaper reports were frustratingly thin. The tide of time had rolled in and swept heedlessly out again, smoothing away the footprints in the sand, but the telephone call had aroused my curiosity.

Looking back, that is where this book began, for it is a book about curiosity, and my attempt to satisfy it.

The Dark Pool

People expect there to be skulduggery in horse racing, and over the centuries the sport of monarchs — and scoundrels — has not failed them. Sometimes, trainers have simply instructed jockeys not to win; sometimes, jockeys have taken the initiative themselves. Few have taken as many initiatives as Pat Sullivan. In the 1950s, after being disqualified for two years by the Australian Jockey Club, Sullivan confessed that he had "pulled," doped, or used batteries or sinkers* on 314 of his 1,043 mounts, an impressive strike rate of 30 percent.

Racehorses have been drugged to go slower and drugged to go faster. They still are. In 2002 Dermot Browne, twice British champion amateur jump jockey, claimed to have doped 23 horses during a seven-week spell in 1990.[1]

Browne, although warned off, fared better than Daniel Dawson. In 1811, when doping was in its infancy, Dawson arranged for arsenic to be put in a water trough on Newmarket Heath, with fatal consequences for several horses, and for Dawson. The "Nobbler King" was hanged at Cambridge a year later.

By the end of the nineteenth century, skulduggery was so sophisticated that in 1898 a group of conspirators invented an entire race meeting. On August 1, a Bank Holiday Monday, *The*

* Lead-lined aluminum horseshoes designed to slow a horse down.

Sportsman published the programs for five English race meetings: Newton Abbot, Hurst Park, Birmingham, Ripon, and Trodmore.

The card for Trodmore opened at 1:30 p.m. with The Farmers' Plate of 10 sovereigns and closed at 4:00 p.m. with The Hunt Steeplechase of 25 sovereigns. The details had been supplied by a Mr. G. Martin, of St. Ives, Cornwall, who helpfully telegraphed the results for the newspaper to publish the following day.

When bookmakers sought confirmation of the results from *The Sporting Life*, the paper lifted them from its rival and sent them to the printer to be reset in the newspaper's own type. They appeared on August 3. Unfortunately for the audacious conspirators, a printer's error resulted in the odds for Reaper, the winner of the handicap hurdle, appearing as 5-2 instead of 5-1.

When attempts were made to contact Trodmore's officials to clarify the situation, neither Trodmore nor its officials could be found. On August 23, *The Sportsman* conquered its embarrassment and published a short statement.

"Investigation has shown that there is no such place as Trodmore and that no race meeting was held on 1 August in the neighborhood of St. Ives, Cornwall.

"It is obvious, therefore, that 'Martin,' by himself or in league with others, invented the program and report in question for the purpose of defrauding bookmakers, several of whom have communicated with us.

"We are endeavoring to trace the fraud to its source, and meanwhile would recommend agents who received commissions in connection with the meeting to withhold payment and to forward to this office the names and addresses of any persons who sent commissions to them."

For some bookmakers it was already too late and, like Trodmore, the conspirators were never found, although a journalist called Archie Sinclair, who worked for *The Sportsman*, played the part of principal suspect.[2]

The choice of a Bank Holiday was not mere chance. Bank Holiday Mondays have proved a popular choice for coups, licit and illicit. They are busy days, with a lot of race meetings and many competing demands and distractions for bookmakers and officials. When another clever set of conspirators planned the most famous of all modern British horse racing coups, they, too, selected an August Bank Holiday Monday.

While Gay Future was being prepared for the sting, steps were taken to conceal the horse's true identity, but the celebrated winner of the Ulverston Novices' Hurdle at Cartmel on August 26, 1974, was not a "ringer." The horse that ran in the name of Gay Future was Gay Future.

That is why the often-told story is not told again here, for this is a plunge into the part of the dark pool of skulduggery occupied by ringers.

The term "ringer," denoting a horse dishonestly substituted for another, originated in the United States in the 1860s, during the years following the Civil War, when many Thoroughbreds were parted from their papers. The papers were sometimes used to provide other horses with valuable credentials. Those horses were said to have been "rung in," and were known as "ringers."

The first serial ringer was Benjamin A. Chilson, a Californian blacksmith who, setting an example for future exponents of the practice, often "rang" himself as well as his horses. In 1902 Chilson, alias Alex Mathieson, alias John Rogers, alias W. Miller, alias various other figments of his imagination, started the year by running Abba L in the name of Spooks at Oakland, California, and ended it by running McNamara in the name of Hiram Johnson at New Orleans.

During the next three years, Abba L and McNamara were joined in the cast by Freckman and Useful Lady and taken on a tour of St. Louis, Baltimore, Chicago, New York, and Rhode Island, where they made lucrative appearances under fitting names such as Untrue and The Fiddler.

Chilson was ruled off in New York in 1905 but popped up again in South Carolina in 1914 and in 1926 was suspected of having indulged in another bout of ringing.[3]

In Britain the pastime was already well established. Its practitioners were active at the very peak of the sport. In 1844 the Epsom Derby, reserved for three-year-olds, was won by a four-year-old called Maccabeus, racing in the guise of Running Rein.

Levi Goldman, the unscrupulous architect of the horses' exchange, ultimately fled to France to escape both the law and his creditors, while Running Rein's name was replaced in the record books by that of the runner-up, Orlando.[4]

Goldman's deception relied on the fact that many Thoroughbreds look similar, which is why racehorse owners proudly visit their horse's stable and then, less proudly, ask their trainer, "Which one's mine?"

An experienced horseman, dealing with many different bay colts every day, may readily identify each one, but casual observers find it more difficult. So, on occasion, do racecourse officials.

Without having its teeth examined, a prime indicator of age, a three-year-old may pass for a well-developed two-year-old, and a four-year-old for a three-year-old. For those pursuing a career in fraud, this is an attractive feature of Thoroughbreds.

Younger, less mature horses are at a considerable disadvantage when raced against older ones, a fact acknowledged in the official weight-for-age scale. Nowadays, if a two-year-old tackles a three-year-old over five furlongs in November, the younger horse is entitled to receive 17 pounds. If a three-year-old takes on a four-year-old over six furlongs in January, it receives 16 pounds.

That is why, in 1920, when a magistrate asked Peter Christian Barrie, the "King of the Ringers," what he meant by "a good thing," Barrie replied, memorably, "A useful three-year-old in a moderate two-year-old race, your honor."[5]

A man can be forgiven a lot for a quip like that. In Barrie's case, there was a lot to forgive.

In those days, with no prying cameras or systematic identity checks, arranging a ringer was a relatively easy matter, although arranging the associated betting coup without provoking suspicion was more difficult.

In the United States immediately after the Second World War, a rash of ringers prompted the newly established Thoroughbred Racing Protective Bureau to promote an identification system based on tattooing horses' lips.

Britain was also experiencing a spate of ringers, but the Jockey Club did not introduce tattooing and it was another fifty years before racehorses were identified by marks other than their own.

Since January 1, 1999, every racehorse foaled in Great Britain and Ireland has had a microchip injected into its neck to provide easy and unique identification. Every two-year-old running in 2001, every three-year-old from 2002, every four-year-old from 2003 can be identified by a chip.

Ringers are an endangered species. In Britain the last known example was Flockton Grey in 1982, although in 1995 Pretty Average did her best to claim the title. Horses' passports still occasionally get mixed up, but in Britain the most recent ringers have been human.

When Bold Faith narrowly landed an amateur riders' race at Newbury on June 11, 1998, the official form book recorded that the winner "was given a fine ride" by Mr. A. Jacobs. It was the personable 29-year-old Puerto Rican's first winner in Britain, and he promptly declared his ambition to win the amateur riders' championship.

Angel Jacobs explained that he had come to Britain because his weight restricted his race-riding opportunities in America. He told journalists that his own family was not involved in racing but that his godfather was Angel Cordero Jr., a fellow Puerto Rican and one of the all-time greats of American race-riding. It was news to Cordero.

Jacobs continued to impress. On June 24 George Dillingham's success at Carlisle was reported to have, "owed a great deal to his highly capable rider. Stylish and vigorous, Angel Jacobs got right to the bottom of Denys Smith's eight-year-old."

After his fifth win, on Gymcrak Flyer — "given a super, confident ride" — at Beverley on August 13, Jacobs posed for photographs. The photographer had been arranged by Peter Murphy, the husband of Sandy Brook, secretary of the British Amateur Jockeys' Association.

Murphy, suspicious of Jacobs' credentials, sent the photographs to Dick Milburn, secretary of the Amateur Riders' Club of America. Milburn identified the beaming jockey as Angel Monserrate.

Monserrate grew up in New York, where one of his schoolfriends was Carlos Castro, later a successful marathon runner. Monserrate's father, also called Angel, was a jockey and work rider.

During the late 1980s and early 1990s, Angel Jr. rode as a professional jockey in several states, but in 1995 he was banned after failing a drug test.

In November 1996, Castro was watching an amateur riders' race at Aqueduct, New York, when he recognized Angel Monserrate on the winner. A few seconds later, he was shocked to hear the commentator announce that the winning rider was Carlos Castro.

For a while, Castro and Monserrate had shared accommodations. Monserrate had stolen Castro's credit cards and other identification and used them to register as an amateur rider. After his exposure, Monserrate's five English winners were disqualified and in November 1998 the Jockey Club handed him a ten-year worldwide ban.

It was a good year for ringers. On July 17 the suitably named Almost Impossible turned over the favorite in a maiden race at Calder, in Florida. The winner wasn't a maiden, and his real name wasn't Almost Impossible, but Forty Two.

In August the former British apprentice Colin Campbell was deported from Canada, where he had ridden five winners under the name of Gary Cruise. In December, Washington state's promising apprentice, Fernando Velazquez, the winner of over 60 races since his arrival from Mexico, was revealed as Cuevas Cuellar, a fully fledged professional.[6]

Horsemen were doing their best to maintain the tradition of ringing but the greatest heroes — or villains — of the genre had gone before them.

part 1

THE ONE AND ONLY...THE KING

Heating Up 1

In a neat, modern building on Myddelton Street, not far from the Angel, Islington, in London, thousands of tall, narrow volumes stand on deep wooden shelves. Some are bound in black, some in red, some in green.

The volumes are arranged by year, each volume covering part of the alphabet, a volume for each quarter: March, June, September, December. Each large page is full of lists of surnames, in the print of an old typewriter, faded and gray.

The room rustles with the sound of volumes being pulled from their shelves, and rested on sloping tables, and opened and closed and replaced. People scurry and scuttle in a suddenly important, anxious search for their past.

The first volumes are dated 1837, the year after the act that introduced the civil registration of births, deaths, and marriages. You would be surprised at what you can discover, if you persevere and are lucky.

I have a name but no date. In June 1920, the man I am interested in was reported to be 32. In September 1920, he was reported to be 30, but, mainly, he was said to be 32. So he was born, let us say, between 1887 and 1891.

The luck is in the name. Jones is an unlucky name, so is Smith. There are so many Smiths. Barrie is a lucky name, luckier than Barry. Peter Christian Barrie.

The indexes of births are bound in red. March 1887 through to December 1891. In some volumes there are no Barries; in others, four or five. None are Peter Christian Barrie.

Perhaps he was neither 32 nor 30 in 1920. Perhaps he had chosen to call himself Barrie, despite having been christened Barry; after all, he used many names. Maybe those who said that Barrie had been born in Australia, or in Scotland, were right.

The 1836 Registration Act covered England and Wales. Scotland had to wait for an Act of 1854, and its register of births is not held in the Family Records Centre in London but in an office in Edinburgh. In the volume for the March quarter of 1888 there is an entry for Peter Christian Barrie. One hundred and fourteen years later, the General Register Office for Scotland supplied me with a copy of his birth certificate.

As a young man, Barrie did go to Australia, and in 1914 he joined the Australian army. Armies are full of orders, duties, regulations, and forms. Name, number, rank, regiment, date. "Australian Imperial Force. Attestation Paper of Persons Enlisted for Service Abroad," "Casualty Form — Active Service," "Proceedings on Discharge."

In Canberra, the National Archives of Australia hold dossiers of forms for First World War personnel, including for Barrie, Peter Christian. You would be surprised what you can learn from them, too.

And from reports of trials, a staple of newspapers since they were first published; murders, scandals, frauds. In 1920 the case of the Turf fraud, first heard at Bow Street Police Court, then at the Old Bailey, whetted the appetite even of *The Times*.

Barrie was there, as chief defendant, but there were no photographs, and reports were starkly factual. Counsel were given neither first names nor mannerisms. Their appearance and character, in company with those of the defendants and witnesses, were not described, although they might sometimes be inferred from the nature of the questions, and the answers.

When he emerged from prison, "Ringer" Barrie, it was thought by some, "disappeared from the Turf with the same suddenness as he had arrived,"[1] but he didn't. Barrie's racing exploits were far from over, for his was an extraordinary tale, one that has been waiting too long to be told.

His story stretches from Australia to England, Canada to Cuba, Mexico to South Africa, and to the files of Pinkerton's National Detective Agency, preserved in the Library of Congress in Washington, D.C. You can't imagine how excited I was to find them, as well as a copy of a letter Barrie circulated in 1939, in which he referred to himself as "the man who wrote his reminiscences in *The People*."

Barrie had already published his confessions, 16 years earlier, in *John Bull*. Were these merely a repeat? When had they appeared? There are no indexes for *The People*. So I took a deep breath, tried to narrow the search, and turned the pages. Eventually, I found them. Later, I found more. It was worth the effort, although there was frustration as well as reward.

As far as I knew then, the last recorded sighting of Barrie was in 1945, when he would have been 57. William Bebbington, the cumbersomely titled Senior Jockey Club Supervisor of Racecourse Detective Personnel, saw Barrie at a racecourse and asked him to leave.

The black bound volumes, appropriately, are the indexes of deaths. I started with the volume for the March quarter 1945 and worked my way through to 1950, when Barrie would have been 62; nothing. To 1960, when he would have been 72; nothing.

Nowadays, we are used to people living that long, we expect it, but a man born in 1888 was still likely to heed the warning in the Prayer Book, that "The days of our age are threescore years and ten." Anything more was a bonus.

Maybe Barrie had moved abroad. I plodded on, to 1970. Barrie would have been 82; still nothing. I had almost given up hope. Then, September quarter, 1973. There he was.

During the summer of 1973, an old man suffering from senile dementia was moved from Carrington House, a lodging house for single men run by Lewisham Council, to the nearby Greenwich District Hospital.

CHAPTER 1

Peter Christian Barrie, once notorious on both sides of the Atlantic, died, poor and alone, on July 6. He was 85, and long forgotten.

Often known to his friends as Pat, Barrie had been regarded by the British as the "King of the Ringers," while Americans knew him as the "Master Horse Faker." Many people on each side of the Atlantic were ignorant of Barrie's exploits on the other, which was surprising, because Barrie was boastful.

He was sometimes said to have been born in England, or Australia, but Barrie was Scottish, born on St. Valentine's Day 1888, at number 12, West Tollcross, Edinburgh, not far from the castle. His father, Edmund Chadwick Barrie, was a master butcher who almost seven years earlier had married Mary Ann Kelly in Aberdeen.

Their son later claimed to have arranged his first ringer when he was 16. Having bought a gray mare from Lady Mary Cameron for 16 guineas, Barrie painted the horse brown and sold it back to Lady Cameron for £300. So he said.

He also said that he had been a veterinary research student in Scotland for three years and later sat at the feet of Professor Ross, in Philadelphia, "the finest vet in the world." Neither was likely to have been true, although it was true that at some point between Barrie being born and Archduke Francis Ferdinand of Austria being shot in 1914, Barrie emigrated to Australia.

According to Barrie, he farmed, worked with horses, and rode as an amateur jockey, although when the Jockey Club contacted its Australian counterpart in 1920 to ask if Barrie was known to them, they replied that he was not.

Nor was he known to the long-serving postman or residents of Walker Street, Lavender Bay, Sydney, the address he gave to the Jockey Club. You see, he was a rascal.[2]

In September 1914, in Sydney, Barrie enlisted as a private with the 6th Light Horse Regiment, describing himself as a veterinary dentist. Later, if not earlier, his speciality was making horses' teeth look more youthful than nature intended.

Barrie was then 26 years old, chunkily built, just under 5 feet 7 inches tall, 11 stone 12 pounds (166 pounds), with a dark, florid complexion, hazel eyes, and black hair. The army's description of their latest recruit is one to cling to, for descriptions and photographs of Barrie as a young man are elusive. You have to picture him in your mind.

War had broken out in Europe the previous month, and on the Western Front a pattern of unprecedented slaughter had already been established.

Early in 1915, urged on by Russia, Britain and France attacked Turkey and attempted to force a passage through the Dardanelles, the narrow straits that are the gateway to Constantinople. When the attempt failed, an expeditionary force, including troops from Australia and New Zealand, was dispatched to the Gallipoli peninsula to seize the land that controlled the Dardanelles. The campaign was a failure, and by January 1916, after suffering heavy losses, the expeditionary force was withdrawn.

Barrie fought at Gallipoli and later claimed that he had been discharged after receiving a serious wound in his right arm, but Barrie and the truth never advanced beyond a mild flirtation. The truth was rather less heroic.

Barrie travelled to Gallipoli on the troopship *SS Lutzow* and arrived at Anzac Cove on May 14, 1915. It was a terrible place. The front line was just inland from a small, overcrowded, and dangerous beach, afflicted by Turkish shells, snipers, and disease, with rudimentary field hospitals dug into the banks beyond the shore.

During the medical examination that led to his discharge, Barrie said that he had been at Gallipoli for four and a half months. He was exaggerating. At the end of July 1915, Barrie was moved to the hospital ship, *Itonus*, suffering from a septic foot. He returned to Anzac Cove on August 19 but within a day was removed by field ambulance, suffering from diarrhea, associated with dysentery.

Barrie was transferred to the troopship *Caledonian* and on

August 22 sailed for England. On September 1, 1915, he was admitted to the military hospital at Lewisham and eight days later, suffering from stomach cramps, was moved to the 1st Australian Auxiliary Hospital at Harefield, Middlesex, from where he was discharged on September 14.

At his medical examination the following March, Barrie played further tricks with the truth. He told the medical officer that he had spent six weeks on board ship, a month at the hospital in Lewisham, and two weeks at Harefield.

After leaving the hospital, Barrie was initially employed at a military base in Weymouth. In January 1916 he was transferred to the Australian army headquarters in Horseferry Road, Westminster, where he worked as a driver.

In March a medical board concluded that Barrie "cannot do strenuous work without suffering from dyspnea," shortness of breath, which the medical officer was inclined to blame on a heart problem. There was no mention of a wounded arm although at the time of Barrie's enlistment in 1914, an oval scar on his right upper forearm was noted. Perhaps he kept that at the ready.

On June 19, 1916, Barrie was discharged from the Australian army, "being permanently unfit for active service." Not wounded in battle, but struck down by dysentery, and shortness of breath.[3]

Barrie was deemed fit for munitions work, and Roberts & George, an engineering company with an office in Westminster, offered to employ him in their munitions factory. If Barrie accepted the offer, his employment was short-lived. In March 1917 he was in Liverpool, being sentenced to two months in prison with hard labor for stealing a checkbook and wallet.

In April 1918 Barrie, then 30, briefly broke off from petty crime to marry Florence Eva Vince, a 23-year-old bandmaster's daughter. He returned to court a year later, at Marylebone, charged with having used a worthless check to obtain £275. Barrie was acquitted, leaving him free to pursue more imaginative deceptions.

Something bold was required, for Barrie, a moderately engaging scoundrel, combined an ambitious lifestyle with inadequate funds to support it.

Well-dressed but only fitfully solvent, in the tradition of con men, Barrie and his new wife established themselves at the Queen's Hotel in Leicester Square, a comfortable journey from Horace Berg's racing yard at Epsom, where eight horses were later stabled in Mrs. Barrie's name. Somehow the Barries, their horses, and the Queen's Hotel had to be paid for.

Encouraged by bookmakers with even fewer scruples than himself, Barrie had dipped his criminal toe into the ringing pool, unsuccessfully, in 1918, when he briefly held a trainer's license in Ireland, but the bulk of his European endeavor was concentrated in a few frenetic months, from the autumn of 1919 to the summer of 1920.

While returning soldiers waited for Lloyd George to fulfill his pledge "to make Britain a fit country for heroes to live in," they indulged themselves in the benefits of a brief post-war boom.

People had money and they wanted to spend it. There was no national radio service, let alone television, to keep them indoors. Half-starved of racing during the war, race crowds returned in packs, filling race trains, car parks, bookmakers' satchels, and card-sharpers' pockets.

Bookmakers had the time of their life, and so did the race gangs who preyed on punters and bookmakers alike at railway stations and racecourse car parks, on the trains, and at the tracks, terrorizing and blackmailing.

"Don't play cards, gentlemen," outnumbered police officers would warn race train passengers, "there are sharpers on the train."[4]

And pickpockets, and three-card tricksters, and gangs of hooligans, the most feared hailing from Birmingham, armed with razors, spanners (wrenches), hammers, and clubs. Sunny Jackson's and Harry Sabini's gangs, and gangs calling themselves Titanic, Nile, Hoxton, and Aldgate.

Some gang members protected dishonest bookmakers from

the need to pay winning customers, while others persuaded honest bookmakers to buy overpriced sponges and chalk, or contribute to a charitable fund. They were necessary contributions, as those who declined to make them could testify.

Barrie, who was well placed to know, described these as "vintage years for turf rogues, when money was plentiful and easy to get, and you could back a selling plater to win you a fortune." [5]

During 1919 and 1920, £119,000 allegedly passed through his various bank accounts, as Barrie launched a furious and reckless assault on the racing authorities' feeble defenses.

The Jockey Club ruled racing with growing authority, but neither its rules nor the manner of their application deterred cheats, and the club viewed the need for change with the suspicious eye of a dedicated miser.

Everything the Jockey Club did, it did belatedly. It was not until 1903 that a rule was introduced prohibiting doping, and there were no investigators or analysts to give force to the prohibition.

Until 1913, horses regularly ran without the benefit of a name, and two-year-olds continued to run in semi-anonymity, identified only by the name of their dam. Until 1920, their owners were allowed to go a step further and present themselves under an alias.

The Jockey Club's intense conservatism was reflected in its response to technological change. In the United States, after various experiments, starting stalls were introduced on a regular basis at Hawthorne, in Chicago, in 1929, and spread rapidly. In Britain, they were not introduced until 1967, and then spread slowly.

Photo-finish cameras were in widespread use in the United States in the early 1930s. They were not used in Britain until 1947. At the end of 1966, the Levy Board proudly announced that it hoped to see photo-finish equipment installed at most National Hunt courses by 1968.

No wonder Barrie exuded confidence. The barrage of ringers he unleashed has never been matched in Britain, and never will be. They were piled up, in overwhelming and overlapping confusion, the full list of their names and exploits now impossible to establish.

In 1918 Barrie had made the dubious acquaintance of Gilbert Marsh, a fellow confidence trickster with an address in Savile Row, who was apt to present himself as a millionaire, although Barrie later described him, with bitter hindsight, as "an unscrupulous, heartless man with few, if any, redeeming features."

They were well matched. According to Marsh, as reliable a witness as Barrie, their first encounter was when Barrie bought a horse called Scylla from him for £400. By the time Barrie's check had bounced, the horse was on its way to Ireland.

Barrie later explained that he had bought Scylla on behalf of a client. Unfortunately, when the *Leinster* was sunk by German submarines in the Irish Channel in October 1918, so was the client. As a fellow con man, Marsh must have admired the explanation.[6]

He also had horses at Epsom, with Edward Godfrey, including a three-year-old filly called Mexican Belle. Several years later, Barrie related that he had selected Mexican Belle for his "first big exploit" because, in size and color, she resembled an unnamed two-year-old filly of his own, out of La Lune. The resemblance did not extend far, since Mexican Belle had two white fetlocks and a big white blaze while the La Lune filly did not.

It didn't matter, because the La Lune filly had never been seen in public. Barrie had no intention of exhibiting her. What mattered was that Mexican Belle must not look like Mexican Belle, who had been seen in public, regularly.

"It was a very simple matter," according to Barrie, "by giving a little additional hair to Mexican Belle's tail, and by a judicious application of dye, to make the three-year-old look as much like the La Lune filly as possible."

Barrie boasted that he had succeeded in changing Mexican Belle's appearance "so effectively and completely that anybody who had seen the horse every day of his life would not recognize her."

In case his audience underestimated the merit of the artist's achievement, Barrie spelled it out. "The changing of a horse's appearance requires a tremendous amount of skill and care. The ordinary dyes which come readiest to the mind would be absolutely useless, because the faked horse might be caught in a shower of rain, and is very liable to be covered with a white sheet, whereupon the dye would come out and the whole trick would be exposed."[7]

Barrie's favored dye was henna, which had the virtue of not being water-soluble. The problem with henna was not how to keep it on but how to get it off.

The powdered leaves of the henna bush had been used for centuries in the Middle East and India, largely to adorn women but also on horses. Sir John Chardin, in his *Travels in Persia, 1673 to 1677*, noted, "They have a way also in winter of painting the horses with henna, that yellow paint, used likewise by men and women."

In 1913, *Webster's Dictionary* offered the following definition. "Henna. (1.) A thorny tree or shrub of the genus *Lawsonia*. The fragrant white blossoms are used by the Buddhists in religious ceremonies. The powdered leaves furnish a red coloring matter used in the East to stain the nails and fingers, the manes of horses, etc. (2.) The leaves of the henna plant, or a preparation or dyestuff made from them."

Green in color, henna powder was mixed with water to produce a paste, which created an orange-brown effect. The trick was to produce the required color. Over 60 years later, in the Fine Cotton case, poorly applied henna produced a ringer the color of a bright red Hereford bull. Barrie was more successful, at least with the dye.

The La Lune filly was entered for two selling races at Doncaster, the first on September 10, the second two days later, and Barrie set to work on Mexican Belle. "Two days before the race, I dyed her from bay to brown," he recalled, "carefully touching up her face and legs to match the La Lune filly. Mexican Belle was not the exact replica, but the resemblance was good enough to pass muster."

It needed to be because Richard Wootton, Mexican Belle's former trainer, was expected to be at Doncaster.

Not content with running a three-year-old in the name of a two-year-old, Barrie proposed to run Mexican Belle in both races, both times doped, first to run slowly and then, when longer odds were available, to run fast.

As a "stopper," Mexican Belle was given a dose of laudanum, a derivative of opium popular with horse dopers and artists. Appearing in the fictitious ownership of Mr. A.P. James, and trained privately, the filly duly finished unplaced but recovered in time to be given four grains of cocaine, administered by syringe half an hour before her second appearance.

Barrie boasted that he had "complete knowledge of the action of cocaine on horses," but on this occasion his knowledge was not equal to the task for, while Marsh executed the betting, at odds of 100/8, Mexican Belle reacted to the drug by chewing her reins, which broke at the start. She raced out of control, finished last, and was eventually caught, appropriately, by Dick Wootton.

Barrie took comfort from the fact that Wootton failed to recognize his former inmate, but it was cold comfort. The plot had failed and money had been lost. It had to be recouped.[8]

Barrie wasted no time, weaving a complex web later partly unravelled at the Old Bailey. Using the alias of Mr. A.W. Pearson, allegedly a resident of the Hotel Victory, Leicester Square, he entered Coat of Mail for the Faceby Plate at Stockton, a five-furlong race for maiden two-year-olds, to be run on October 25, 1919.

Coat of Mail was, indeed, a two-year-old, and a bad one. That June, Newmarket trainer Dawson Waugh had sold the bay colt to Walter Hopkins, a bloodstock dealer, for about £90, with the stipulation that it was not to race in England.

Hopkins was a former jockey and trainer who had twice

been warned off. Despite his subsequent denials, he was now working in tandem with Barrie.

According to Hopkins, Coat of Mail never raced and never left his stables at Ashstead, near Epsom. "In fact," he testified, "it has been ill the whole of the time, not fit to run or to be in training." That assertion, at least, was convincing, since a judge would soon be shown a photograph of Coat of Mail impersonating a toast rack.

Barrie was unconcerned. Cheekily, he claimed, "In my handling of Coat of Mail, I was a public benefactor and there are certain fashionable trainers who might profitably follow my example. He was useless for racing, and I did not run him. If all the useless horses that are now being entered for expensive races were similarly treated, the public would lose less money."

Coat of Mail's value to Barrie was that he existed. When it came to actually racing, he had a very different horse in mind. "It was my intention from the very start to substitute an older horse for that race, and so to doctor and paint him that his own mother wouldn't have known him."

A few days before the Stockton race, Hopkins bought a three-year-old called Jazz from trainer Atty Persse for £800, again with the stipulation that the horse would not race in England. Two months previously, Jazz had finished second in a five-furlong handicap at Stockton.

Hopkins said that he had bought Jazz on behalf of William Collis, a jockey looking for horses to race in India. Hopkins asked Persse to send the horse from his yard at Stockbridge, in Hampshire, to Waterloo Station. He claimed that he had informed Collis and assumed that Collis had collected the horse.

On October 23, Jazz did arrive at Waterloo, but it was Barrie who collected him. He promptly transferred the horse to King's Cross station and on to a train to Stockton.

With characteristic self-satisfaction, Barrie recalled, "He went into the horsebox Jazz, a brown colt by Mushroom out of Fizzer. He came out Coat of Mail, a bay colt by Roquelaure out of Queen of the Dell. I did all the faking in the box on the journey."[9]

That was not the story Barrie told the police. He told them that he didn't know who had taken Coat of Mail to Stockton, that the horse was already there when Barrie arrived, and that he had not backed the horse, although he believed Hopkins had. There was the traditional lack of honor among thieves.

When the horsebox arrived at the racecourse, it was snowing, a useful excuse for keeping Coat of Mail in his box and out of the parade ring. According to Barrie, Marsh had arranged for William Griggs, a leading jockey, to ride, but Griggs testified that it was Barrie, representing himself as Mr. Pearson, who approached him. When Griggs declined, Barrie offered him £25, and told him that the horse was sure to win. That was a good enough reason for Griggs to change his mind. He dashed to the box, just in time to get to the start.

Backed from 20-1 to 5-2 favorite in the eight-runner race, the supposedly unraced Coat of Mail led from start to finish, and won by an easy three lengths. "I thought it was a very good two-year-old," said the unknowing jockey, "and tried to buy it."

Collis had travelled to Stockton and backed Coat of Mail, but later insisted that he was ignorant of the substitution. It was only after the race that Barrie told him that the winner was Jazz, adding, "It is easy to ring horses in this country." Collis was angry. To appease him, Barrie promised Jazz's owner £1,000 as his share of the winnings. Collis was appeased but only temporarily. "I never got a halfpenny," he complained.[10]

Perhaps Barrie never intended to pay, or perhaps the winnings were less than he had expected. It was Marsh's job to organize the betting, and Barrie had a low opinion of Marsh's competence. The conspirators should have netted £40,000 but made only about £5,000, of which Barrie claimed to have received only £500. Marsh said that he himself had won about £750.

"The truth," a dangerous way for Barrie to start a sentence, "was that Gilbert Marsh was so broke, and owed so much money to bookmakers, that he had no credit at all. So far from there only being a few people in the swindle, there were 75!"

Marsh had been spreading the word, in return for a share of the winnings, and Coat of Mail had become the subject of a public gamble, destroying the odds, and the secret.

The *Sporting Life*'s "Special Representative" reported, slightly peevishly, "By far the easiest victory was gained by the little known Coat of Mail in the Faceby Plate. It was not until later on that W. Griggs's services were enlisted. Judging from the 'inspired' money that came into the market from all sources, it is obvious those concerned were not entertaining an angel unawares, and the colt won from flag fall with a considerable amount in hand."

To Barrie's dismay, rumors of a substitution were soon circulating. "After the event," he recalled, "whenever I walked down Coventry Street (near Piccadilly), I was certain to meet half-a-dozen people who would pull me up and, fingering my jacket, would say, 'That's a nice coat of mail you've got on, Barrie, but you've had it dyed?' "[11]

On November 7, Weatherbys wrote to Mr. Pearson, asking for the name of Coat of Mail's trainer. They received an evasive reply, written on the Hotel Victory's notepaper, together with a request for the prize money.

A check was issued for 167 pounds, 19 shillings, and 6 pence, which Barrie promptly took to a tailor's shop in Regent Street. He endorsed the check "Arthur Pearson," bought a fur coat and a rug, and took the balance, 138 pounds, 9 shillings, and 6 pence, in cash.

Pressed by Weatherbys, Mr. Pearson informed them, "Coat of Mail has been at my farm for some two months and has been, not exactly in training, but out at exercise with the hunting horses under the charge of my groom. About a fortnight previous to his winning the race at Stockton, I asked several trainers to take him, but unfortunately they had no boxes vacant. A friend of mine intended asking Berg of Epsom to take him over at Stockton but he (Berg) never arrived to do so, hence the mistake. The colt is at my place now.

"I am extremely sorry if I have inadvertently transgressed

any of your rules, but I was led to understand that any horse trained by the owner, on his own private grounds, could be classed as trained privately."[12]

Barrie rarely waited for one dish to cool down before heating up another and was already plotting his next deception. A few days after Coat of Mail's success, he arranged for the purchase of The Squire, a six-year-old who had won an apprentice race at Newcastle on October 22.

The Squire had been entered for the Ford Welter Selling Handicap at Liverpool on November 5, and James Burns, its Scottish trainer, was asked to send the horse to meet its engagement.

In the meantime, Barrie secretly watched The Squire at exercise, in preparation for producing a replacement. When The Squire arrived in Liverpool, his place was taken by an unidentified ringer, and the champion jockey Steve Donoghue booked to ride.

"You've got a winning ride here," Barrie told him in the parade ring. Well before the finish, Barrie turned to Marsh and said, "Go and collect your money." The ringer won easily, at 2-1.[13]

The race following the Ford Welter Selling Handicap was another seller, the Wavertree Selling Plate. The winner, D.N.P., was sold to a Mr. Bazley for 520 guineas. It was probably Barrie spending his winnings, for the following month he persuaded Norman Weisz to buy a half-share in D.N.P., who never ran in Britain again, at least not in his own name.

Weisz was a Hungarian-born jeweler whose thriving business at 1 Hatton Garden produced a massive income of £10,000 a year. Weisz's wealth was matched by his gullibility, an irresistibly attractive combination to con men.

The jeweler's barrister later related that, "In 1919, Mr. Weisz determined to go in for racing, but he knew no more about racing than the man in the moon."

Ernest Stephens, an insurance broker who knew Weisz well, stated that, on the racecourse, he was "a most absolute ass," while another friend, Hugh Thomas, favored the description, "a good-natured fool." Barrie himself, not to be outdone, depicted Weisz as "the prize mug of the world, a pigeon ready for plucking."[14]

Weisz relied heavily — and indiscriminately — on tips, regularly putting £500 or more on a horse purely because he had been told that it would win. Marsh and Barrie promptly set about parting the fool from his jewelry.

Weisz met Marsh in October 1919, when the enthusiastic recruit agreed to take a half-share in a horse called Le Connetable and to back Coat of Mail on Marsh's behalf. The following month Weisz met Barrie, who warned him to be wary of Marsh, who had presented himself as a millionaire metal merchant.

Perhaps as a result, the jeweler declined to pay £5,000 for a half-share in Marsh's two-year-old Bruce Lodge, despite Marsh's assurance that the colt would win the Derby.

Undeterred, on November 22, Marsh maneuvered Weisz to his West End flat on the pretext of introducing him to an Indian maharajah, who wanted to buy some pearls. When Weisz arrived, there was no maharajah but a game of cards, at the end of which Marsh claimed that Weisz owed him £2,200. Weisz gave Marsh £94 and consulted ex-Police Chief Inspector Drew, who told him that Marsh was "a crook and a card sharp."

Marsh insisted that Weisz had lost the money to a friend of his, not to Marsh. "My friend never got his money. Weisz gave me a gold cigarette case and my wife a few trinkets some days afterward, which showed that he could not have thought that I was trying to cheat him."[15]

Shortly afterward, during a visit to Horace Berg's yard at Epsom, Weisz was introduced to Cyril Lawley, a friend of Barrie's who had a car repair business in Hampstead, called The Silver Badge Motor Works.

On December 28 Weisz was at his flat with his friend Hugh Thomas when Barrie appeared. He told Weisz that he expected to have a winner at Cheltenham the next day but would not tell him the horse's name.

Curious, Weisz and Thomas went to Cheltenham and sought out Barrie. They found him, but Barrie still refused to name the horse unless Weisz promised to buy it afterward. Weisz agreed and Barrie told him that the horse was Silver Badge.

Silver Badge had come into the world very recently, on December 16, when Cyril S. Lawley, Lt., RE (Corps of Royal Engineers), retired, wrote to Weatherby & Sons requesting that a mare he had bought at a sale of army horses at Bristol in March be registered as Silver Badge, and entered for the Malvern Selling Hurdle.[16]

Weatherbys obligingly agreed, and shortly before the race, a rugged-up and hooded horse, with bandages on all four legs, appeared in the parade ring, along with Barrie and jockey Tom Hulme.

Barrie told Hulme that Silver Badge had won army competitions and was a good jumper. He promised the jockey £50 if he won. Silver Badge did win, by an easy six lengths, at 10-1, and Weisz kept his part of the bargain and bought the winner at the subsequent auction for 510 guineas, bidding as Mr. Norman.

To ensure that Weisz didn't waver, Barrie allegedly told him, in a manner revealing total confidence in the jeweler's ignorance, "If you buy it, it will certainly win the Chester Cup and very likely the Grand National. Wouldn't you like your friends to see you win the Grand Prix at Auteuil?"

The purchase was no great hardship, since Weisz and Thomas had won £3,000 in bets. Barrie had won a lot more. He told Cyril Targett, the manager of the racecourse stables, that he had won £7,000, but, ominously, there was a hint of suspicion in *The Sporting Life*'s report of the race.

"The winner, and an easy one at that," it observed, "turned up in Silver Badge. She, it appears, was an Army 'surplus,' and one wonders who she really was before the War. In present circumstances, her pedigree is unknown."[17]

A few days later Weisz took a party of friends to Berg's yard to show off his new racehorse. He was doomed to disappointment, since Silver Badge did not exist. Thinking quickly, Barrie told Weisz that Silver Badge was at his own stables in Hampstead, getting used to the sound of traffic.

Barrie could have shown Weisz another horse at Berg's yard, called Shining More. On November 10, Shining More, then owned by Herbert Rich, had won an amateur riders' handicap hurdle over the same course and distance as Silver Badge. After finishing second in a selling hurdle at Cardiff on November 21, the six-year-old was sold. When Shining More reappeared at Sandown on December 6, she was carrying Mrs. Barrie's colors.

On December 27 Shining More, a bay with a white star on her forehead and white hind fetlock, was dispatched to London and taken to Hampstead to be given Barrie's unique attention. Her tail was pulled and dye applied to produce a dark brown color, and the hair on the mare's quarters was singed, to give the impression of an army brand. Military numbers were burned on her hooves.

After triumphing in the name of Silver Badge, Shining More returned to Epsom, where Barrie tried to remove the dye with petrol. When that didn't work, he bought a dozen bottles of peroxide which, according to Alexander McFarlane, who worked at Berg's yard, were "pretty successful."

"When I dye, I dye," bragged Barrie, turning the problem into self-congratulation, "and neither rain nor thunder nor lightning can change the horse's color. Nothing but week after week of hard rubbing, with special chemicals, can change his appearance."

Weisz, mercifully, had disappeared to Switzerland on business. When he returned, Barrie told him that Silver Badge had broken down on the gallops and been sent to Ireland, for breeding. As if to prove it, he presented Weisz with a bill for £92 for Silver Badge's keep.

When Weisz asked him about rumors that the Cheltenham winner was actually Shining More, Barrie protested, "How can you be such a silly as to believe in rumors of that kind?

Shining More is a veteran race winner, and is as well known to these racing men as a champion boxer or a famous footballer would be to you."[18]

Weisz apologized, while Barrie looked for another horse suitable for another fraud. There was a wide choice. Bad horses could be made better by means of a ringer and all horses by the application of dope.

Barrie had further plans for Shining More, but the police were on the trail and it was time to dispose of Coat of Mail.

In February 1920 Edward Hardie, a former jockey, returned to England after six years in India, with the intention of buying some horses for export. He met Barrie and Hopkins in London, and the following month Hopkins took Hardie and his friend Joseph Wise to Berg's yard at Epsom.

Hardie agreed to buy Coat of Mail for £1,000 but changed his mind after Albert Bowley, a jockey who knew that the Stockton race had been won by a ringer warned him against it. Later, when Wise was shown a photograph of Coat of Mail, he testified that it was nothing like the horse Hardie had been shown.

If the deal had gone through, the real, sickly Coat of Mail would have been shipped to India, along with the five other horses Hopkins had already sold to Hardie. They included Headland, a winner at Brighton the previous season. When Alec Law, Headland's former trainer, was shown the horse sent to India, he stated that it was nothing like Headland. That was a ringer, too. There were so many, it was difficult to keep track.

While Hopkins pursued one set of frauds, Barrie warmed up for another. Shining More was to be given the unique distinction of having been both raced as a ringer and replaced by one.

The mare was entered for two hurdle races, the first on Easter Saturday, April 3, 1920, at Plumpton; the second on Easter Monday, at Manchester. For her first outing, Barrie engaged Captain Geoffrey Harbord "Tuppy" Bennet, a successful amateur rider who three years later won the Grand National on Sergeant Murphy.

Barrie fancied Shining More's chances at Plumpton, and "to leave nothing to chance, half an hour before the race I gave her just a gentle gee-up with a couple of grains of cocaine." Shining More finished a creditable, albeit doped, third.

Barrie now prepared "the most audacious piece of villainy in my career. Whilst I had taken Shining More to Cheltenham and called her Silver Badge, I was now going to take another mare to Manchester and call her Shining More!"

Barrie was never charged with this deception, and he did not identify the ringer, beyond stating that she was a superior mare who had been racing successfully in Ireland.

At Manchester, Barrie rode the ringer himself and was surprised but claimed not to have been discomforted to see that Captain Bennet was riding The Wisp in the same race, the Cheetham Handicap Hurdle.

"That's a nice little thing you're riding, Barrie," Bennet said. "What is it?"

"Well, you ought to know," Barrie replied, "You rode her on Saturday."

Bennet's eyebrows rose. "Is that Shining More? I thought she was a bigger animal than that."

Bennet must have known that one of his four opponents was Shining More and the conversation was doubtless invented by Barrie for effect.

The ringer won as ringers can, by an easy 10 lengths, at 6-1. Many years later Barrie claimed that the doped winner had provided him with the most lucrative win of his life.[19]

There would soon be another. On April 20, Jazz, now a four-year-old, appeared in the Nork Park Plate at Epsom in the guise of The Clown, a three-year-old owned by Gilbert Marsh and trained by Edward Godfrey. "He was a brown colt," Barrie recalled, "practically the same color as Jazz, so there was no dyeing required, though it was necessary to make some 'structural alterations,' by trimming the mane and tail."

Despite facing only three opponents, The Clown started at 100/14, with Atty Persse's Mapledurham the odds-on favorite.

The Clown had one major advantage over Mapledurham; as a theoretical three-year-old, he was carrying 16 pounds less. Barrie was confident enough to stake £200, after which he watched the ringer win "very handsomely, in a canter." Six days later, at Alexandra Park, The Clown, alias Jazz, overturned another odds-on favorite, Silver Jug, in a race meant to be confined to three-year-olds.[20]

Flush with success, Barrie and Berg visited Epsom trainer Stanley Wootton and bought a three-year-old called Homs for £350, although Weisz paid for it. It was an unusual purchase, because Homs had never raced.

Barrie's new acquisition made only a fleeting visit to Berg's stable before being dispatched to Euston and rapidly converted into an imaginary two-year-old called Golden Plate.

An equally imaginary Mr. J.H. Hawkins, blessed with an address in Berkeley Square, had entered Golden Plate for the Wynn Two-Year-Old Selling Plate at Chester on May 6. Since neither Barrie nor Berg wanted to be associated with the ringer, Barrie introduced himself to another Epsom trainer, George Gray, who was going to Chester.

Barrie told him that Mr. Hawkins was a wealthy American, a potential owner for Gray, and, with Berg abroad, offered to pay Gray £15 expenses to make the necessary arrangements at the racecourse. He gave Gray a note, purportedly written by Hawkins, giving Gray the authority to act on the owner's behalf.

Barrie travelled with Gray to Chester, then asked the trainer to engage a jockey, along with an offer of £25 if he won and £10 if he was placed. Neither sum had to be paid.

Sensitive about his reputation, when Barrie later produced his own, largely fictional, account of the Golden Plate affair, he claimed that it had not been his plan but that of Marsh and an unnamed bookmaker. Barrie had disliked the choice of Chester, a notoriously tight track where a good draw and a fast start were often crucial.

Tommy Weston, then a promising apprentice, later champion jockey, had already been booked by Barrie's fellow conspirators, and Marsh stood to win a fortune from the punters he had tipped off. "Thousands of pounds were invested in London and in Manchester," said Barrie, "and even Ireland was not neglected." Nevertheless, Golden Plate started at 10-1.

When the starting gate went up, Golden Plate, who was drawn on the wide outside, was standing sideways and was badly left. First Out, the second favorite, got a flying start and although the ringer got to the heels of the leaders, he then faded.

"I saw the horse unsaddled," said Barrie, "and then hurried into the ring to draw my money. For when I saw how Golden Plate was drawn, I took the liberty of backing the winner." It was typical of Barrie to say so, but whether he did so or not ...[21]

Barrie was a plausible and sometimes charming crook. He was certainly good at disguising horses, a talent of which he was enormously proud. It wasn't the ringers' make-up that attracted the authorities' attention but Coat of Mail's and Silver Badge's mysterious backgrounds, and the enthusiasm with which these unlikely winners were backed.

Once the Jockey Club and the police started to ask questions, the conspirators were doomed, for there were no satisfactory answers.

On Saturday June 5, 1920, as Barrie stepped off a train at Charing Cross station, Detective Inspector George Cornish was there to greet and arrest him. The following Tuesday, Barrie, described as a horse dealer, appeared at Bow Street Police Court, charged with having obtained a check for 167 pounds, 19 shillings, and 6 pence by false pretenses. It was the check for Coat of Mail's prize money, made out to A. Pearson.

The following day, Walter Hopkins appeared at Bow Street, charged with conspiracy. Both men were bailed while the police pursued their inquiries.

On July 2 Barrie was arrested again and charged with conspiring to obtain money under false pretenses, this time in connection with Shining More.

During the following days and weeks, Norman Weisz, Cyril Lawley, William Collis, and Horace Berg were added to the list of conspirators and the case of Golden Plate added to the list of suspect horses.

To Barrie's lasting disgust, Gilbert Marsh's name was missing, an omission that colored all Barrie's future references to his co-conspirator. "Why he did not appear with me," Barrie complained, "a police official could tell. I could also tell, for I know very nearly the amount of money that Marsh paid to keep out of the 'boob,'* though all his bribery did not serve him, for he was later arrested on another charge and went to prison for a much longer term than was awarded me."

Peter Barrie

In a statement produced in December 1920, Marsh wrote, "I am told that there is a story going round that I gave £2,000 to Sergeant McCooey to be kept out of this case. This is absolutely untrue." McCooey was one of the investigating officers.

A note by the Jockey Club's lawyers, Charles Russell & Co., observed, "Gilbert Marsh was obviously in some way connected with these frauds, although there was no very definite evidence."[22]

The six defendants were committed for trial at the Old Bailey. Proceedings opened on Monday, September 13, 1920, before Mr. Justice Greer and attracted considerable attention, with *The Times* providing daily coverage.

Barrie, sensibly, but to the surprise and disappointment of those hoping to see him in the witness box, pleaded guilty. The other five defendants all pleaded not guilty.

* Police cells or prison.

Arthur Greer, 56, a tall, bent-shouldered figure with a keen, sharp face lined with the pain of arthritis, had been appointed as a judge only the previous year but was a well-regarded figure with a reputation for fairness.

The dominant legal presence in court was a less sympathetic figure, Charles Frederick Gill, the leading counsel for the prosecution. Gill, 69, was nearing both his retirement and knighthood. Hugely experienced, he had been senior counsel to the Jockey Club since 1903 and was relentless in his pursuit of the defendants as he had been of Robert Sievier, whom he had hounded with "plodding ruthlessness."[23]

The defendants did not deny that the races under scrutiny had been won by ringers but claimed to have been innocent dupes. It was all Barrie's doing.

Photographs of Coat of Mail and Jazz, presented in court, revealed two very different horses. Mr. Justice Greer remarked that they looked like an advertisement of "before treatment and after treatment," and Jazz was identified by both Atty Persse, his former trainer, and William Griggs, who rode him at Stockton.

Walter Hopkins insisted that although he knew Barrie, he had had no dealings with him over Coat of Mail. He had been made a dupe, and "it was a disgraceful fraud to run a three-year-old as a two-year-old."[24]

Hopkins' high moral tone failed to impress the judge. When Hopkins claimed that he had not heard of Coat of Mail's victory until April 1920, Greer, clearly skeptical, intervened with his own set of questions.

Hopkins conceded that the race result would have appeared in every national newspaper but claimed that he was too busy to read newspapers. He employed four stable staff, but none had mentioned Coat of Mail's success, and nor had anyone else.

One person who had definitely drawn Hopkins' attention to the Stockton race was Dawson Waugh, the trainer who had sold Coat of Mail to Hopkins on the condition that the horse was not raced in England. After Coat of Mail won, Waugh wrote to Hopkins to ask for an explanation but received no reply.

Hopkins had purchased the ringer, Jazz, as well as Coat of Mail, and it was Hopkins who asked Persse to send Jazz to Waterloo station, where Barrie was waiting to collect him. Who, other than Hopkins, could have informed Barrie of Jazz's travel arrangements?

The only plausible alternative was William Collis, who had just bought Jazz, but no one suggested that Collis was deeply involved in the conspiracy.

On his own admission Collis had accepted Barrie's belated offer of £1,000 as his share of the winnings. The main question in Collis's case was whether or not he was aware of the substitution before the race. The judge specifically asked the jury, should they find Collis guilty, to indicate whether they judged his involvement to have started before or after the race. The jury gave Collis the benefit of the doubt.

He was bound over to keep the peace while Hopkins, who was found guilty of conspiracy and with having obtained money by false pretenses from Edward Hardie, was sentenced to 15 months imprisonment and ordered to pay costs.

In the Silver Badge and Shining More case, Lawley's guilt was deemed to have been restricted to having obtained the prize money by false pretenses. The jury and Mr. Justice Greer were inclined to take a lenient view of Lawley's readiness to write letters and pose as an owner on Barrie's behalf. He escaped with a £100 fine.

The jury could not agree about trainer Horace Berg's involvement, but in the case of Golden Plate and Homs, Berg was found guilty of conspiring with Barrie to obtain money by false pretenses. He was sentenced to nine months in prison.

The only contentious judgment concerned Norman Weisz. There appeared to be strong evidence that Weisz was telling the truth when he insisted that he had no idea that Silver Badge was actually Shining More, and several bookmakers, as well as business associates, testified to Weisz's honesty. Yet

Weisz was found guilty of conspiracy and sentenced to 15 months imprisonment, the same sentence as Hopkins.

Weisz's counsel immediately declared that there had been "a grave miscarriage of justice," and lodged an appeal.

The appeal hearing began on November 15 and was dismissed two days later. The appeal court ruled that the jury were entitled to reject Weisz's story, which required excessive faith in Weisz's stupidity. Could a successful businessman really have been, and remained, such a total innocent?

"Poor Norman Weisz," Barrie declared, in 1923, "A man holding a good position, a rich man, an innocent man, whose only offense was that he was a tool for rascals like myself and Marsh. The truth is, Weisz knew nothing! He was as innocent as you. I declare on my oath that Weisz knew nothing of any swindle."

Weisz may have been harshly treated, but he was not entirely without guile. In September 1919 he had written to Weatherbys to register his assumed name of Mr. Norman, which he was entitled to do. When, from January 1, 1920, this was no longer permitted, Weisz preserved his anonymity by arranging for Ernest Stephens' wife, Rena, to inform Weatherbys that his horses were now hers, with Weisz managing them for her.

Barrie, the central figure in what prosecution counsel Charles Gill described as "a gross and scandalous fraud," was sentenced to three years in prison.

The Times, greeting the sentences with approval, remarked, "It is a part of the national honor of England that one of the greatest of her sports should be conducted with clean hands. The frauds which led to the trial were unusually audacious, even for the Turf."

The Sporting Life reassured its readers, rather confusingly, "That the substitution of horses is of anything but very infrequent occurrence is certain. The Jockey Club are to be congratulated upon bringing the case to light, and it is to be hoped that the smart sentences imposed will prove a deterrent to others inclined to abuse the Turf."[25]

The Jockey Club may have helped to bring the case to light, but its rules and their administration were an invitation to rogues. During the trial a Weatherbys' employee admitted that entries had been accepted for both Silver Badge and Golden Plate with little evidence that either horse existed. When the employee, squirming under cross-examination, was asked if there was anything to prevent "an old bus horse" being entered and raced, he finally, reluctantly, conceded that there was not.

Barrie served his sentence in Dartmoor prison, where his resentment against Marsh festered. In January 1923 he returned to Bow Street Police Court in an abortive attempt to initiate action against police officers for allegedly accepting bribes.

Five months later his wife, Florence, gave birth to a girl, Angela June. Barrie was out of prison in time for the birth but not, apparently, for the conception. The space on the birth certificate reserved for the name of the father was occupied by a dash.

Barrie may not have renewed his association with his wife, but he did make contact with Edgar Wallace, who was busy establishing himself as Britain's most popular writer.

Wallace, then in his late 40s, was an extraordinary figure, the illegitimate son of an unsuccessful actress, brought up by an illiterate Billingsgate fish-porter's wife. As a writer, his output was phenomenal, as were his methods.

Since he possessed a head full of ideas and an enormous capacity for spending money, much of it backing racehorses, the object of the exercise was not to be a great novelist but a financially successful one.

Wallace came to writing through journalism and viewed books like newspaper articles, to be produced quickly, for immediate consumption. When a friend tried to persuade him to concentrate more on quality and less on quantity, Wallace retorted, "The good stuff may be all right for posterity, but I'm not writing for posterity."

Often, strictly speaking, Wallace wasn't writing at all but dictating, at breathtaking speed. He would surround himself with cigarette smoke and cups of sweet tea and launch himself at the dictaphone, reaching speeds of up to 70,000 words in 72 hours.

When the plot became overcrowded, characters would be summarily dispatched. The jockey Jack Leach, a friend of Wallace's, once asked the author's daughter, Pat, whether a book called *Murder on the Second Floor* was by her father. "Of course not," she replied. "Daddy would have had a murder on every floor."

As far as Wallace was concerned, the conclusion of a book's dictation brought his literary responsibilities, and interest, to an end, and he retired to bed, or to *Racing Up To Date*. It was left to his secretary to produce a tidy manuscript from the dictaphone cylinder recording and to send it off to Hodder and Stoughton, who had conveniently agreed to publish Wallace's books as fast as he could write them.

Sir Ernest Hodder-Williams introduced Wallace to the joys of royalties, curing him of his earlier, unfortunate habit of selling all the rights to his latest work for a pittance. Wallace had actually managed to lose money on his first and one of his best-known books, *The Four Just Men*, published in 1905, and sold the rights to many of his early novels for less than £100 each.

By the time Wallace had agreed to "ghost" Barrie's confessions, a decision likely to have occupied a moment's thought, his interest in racing and gambling was already well established. He had worked as a racing journalist before the war and in 1913 published the first of a number of racing novels, *Captain Tatham of Tatham's Island.*

Meyrick Good, the long-serving chief racing reporter for *The Sporting Life*, claimed to have introduced Wallace to racing and for a few years shared a Newmarket apartment with him during race meetings. "I have known many Turf enthusiasts," Good recalled, "but none to compare with Edgar. He dabbled in many things, but racing was his first and greatest love, his ruling passion."

Unfortunately, his expertise failed to match his enthusiasm. Leach thought Wallace a "fantastic man," but "there was one very weak link in his make up. He thought he knew everything about racing. I never met a man who knew less. He fought a continuous battle against the bookmaker, and hardly won a round."[26]

Another racing novel, *The Flying Fifty-Five*, came out in 1922, along with a successful thriller, *The Crimson Circle*. At the time Wallace was writing Barrie's story, he was already at work on his next thriller, *The Green Archer*.

Following his release from prison, "Ringer" Barrie set up a tipping business in a street off Piccadilly. Wallace was intrigued and arranged to take it over, but the arrangement foundered after six months, as customers fled in the face of Wallace's selections.

The two men remained on friendly terms, with Barrie introducing Wallace to his dubious associates, an experience that later prompted the appearance of Educated Evans, a fictional cockney tipster who made his debut in 1924. The following year, Wallace wrote a successful play called *The Ringer*, although the ringer was a person rather than a horse.

John Bull, a populist weekly magazine, was the chosen outlet for Barrie's confessions and a particularly appropriate one, since its editor, until recently, had been Horatio Bottomley.

Bottomley and Barrie may well have met at the racecourse, one fraudster introducing himself to another. Bottomley, who had been brought up in an orphanage, made his initial fortune through the promotion of highly suspect companies, surviving a steady stream, later a flood, of bankruptcy and other legal actions.

Always attracted to an audience, particularly an admiring one, Bottomley was strongly drawn to racecourses, where he could indulge three of his enduring passions, champagne, mistresses, and gambling, all of which he pursued to near fatal excess. The champagne tended to be Pommery, the mistresses chorus girls, and the bets £1,000 each.

In 1897, aged 37, he had decided to win the Derby, Grand Steeplechase de Paris, and Grand National, and bought three horses for the purpose. Hawfinch had won that year's Dewhurst Stakes, Count Schomberg the Goodwood Cup, while Gentle Ida was the well-regarded half sister of the 1897 National winner, Manifesto.

Hawfinch was well beaten in the 1898 Derby, Count Schomberg well beaten in the Grand Steeplechase de Paris, while Gentle Ida, sent off at 4-1 favorite for the 1899 Grand National, fell at Valentine's.

There were compensations, often in selling races but occasionally at a more exalted level. In 1899 Bottomley won the Stewards Cup at Goodwood with Northern Farmer, along with a reputed £70,000 in bets; in 1902 Wargrave won the Ebor at York and two years later, backed down to 5-1 favorite, won the Cesarewitch, and Bottomley the contents of several bookmakers' bags, said to total £80,000.

For once, and it was a rare occasion, Bottomley's prediction to the electors of South Hackney proved correct. "Bottomley for South Hackney and Wargrave for the Cesarewitch."

By the time he founded *John Bull* in 1906 Bottomley was an MP (Member of Parliament), representing largely himself, while continuing to fight off a persistent assortment of discontented creditors and mistresses. He treated both in the same way, by disappearing out of a secret exit from the magazine's offices.

Bottomley treated the office boy rather better, rescinding his dismissal for having stolen some stamps with the observation, "We've all got to start in a small way."

In 1907 Bottomley insisted on running a selling plater named after the magazine in the Derby and instructed the jockey to make sure that he led the field, even if not for long. The next day, posters appeared — "John Bull Leads The Field."

The magazine gave Bottomley better access to the gullible, whom he exploited through lotteries and sweepstakes, but in 1912 he was temporarily pinned down in the London Bankruptcy Court, providing intermittent amusement.

Counsel: You keep racehorses, Mr Bottomley?

Bottomley: No.

Counsel: You do not keep racehorses?

Bottomley: Certainly not.

Counsel: Then you did keep racehorses?

Bottomley: No, never.

Counsel: You have a place in Sussex called 'The Dicker'?

Bottomley: Yes.

Counsel: You have stables there, large stables?

Bottomley: Yes.

Counsel: You breed horses there, racehorses?

Bottomley: Yes.

Counsel: Then why did you tell me that you never kept racehorses?

Bottomley: I gave you the correct answer. I never kept racehorses. They keep me.

Bottomley was obliged to resign as an MP, but his fortunes were temporarily revived by the war, which enabled *John Bull* to play the part of popular patriot and hater of Germans, while its editor embarked on a lucrative "patriotic lecture tour," with the fervor of Bottomley's patriotism determined by the fee received.

In 1918 Bottomley triumphantly returned to the House of Commons, buoyed up by a wave of patriotic fervor and the income from a Victory Bond scheme in which Bottomley was the prime victor.

Some of the income was converted, not into Victory Bonds, but racehorses, which helps to explain why, at Manchester's race meeting on the first two days of 1919, Bottomley's colors were carried by seven different horses.

Both Barrie and Gilbert Marsh would have been well aware of Bottomley's racing interests. In March 1919, at Sandown, Bottomley's Royal Signet narrowly beat Marsh's Doctor Ryan, avenging an earlier defeat at Gatwick. At Kempton, in November, Bottomley's prolific winner, MacMerry, finished second in a race in which Mrs. Barrie's The Squire also ran.

MacMerry's jockey lodged an objection to the winner, which the stewards regarded as frivolous. Bottomley may have encouraged the objection because he always put a special betting hat, a bowler hat, on when MacMerry was running, and raised his stakes.

That may have been because, according to former jockey and trainer Frank Brown, Bottomley had a habit of waiting for a selling hurdle with only three or four runners, then buying them all and arranging their finishing order.[27]

At the end of 1921, Bottomley was replaced as editor of *John Bull* by Charles Pilley, a prelude to a worse setback. In May 1922 the Independent MP for South Hackney appeared at the Old Bailey, charged with fraud.

When the judge sentenced him to seven years in prison, Bottomley responded, "I was under the impression, my lord, that it was sometimes put to an accused person, 'Have you anything to say before sentence be passed upon you?' "

"It is not customary in cases of misdemeanor," the judge replied.

"Had it been so, my lord, I should have had something rather offensive to say about your summing up."

Bottomley's conviction earned him the rare distinction of being expelled from the House of Commons and the chance to create two famous anecdotes. In the first, a prison visitor, whose identity varies in the telling, sees Bottomley making a mailbag. "Ah, Bottomley, sewing?" "No, reaping."

In the second, Bottomley spots a former acquaintance, imprisoned for defrauding bookmakers, cutting the lawn. "Still on the Turf, I see."

If Bottomley had still been editor, he would surely have been keen to run Barrie's confessions, but when the first installment appeared, on February 17, 1923, he was in Wormwood Scrubs. Perhaps he read them there.

"For the first time in Turf history," trumpeted *John Bull*'s new editor, "the veil which has hidden the modern methods of rascality practiced by the unscrupulous underworld of the

Turf is torn aside, and there is revealed, by a master practitioner, the notorious Patrick Barrie, a story which is as enthralling as a novel and is as informative as a confession."

Described, modestly, as a "good-looking, raven-haired young man" with "the coolest, most brilliant mind of the Turf underworld," Barrie promised to tell "the true and inside history of the racecourse swindles which, if I was not the instigator, I was one of the principal instruments of carrying out."[28]

The articles, 15 in all, were bright and breezy but brief and often begging questions, left unanswered thanks to a combination of Wallace's rapid production methods and Barrie's concern for effect rather than accuracy.

The experience further whetted Wallace's appetite for racing. While Bottomley was selling horses, Wallace was buying them. His first two purchases, Sanders and Bosambo, were named after characters in an early series of stories, *Sanders of the River*, although the horses were less successful than the characters.

Like Bottomley, Wallace was an extravagant and ill-disciplined punter, addicted to tips and prone to backing his own generally talentless horses.

On, appropriately, April 1, 1924, Bosambo made his debut at Warwick. Wallace, characteristically full of misplaced optimism, booked both champion jockey Steve Donoghue and a Daimler for the great day. On his way to the racecourse, he drafted a telegram booking a trip to America, to be funded by Bosambo's imminent victory. The trip was cancelled.

Ten months earlier, in his final confession, published on June 9, 1923, "Ringer" Barrie declared that, "with me, ringing is a thing of the past. My mind is made up. Never again!"

But Barrie changed his mind. A con man has to live. By the time Barrie was released from prison, boom had turned to slump, and although London escaped the brunt of the depression, the future was uncertain, especially for Barrie.

His story sold, what was he to do? He had no trade or profession, was unfit for the army, and had a criminal record.

There were even signs that the Jockey Club was stirring.

In 1921, at Surrey Assizes, over 20 men were imprisoned following violent clashes between race gangs. Walter Beresford, president of the newly founded Bookmakers' Protection Association, denounced the "terrorism and blackmailing" to which his members were subjected.[29]

After consultations with the Home Office and police, the Jockey Club appointed Major G.P. Wymer to head a team of ring inspectors, many of them former policemen, to tighten racecourse security and protect the public.

They began operations in 1925 and, with police help, gradually eliminated the threat from race gangs. In 1936, when there was a late flowering of gang warfare at Lewes racecourse, it was quickly suppressed.

Barrie had long since crossed to the other side, where he would have one final meeting with Edgar Wallace, in Mexico.

Hot 2

Peter Barrie arrived in Canada in 1923, bribed his way across the border, and moved on to New York. Broke, a condition he came to know well, Barrie got a job as a groom with Sam Hildreth.

Hildreth was top of the East Coast training tree, the leading money winner nine times between 1909 and 1924, and the trainer of Zev. In 1923, having won the Kentucky Derby, Zev famously defeated Papyrus, winner of the Epsom Derby, in a match at Belmont.

There were more obvious reasons for Zev's victory than Barrie's wild allegation that he was "shot full of dope," but Hildreth, a big gambler who had once employed Jesse James's brother, Frank, as his betting commissioner, was not above reproach. In 1900, before his glory days, he had been warned off by The Jockey Club.

After Hildreth's death in 1929, Barrie, an unreliable witness but generally more prone to exaggeration than bald falsehood, claimed that the "Big Boss" had regularly administered both drugs and electric shocks to his horses.

"Racing in America was rotten with doping," said Barrie. "At that time, it is my honest belief that three horses out of every four running on the American tracks were drugged. I don't believe anybody but a crooked man could possibly make money on the American Turf, and when Sam Hildreth died he left over a million dollars!"[1]

Barrie's scurrilous allegations were made when he was back in England and safe in the knowledge that Hildreth was dead, but he had made similar, more general allegations while still in the United States.

In 1932 Barrie claimed that "fully 60 percent of the horses racing on the American turf are stimulated," and that on many tracks doping was condoned. Since poor horses were doped more often than good ones, and the final races on a card tended to be for moderate horses, "the sixth or seventh events at almost any track are known as drug store races."

Doping was certainly commonplace. Toney Betts, a New York racing journalist, recalled that during the 1920s "many stables, including those of millionaires, stimulated horses with narcotics and other drugs."

Sam Hildreth

Barrie cited a raid on Arlington Park by the Narcotic Bureau in 1933 as evidence of the extent of the practice. Inevitably, he exaggerated, but the bureau claimed to have "conclusive evidence that at least 200 Thoroughbreds, competing in as many races on American tracks in the last eight months, had been doped."

Ralph Oyler, head of the Chicago Narcotic Bureau, produced a list of 15 horses allegedly doped either at Arlington or at Hialeah in Florida, both high-profile tracks.[2]

Barrie was hardly in a position to condemn the practice, since he was an exponent of it, and he soon adjusted to the demands of the American criminal system.

It was the age of prohibition and gangsters. From January of 1920 until December of 1933, the manufacture, sale, transportation, import, export or possession of intoxicating liquor was prohibited, providing a lucrative opportunity for criminals and a hopeless task for law enforcement agents.

Gangsters added bootlegging, the illegal supply of liquor, to their standard fare of robbery, extortion, prostitution, and gambling and battled each other for control of this new and valuable activity.

Barrie soon became acquainted with members of the Purple Gang, a vicious collection of bootleggers who hailed from Detroit and later played a part in the notorious St. Valentine's Day massacre of 1929.

He became Hildreth's chauffeur, and when his gangster associates asked him to find out what dope the trainer was using, Barrie switched three of the bottles Hildreth kept in the car's glove compartment and had the contents analyzed. All three contained heroin and cocaine.

Hildreth's new driver became friendly with two of the stable's jockeys, Mark and Laverne Fator. Laverne was at the height of his considerable career in the mid-1920s, but Barrie was closer to his brother. "Mark Fator, as clever a jockey as ever pulled a horse or won a hard race," Barrie wrote, "was in with us."

Although less famous than Laverne, Lester Mark Fator was also a talented rider. In 1922 he topped the jockeys' table with 188 winners, but the *New York Times* described him as "one of the stormy petrels of racing," forever in trouble with the authorities.

When Hildreth wanted to back Celidon, a talented horse but a chronically slow starter, he issued Mark Fator with a "buzzer," a battery-powered device to encourage Celidon to jump smartly from the gate. It was Barrie's job to collect the device from the point on the track where Fator had arranged to drop it.

Since Hildreth didn't usually give the jockey his riding instructions until the last minute, Fator and Barrie arranged a "little private sign" to indicate whether or not Fator would be trying to win.

On October 22, 1925, at New York's Empire City track, Hildreth encouraged Fator to win a small sprint race with

Euclid. Barrie passed the information on to members of the Purple Gang, who promptly backed Euclid from 4-1 to odds on. When Hildreth saw the tumbling price, he decided to back Teak, Euclid's only serious rival in the seven-runner race, instead, and amended his riding instructions accordingly.

Mercifully for Barrie, Fator managed to pass on the change of plan, and Barrie quickly told gang member Murray Marks. The gang were able to back Teak, who duly won at even money. Euclid, who ended up at 6-5, finished third. *The New York Times* observed that Fator gave the two-year-old a ride, "that the mildest comment of the spectators labeled 'raw.' "

John J. FitzGerald, a respected reporter with *The Morning Telegraph*, was more expansive. "Euclid broke on top," he wrote, "and rated in a position close to Claptrap and Teak until making the turn for home. Then Fator went out to take a look at the folk in the grandstand and tossed off the race. Had he held the colt to a straight course he would have been the winner."[3]

KEENELAND-COOK

Mark Fator

Barrie must have heaved a huge sigh of relief. His description of Marks as the Purple Gang's chief killer, "an elegant gunman who once 'bumped' eleven men in a row within fourteen days," was fanciful, but Marks, alias Murray Miller, alias Martin Marks, was real enough for a while.

In 1933, age 32, he stepped off a bus in New York and into a gun chamber of bullets, a victim of Arthur "Dutch Schultz" Flegenheimer's feud with Waxey Gordon, Marks' bootlegging boss.[4]

FitzGerald observed that although Fator's performance "brought much condemnation from the crowd," it "evidently failed to attract official attention." Not, perhaps, entirely.

Two days later another unsatisfactory effort, this time on Siren, also trained by Hildreth, provoked the Empire City stewards into suspending Fator for the rest of the season. Siren, coupled in the betting with stablemate Mayne, had started a heavily backed 2-1 favorite but finished fifth in a field of six, with Mayne a place in front of her.

The following March, The Jockey Club turned down Fator's application for a license. No explanation was given, but *The New York Times* remarked that the decision came as "little surprise."[5]

Barrie eventually fell out with Hildreth, which may have fueled his later accusations. In 1926, perhaps influenced by Fator's disqualification, he moved to Minneapolis and persuaded a local man to fund the purchase of several horses in Canada. Barrie stayed over the border just long enough to be charged with having obtained $1,800 by false pretenses.

Rather than appear in court in Winnipeg, he changed his name to Patrick Christie and appeared in Chicago, together with two recent purchases, the $2,500 Kalakaua and the $100 Bobby Dean. Barrie disguised the former as the latter and on September 6, 1926, lined him up for a six-furlong claiming race at the recently opened Lincoln Fields racetrack at Crete, just south of Chicago.

It was Barrie's first ringer, of many, in the United States. A Labor Day crowd of nearly 30,000 braved the rain, but the heavy track did not suit Kalakaua, who allegedly stood to win his backers $250,000. Having led into the straight, "Bobby Dean" tired badly but managed to hang on to third place. According to Barrie, the show dividend of $6.20 almost covered the gang's losses.

Retaining his adopted surname of Christie, Barrie moved

Kalakaua and the rest of his small stable, including Hot Dog and Little Archer, to Cuba. Barrie was never afraid to travel; often, he had to.

From the corner of Galiano Street and Zanja Street in Havana, it was a 10-cent ride on the United Railways of Havana's electric train to Marianao and the Oriental Park racetrack. They raced through the winter, every day except Mondays, for 90 days, from December 11, 1926, to March 20, 1927, six or seven races a day, almost all of them claiming races, each for a purse of $700.

Cuba's President Gerardo Machado was sometimes a spectator, along with James Walker, New York City's mayor. Both were corrupt, and a few years later both were forced into exile.

Standards at Oriental Park were not high, although Barrie considered the rogue-count to have been even higher at Agua Caliente, a future hunting ground across the Mexican border. He should have known.

With typical exaggeration, Barrie claimed to have won 12 races in Cuba with Hot Dog and Kalakaua, proudly adding that, "apart from doping, those races were on the level."[6]

He certainly got off to a cracking start. On December 15 *The Havana Post*, a most enthusiastic supporter, reported, "Hot Dog, racing for P. Christie, was the juicy-priced winner of the afternoon. Six to 1 was his quotation. L. Hardy, Indiana whirlwind rider, brought him home with four lengths to spare. The mutuel reward on this one was $27.60 for a two spot."

Perhaps that was the race that landed one illegal New York bookmaker in court. A police officer testified that the previous day he had arrested the bookmaker as he took a bet on Hot Dog. The magistrate looked at the racing results and, on seeing Hot Dog's odds, dismissed the case. "This man can't be making a book any more," he said. "If he took a bet on Hot Dog, he's broke."[7]

Hot Dog went on to win another four races at Oriental Park, but Kalakaua won only once, as did Little Archer. Kalakaua's record might have been better if the horse had not been barred by the

THE BLOOD-HORSE

Oriental Park

stewards of the Havana-American Jockey Club, who decided that he had been doped. P. Christie escaped with a $100 fine.

He had already got away with running a dark bay called The Import in the name of a less able light bay mare called Bellfont. On January 15, when Bellfont won at 6-1, Barrie claimed to have collected the equivalent of £3,000, but Barrie's claims always needed to be treated with caution.

In 1932 he told Bob McGarry, of the *New York Daily News*, that he had won seven races with Bellfont, alias The Import. Three years later, he had reduced the total to six, five of them in a row.[8] In fact, Bellfont won five races at Oriental Park, the last three consecutively, including the final race of the season.

Barrie moved back to the United States, accompanied by the real Bellfont. Having sold the supposedly multiple winning mare for a bargain price, Barrie then happily laid against her.

In a Chicago pool room, he met a tipster who suggested running a ringer and making money by tipping it to his clients. Barrie bought a cheap five-year-old called Infante and made plans to race a good sprinter called Gibbons in its place.

He was taking an enormous risk, because Gibbons was owned by Terry Druggan, who had sent the horse to Barrie to treat Gibbons' suspect leg. "Terrible Terry" Druggan was a very small man, capable of providing very big trouble.

He and his partner, Frankie Lake, were the leaders of Chicago's Valley Gang, who allied themselves lucratively with Johnny Torrio and Al Capone. When the pair were sent to Cook County jail in 1924, their influence enabled them to reduce the inconvenience to a minimum.

They bribed Sheriff Peter Hoffman to relax restrictions. When a journalist asked to interview the prisoners, he was told, "Mr. Druggan and Mr. Lake are out right now — an appointment downtown. They'll return after dinner." "Well," said Druggan, when asked to explain his absence, "it's awfully crowded in there."

The arrangement worked out better for the bootleggers than for Sheriff Hoffman, who ended up being imprisoned in his own prison. Druggan, on the other hand, made a fortune, which he spent on palatial homes in Illinois and Florida, a fleet of cars, and a string of racehorses, which raced in the name of Sanola Stock Farm and sported the Irish-American's Celtic colors. It didn't last. Eventually, Druggan was sent back to prison for tax evasion, the Achilles' heel of gangsters.

During Barrie's spell as Hildreth's driver, Mark Fator had introduced him to a trainer called Steve Mabey. In 1927 the two men met again, at the Morrison Hotel in Chicago, where Barrie, according to Mabey, "seemed to be putting on a great deal of dog* for an ex-chauffeur."

Nevertheless, Mabey agreed to train Infante for him and to take the horse to Wheeling, West Virginia. He also agreed to present himself as the horse's owner. On September 5, 1927, Infante ran in the five-furlong Labor Day Purse.

Mabey probably didn't know that the horse that won easily that day, paying $11.80 for $2, was Gibbons, the same horse that four days later, again in the name of Infante, won another small race at Batavia in New York.

It was the only time that Barrie risked running a ringer in the state of New York, and then it was at a small "outlaw" track,

* To make a flashy display of wealth or importance.

away from the scrutiny of The Jockey Club. "Barrie never was so clever as he has pictured himself," Mabey reflected, sourly, adding that each time Infante won, Barrie bet only $200. Barrie didn't claim to have won much from his own bets but said that after the first race he and the tipster split $8,000, and the equivalent of another £2,000 after the second.

When the connections of Taudlane, the runner-up at Batavia, questioned the winner's identity, Barrie disappeared, leaving an aggrieved Mabey to face the music.

Having discovered that the winner was Gibbons, Mabey contacted Druggan, visited him in Chicago, and managed to persuade the outraged gangster that he was not to blame, Barrie was. To Mabey's amazement, Barrie was also in Chicago, broke and seeking a loan.

"The fact that Barrie, after he had pulled off two successful ringing coups, was flat broke, shows even more clearly that the man did not make real money through his crookedness," said Mabey, adding, presciently. "Most of the ringing coups he executed brought him very little money. Other people may have profited a great deal by them, but Barrie didn't."

Mabey lent Barrie some money and a few days later received another phone call. Barrie told him that he was working for a Minneapolis man who owned several horses, including The Roll Call. Barrie wanted Mabey to train them. Despite his recent experience Mabey agreed.

Having doped The Roll Call before the horse won at Lincoln Fields, Barrie arranged for him to be entered at Pimlico in Baltimore, where he started favorite. According to Mabey, Barrie introduced the horse's owner to a bookmaker and told him that he could make a killing by backing The Roll Call off-track; the bookmaker would place the bets for him. The owner produced the stake money, but Barrie then arranged for the horse to be stopped and split the stake money with the bookmaker.

The trainer's tale may have been true, for Barrie himself confessed to having given the horse a chlorine capsule as a "stopper," and then laid against it.

Mabey told his story with a purpose, to dispel the popular illusion that Barrie was a largely harmless, cheeky, charming rascal. "I know Barrie," he said. "He is the sort of fellow who fancies himself in the role of a suave and daring confidence man. He's not nearly so romantic as he seems. Indeed, he proved himself to be just a cheap, petty crook, but like most of his ilk, he likes to build himself up as a colorful, romantic figure."[9]

Mabey wasn't perfect himself. He was later imprisoned for murder.

Barrie may or may not have stolen, then pawned Mabey's binoculars, but he was certainly wanted by the police in the unromantic sounding town of Mechanicville, New York. On November 24, 1927, he was arrested in Baltimore.

Barrie was wanted in Mechanicville for having obtained $900 by false pretenses, having allegedly sold someone else's horse to the Chief of Police. Fortunately for Barrie, the Baltimore police arrested him on a different charge, that of being a fugitive from Winnipeg. When the Winnipeg authorities declined to pay the cost of Barrie's extradition, he was released.

Barrie then moved to New York, where a Mr. Hermann offered him £500 for an equine "painting" commission in South Africa. Barrie sailed on the *City of York*, traveling on forged papers, dyed a chestnut horse black, and returned to New York without knowing the outcome of his efforts. Several months later Mr. Hermann paid him another visit and gave him £300 as a present. At least, that was Barrie's story.

Barrie's movements between 1928 and 1931 are a mystery. He may have been based at a stable at the Lake County Fairgrounds at Crown Point, Indiana, just south of Chicago, perfecting his doping and disguising techniques;[10] he may have spent periods out of the country. In 1934 Barrie told a district attorney that he had entered the United States illegally at least four times, and was said to have admitted entering the United States in August 1931 as a seaman. Whatever he was doing, it was unlikely to have counted towards a good citizen's medal.

The trouble with Barrie, one of several, was that he kept even worse company than his own. Sometimes he had money, but often he didn't. Paul Gallico, later famous as the author of *The Snow Goose*, but at that time sports editor of the *New York Daily News*, once lent Barrie $80 and, amazingly, got it back. Later, he bumped into Barrie at a prize fight and asked how he was doing. "Oh, all right," Barrie replied. "I'm doing a little better now," then opened his jacket to reveal fifteen $1,000 bills pinned to the lining.

Gallico, writing in 1934, pinpointed Barrie's real problem, apart from having, as Mabey put it, "so much larceny in him." The problem was that, "For the last three years, he has been the tool of the gangsters of New York, Cleveland, Pittsburgh, and Chicago." The price of consorting with gangsters was to be controlled by them.[11]

In the fall of 1931, Barrie was consorting with them on West 44th Street, New York. At number 59, the Hotel Algonquin, Dorothy Parker was spasmodically blowing on the embers of the Algonquin Round Table and drinking huge quantities of liquor. Down the street, at number 107, Duffy's Restaurant, Barrie's acquaintances were also into liquor, but less wittily.

Duffy's, reputedly owned by "Nate" Raymond, was the unofficial headquarters of the gang that, for the time being, controlled Barrie. "I'm a speculator in cards," Raymond told a court a few months later, "and sometimes I bet on horses. I'm a betting commissioner and a sucker; they're the same thing."[12]

He forgot to mention that he was also a crook. As early as 1912, under the name of Harry Cohn, Raymond had been ordered to leave Sacramento for playing with doctored dice. In 1923 in Vancouver, under the alias of John Harris, he was fined for the illegal possession of firearms.

Raymond was best known as one of the gamblers linked to the murder of Arnold Rothstein, a bigger gambler and a bigger crook. On Rothstein's wedding night, during a Saratoga meeting in 1909, he had borrowed his wife's jewelry as collateral for a bet.

By 1921 Rothstein didn't need to borrow jewelry, having become a major league criminal. That year he joined forces with Max Hirsch, later the trainer of three Kentucky Derby winners, to land a record-breaking $770,000 coup on Sidereal at Aqueduct. He won another $450,000 when Sporting Blood won the Travers Stakes at Saratoga, helped along by Hildreth's late withdrawal of Grey Lag, who had beaten Sporting Blood in the Belmont.[13]

Seven years later, Rothstein sat down with Raymond, "Red" Martin Bowe, George McManus, "Titanic Slim" Thomas, Meyer Boston, and others at a 24-hour card game that ended with Rothstein handing out IOUs for several hundred thousand dollars. Raymond claimed to hold pledges for over $200,000.

It was allegedly Rothstein's failure to pay up that provoked McManus into shooting him at the Park Central Hotel in November of 1928, although the prosecution against McManus subsequently failed.

In September of 1931, Raymond may have helped fund Barrie's most famous ringer. For a sum variously reported to have been from $3,500 up to $5,000, Barrie bought Aknahton, owned by Marshall Field and trained in New York by George Odom. A three-year-old chestnut colt, Aknahton had been foaled on April 14, 1928.

For between $300 and $500, Barrie also bought two not decent two-year-olds, Shem and Ep, from John Hastings. Shem, a chestnut gelding foaled on March 15, 1929, had been sold as a yearling for $9,500 but had shown no promise in his work, had never raced, and therefore never been seen on a racetrack. For Barrie, that was a virtue.

Aknahton was moved to William Baird's barn and on September 17 ran in the ownership of J. LeBolt. Baird's involvement was brief. A note to the trainer, dated September 29 and signed Julius Debott, read, "Please hand to bearer my

PINKERTON'S NATIONAL DETECTIVE AGENCY

Aknahton as himself

KEENELAND-COOK

Aknahton in disguise

racehorse Aknahton, three-year-old by Stimulus out of Scarab, on payment of board due."[14]

Officials later decided that the man's real name was Julius

DeLott, who ran the Aviator Rail Restaurant at 245 West 42nd Street.

A new trainer, Arthur Kennedy, had already been chosen. Kennedy and his father had met Barrie several years earlier, when Barrie had introduced himself as Peter Westley. Westley now asked Kennedy to train Shem and Ep for an owner called William Marino. He brought Marino, a short, fat man, in his early thirties, to Kennedy's father's chicken and steak grill. Kennedy soon formed the opinion that Marino knew very little about horses.

He didn't need to. Marino, who gave his address as Duffy's Restaurant, or the Hotel New Yorker, was the front man for the gang.

Shortly afterward, Peter Lehrer, a horse transporter based at Elmont, Long Island, was contacted by Westley, who wanted some horses shipped to Maryland. Although Lehrer didn't know it at the time, he had done business with Westley before, when Mr. Westley was Mr. Christie. On that occasion, his $50 check had bounced.

Kennedy was sent on ahead to arrange stabling. On about October 1 Pete Sylvester, one of Lehrer's drivers, collected two horses from Belmont and one from Aqueduct and set off for Havre de Grace racetrack near Baltimore, 200 miles away. They were accompanied by Barrie, in his guise as Christie, a stable hand. While the unwitting Sylvester drove, Barrie painted.

"Considering horse-faking as an art, then the changing of Aknahton into Shem was a masterpiece," Barrie recalled, with characteristic conceit. "I worked on him in the van, doctored his three-year-old teeth to make them a year younger, and then dyed him, marking for marking, until he was the exact replica of Shem. I had to change his entire color and put two white legs on him, and all this in a moving van."[15]

Near Havre de Grace, the van stopped at Dr. Tubbs's farm, where Barrie had arranged for a horse to be lodged for a few days. The real Shem was unloaded, and the van drove on to the racetrack, where Ep and Aknahton were delivered to

Kennedy, who was told that they were Ep and Shem.

On October 3, 1931, Shem's impersonator lined up against eleven opponents in the opening contest of the day, a $1,300 maiden race for two-year-olds, over six furlongs. Since Shem was a gelding and Aknahton a colt, the ringer had been subjected to the indignity of having ice applied to his testicles, to retract them. Aknahton was to become familiar with indignities.

While associates spread their money off-track, Marino and Raymond were among the 20,000 strong crowd, busily ruining Shem's pari-mutuel dividend, which shrank to $13 for a $2 stake. "Believe me," said Barrie, "he carried all that the traffic would bear."

PINKERTON'S NATIONAL DETECTIVE AGENCY

Aknahton as Shem winning at Havre de Grace

Ridden by R. Leischmann, an innocent borrowed from the stable of George Widener, a future chairman of The Jockey Club, Shem skated home by four lengths. "Good God," said Leischmann, "I thought I was on an airplane. What a horse!" Maryland's Governor Albert Ritchie stepped forward and placed a garland of flowers around the winner's neck.[16]

Eyebrows rose, but no official questions were asked. Next day *The Morning Telegraph* published a lengthy report of the day's racing, by John FitzGerald, but his account of Shem's victory was tucked away towards the end of the piece.

"Supported by one of the heaviest come-back* orders of the meeting," FitzGerald wrote, "the first-time juvenile starter, Shem, running in the silks of William Marino, galloped off with the six-furlong dash for maidens of his age. Close to the early pace, he drew off to a commanding lead turning for home, and breezed on to the judges in 1:13, well in advance of his nearest rival."

Although FitzGerald had not given Shem's facile success much prominence, he was suspicious, and it was Raymond, loud in victory and flashing his winning tickets, who had fueled his suspicions. The veteran reporter started to investigate.

On October 6, writing under the pen name of "Beau Belmont," FitzGerald reported, " 'Nate' Raymond journeyed over to Havre de Grace to drop $2,400 in the machines on Shem, and the country was flooded with money for this first-time starter. The clockers never had seen him on the track prior to his appearance under colors."

PINKERTON'S NATIONAL DETECTIVE AGENCY

Nate Raymond

Barrie, exaggerating hugely, claimed that Raymond had won $50,000 and the gang $500,000 or $1 million.

Three days later, FitzGerald, and his editor, were confident enough to turn his suspicions into a front page splash. The curiously worded headline read, "Killing Made on 'Ringer' at Havre, Belief."

Beneath, a subsidiary line read, " 'Shem' Not Shem? That's Question Officials Are Now Investigating." Above a photograph of the race, *The Morning Telegraph* asked, "What Horse Won This Race?"

"Who was the winner of the first race on the closing day at

* Money sent to the track from off-track sources.

the recent Havre de Grace meeting?" asked FitzGerald. "There is a strong suspicion that the most important 'ringing' of many years was consummated in this event."[17]

By the time racing officials attempted to examine the winner, he had disappeared. According to Barrie, within an hour of the finish he phoned a gangster supposedly called "Big Tim" Maloney, who arranged for Vincent Coll to take a horsebox to Havre de Grace. It arrived at 2:00 a.m. and whisked Aknahton back to New York.

PINKERTON'S NATIONAL DETECTIVE AGENCY

Aknahton as Shem

Coll had some experience of racing. Earlier that year he had visited Saratoga and with Fats McCarthy and Frank Giordano confronted Billy Warren in the racetrack car park. Warren, a punter who also acted as a banker for bookmakers, often carried a lot of cash. Coll, a violent man even by gangland standards, had developed a habit of kidnapping people. Warren handed over $83,000. It was the sensible thing to do.

The Irish-born gangster had been one of Dutch Schultz's gunmen, but a few months before the ring-in at Havre de Grace, he fell out with Schultz, formed a breakaway gang, and engaged in a murderous war with his former boss.

On July 28, during a failed attempt to shoot Joey Rao, an ally of Schultz, Coll and Giordano accidentally killed a five-year-old boy, Michael Vengelli, and wounded four other children. There was a public outcry, and "Mad Dog" Coll picked up another nickname, "Baby Killer."

Shortly afterwards, when Mafia boss Salvatore Maranzano decided to eliminate Charlie "Lucky" Luciano and Vito Genovese, he chose Coll as their executioner, but on September 10 the intended victims got to Maranzano first.

If Coll was involved in spiriting Aknahton away from Havre

de Grace, Barrie was in the company of the most-wanted man in America, but Barrie was writing over three years later, and his imagination and desire to spice up his story had got the better of him.

By early October, Coll wasn't taking orders from anyone; he was hiding in Albany and making secret trips to New York. On October 2, the day before Shem's victory, members of Coll's gang murdered another of Schultz's men, Joe Mullins. Two days later Coll was arrested at the Cornish Arms Hotel and, the next day, he and Giordano were charged with Vengelli's murder. It is highly unlikely that, between Mullins' murder and his own arrest, Coll took time off to pick up a racehorse in Maryland.

In December, the "Baby Killer" was tried for the murder of Vengelli and acquitted, but it was a temporary reprieve. On February 9, 1932, Coll was shot to death while making a phone call from a drugstore across the road from the Cornish Arms.[18]

Barrie himself was on the run, pursued by investigators from Pinkerton's National Detective Agency, widely used to provide racetrack security services.

Within a day of the race, Aknahton and Ep had been driven from Havre de Grace to New York, where they briefly occupied stables used by a travelling circus. On October 13 Charles Hall, yet another of Barrie's aliases, arranged for both horses to be shipped to the Lake County Fairgrounds at Crown Point, Indiana, where they were looked after by stable hand Vladmar Sulick.

Meanwhile, Leo Kammerman, said to be the head waiter at Duffy's Restaurant, had arranged for Shem to be shipped from Dr. Tubbs's farm to A. Ray, alias "Nate" Raymond, in Jersey City. Shem was then taken to a converted garage at Connor's Hotel, in Water Witch, Highlands, New Jersey, under the supervision of Herman Brackenheimer.

Brackenheimer, known as "Blackie," was the hotel owner's son-in-law; a bootlegger who, the previous year, had managed

Max Schmeling's training camp during his preparation for a world championship fight with Jack Sharkey.

There were soon rumors that the ringer was Aknahton, but racing officials could not find either Aknahton or Shem. On October 15 *The Morning Telegraph* reported, "It has been common gossip on the racetrack for the past week that Aknahton, a three-year-old that formerly raced for Marshall Field, and which has since passed into the hands of J. Lebolt, ran in the name of Shem on October 3." Officials had been "attempting to solve the riddle of the 'Shem' case for several days now, but have so far encountered a stone wall at nearly every turn."

Shem's owner, William Marino, provided one wall. According to the *New York Daily News*, "He could speak only three words of English — 'I don't know.' "[19] Before long, Marino had removed his moustache and his surname, replacing it with Martin, and moved on.

On October 14 Kennedy submitted a statement to the stewards in which he explained that after the race Marino had told him that, because of a shortage of stabling and lack of suitable races for Shem, he would be shipped back to New York to race there.

When doubts were expressed about the winner's identity, Kennedy went to New York to look for Shem and Ep. Lehrer, the horse transporter, told him that they had been left at the receiving barn at Aqueduct. Someone had removed them.

On October 21 a Pinkerton's investigator found Shem at Connor's Hotel, and a week later another Pinkerton's operative discovered two heavily blanketed horses and Vladmar Sulick at the Lake County Fairgrounds.

Barrie was apparently unperturbed by the post-race furor. From his new base at Stevens Hotel in Chicago, "Mr. James" and Marino put together another small stable of horses, including Stick Around and Hickey. They invented a fictitious owner, G. Martin, and on October 21 gave Stick Around a dose of heroin and cocaine before running him at Hawthorne.

Ridden by M. Lewis, Stick Around responded as they hoped

he would, paid $21 for $2, and allegedly won the gang the equivalent of $10,000.

Meanwhile, at the Lake County Fairgrounds, Pinkerton's man watched Sulick and the two horses but could not establish their identity. He discovered that their owner was called Pat and drove a Lincoln car with red wheels, but neither Pat nor the Lincoln appeared.

On November 2 one of the two horses disappeared, along with Sulick, leaving a local man, Leslie Miller, to look after Ep. Barrie had given a friendly police officer $500 to let him spirit Aknahton away. The $1 million ringer was taken by a circuitous route to Pimlico where, under the alias of Sir Johren, he was stabled with A.F. Tavener, "a well known Western horseman."[20]

While Barrie frustrated Pinkerton's detectives, the Maryland Racing Commission reached the conclusion that the horse that had won the first race at Havre de Grace on October 3 was not Shem, but Aknahton. On November 18, in all their absences, seven men and three horses, Aknahton, Shem and Ep, were ruled off all the courses under the commission's jurisdiction.

Raymond, Kammerman, Marino, DeLott, Brackenheimer, and Sulick were listed, but Barrie's aliases confused the commission sufficiently for him to be cited as Patrick Christie.

The unfortunate Arthur Kennedy had his trainer's license revoked. "There is no evidence that Kennedy was a party to this fraud," the Commission acknowledged, "or that he knew that it was being perpetrated, but because he accepted without properly identifying either the owner or the horse, and saddled a three-year-old colt when the entered horse was a two-year-old gelding, indicates such carelessness that we do not consider that he is entitled to a license to train on Maryland tracks."[21]

Barrie wasted no time in breaching the ban. On November 25 Aknahton, dressed up as Hickey, owned by the imaginary G. Martin, with M. Lewis again on board, won a maiden race at Bowie, Maryland, at the satisfying odds of 9.1 to 1. Barrie claimed that the conspirators' winnings totaled about $200,000.

There was again a lot of come-back money, the stewards were suspicious, and two days later they arranged for Hickey's former owner to examine the winner. The real Hickey was produced for his inspection.

When Barrie went to New York to collect his share of the winnings, he was told that the money had been lost in a dice game. "We've all had a tough break. Never mind, limey, you'll get your money some other time."[22]

Some other time soon. On December 13 a man walked into a drug store in Baltimore and asked the assistant manager, Mr. Hunter, for a dozen cans of dark brown hair dye. He told Hunter that he wanted them in order to play a trick on a newlywed couple.

That day or the next, a Mr. Crawford and a Mr. Williams bought a three-year-old gelding called Gailmont from his breeder, L.N. Blackwell, for $100, with the promise of $100 more from the first purse Gailmont won. That wasn't likely since, according to one trainer, "I can throw my hat faster than that bum can run."[23]

Yet Crawford returned a few weeks later and gave Blackwell his money, which was a special stroke of good fortune, because John P. Crawford's real name was Peter Barrie, while Williams was probably William Marino.

They doubtless paid Blackwell to avoid him making a fuss. They could afford to because, on January 23, 1932, Gailmont had been heavily backed when winning a race for maidens at Agua Caliente, just across the Mexican border. Three days later, Gailmont won there again.

It was too late for "Nate" Raymond. On January 14 a New York court had sentenced him to prison for a minimum of five years for grand larceny and forgery.

Barrie had a new boss. A Pittsburgh gangster and his "nice boys" were said to have won almost $1 million on Gailmont.

It would have been hard to believe, even if it hadn't been Barrie who said it.

The "nice boys" won something because Barrie knew that the horse they were backing was not the untalented three-year-old Gailmont but the talented four-year-old Aknahton. The real Gailmont was at Howard Parks' barn near Pimlico, where he had been since the day Barrie bought him.

Perhaps Edgar Wallace won a little, too, because Wallace, taking time out from working in Hollywood, was at Agua Caliente, accompanied by jockeys Steve Donoghue and Michael Beary. To Wallace's delight, a race had been named in his honor.

"Edgar, would you like me to slip a ringer into your race?" Barrie asked him. "I don't know what you are doing in this part of the world," Wallace replied. "Keep out of my sight and don't give me any chance to guess."

It was to be Wallace's final racing fling; within a month, he was dead, aged 56.[24]

PINKERTON'S NATIONAL DETECTIVE AGENCY

Gailmont, aka Aknahton, at Agua Caliente in 1932

PINKERTON'S NATIONAL DETECTIVE AGENCY

Clovis Duhain

Pinkerton's frustrated detectives, led by Captain Clovis E. Duhain, had lost the trail but picked it up again when Gailmont, alias Aknahton, resumed his tour of the United States with a trip to Florida.

Barrie had intended to stable his horses at the new Tropical Park track in Miami, but manager Frank Bruen refused to give him stalls because they had been reserved in the name of a known gangster. Barrie and Tavener moved on to nearby Hialeah Park.

On February 23 Gailmont ran there in a six-furlong race restricted to three-year-olds. He moved into the lead two furlongs out but then faltered and dropped back. Aknahton's suspect tendon had given way.

Officials were suspicious. Of $8,489 wagered on Gailmont on the tote, an unusually high proportion, $7,000, was comeback money. The Hialeah stewards watched Gailmont closely. His color seemed strange. They took the horse into custody and contacted officials at Agua Caliente.

They discovered that the scale of betting there had also aroused suspicion, but the horse's owner, who presented himself as Willis Kane, had provided satisfactory answers to the officials' questions.

One of the officials, Judge Francis Nelson, told the Hialeah stewards that Kane had produced Gailmont's registration papers and that The Jockey Club had verified the horse's markings. "The horse had been thoroughly washed in the presence of officials," stated Nelson, who insisted, "the horse that raced at Agua Caliente was unquestionably Gailmont."

It was persuasive testimony, until Blackwell pointed out that the Gailmont he had sold was a gelding, while the winner at Agua Caliente was a colt. Also, Kane had claimed that Dr. H.J. McCarthy had examined Gailmont on his behalf before he bought him. When McCarthy, a Baltimore vet, was approached, he said that he had never seen Gailmont in his life.[25]

At Hialeah, when the horse's teeth were examined, they were found to be the teeth of a four-year-old. The colt was reminiscent of the horse that had won in the name of Shem at Havre de Grace the previous October. Aknahton had more white around his feet but, by dawn, so did Gailmont, who was shedding dye.

George Odom, Aknahton's former trainer, was not sure whether the horse was Aknahton or not, but Bill McKnight, Odom's foreman, and Harold Thurber, who had ridden Aknahton for Odom, were certain it was.

Exposure was quickly followed by disciplinary action. On February 26 the stewards of the Miami Jockey Club, not quite knowing who was who, suspended Crawford, Kane, and Tavener, along with five horses, Gailmont, Dunrock, Polish Prince, Danish Prince, and Lindby.

Neither Crawford nor Kane had been seen since the day of the race, although Tavener told the stewards that he had received messages from Crawford, in New York, and Kane, in Savannah, instructing him to sell the horses and settle outstanding bills. On February 27 the Florida Racing Commission ruled off the three men and five horses.

Barrie wasn't in New York, nor in Savannah, and Tavener knew he wasn't. He was still in Miami, first at the Shoreland Hotel, in the name of Patrick Williams, then at the El Comodora, in his own name.

According to Barrie, his fatal mistake was to have done someone a favor. Driving to Miami in his red-wheeled Lincoln, he gave a man a lift. When they got to Miami, the man promptly got himself arrested while stealing a watch. Barrie had probably talked about horse racing, and the man knew that the Lincoln had been taken to a garage for repairs.

Both the police and Pinkerton's men were looking for Barrie. They recognized him, and his car, from the man's account. Barrie's Lincoln, booked in the name of Mr. Williams, was at the Dade Motor Company's garage. Williams was due to collect it on Saturday, February 27.[26]

That day, Pinkerton's Edward Grogan was joined by Edward Weiss and Clovis Duhain. Williams phoned the garage to say that he would be there by 7:00 p.m. As the time approached, he phoned again; he would collect his car on Monday morning, February 29, between 8:00 a.m. and 9:00 a.m.

The Pinkertons, the police, and the Lincoln were ready. No one came. At 6:45 p.m., Williams phoned. He would collect the car tomorrow.

The waiting detectives were suspicious. They arranged for Detective William Driggers to sit in his car with his wife and keep an eye on the garage. At 8:00 p.m. Barrie and Tavener drove up and were arrested.

Barrie was at his best, and worst, in custody. Boastful, he enjoyed having an audience to boast to, while the audience found his frankness endearing. He readily admitted owning and dyeing Aknahton.

"Barrie is an engaging little cuss," E. Phocion Howard reported for *The New York Press*. "You could not help but admire his brazen frankness. He's the best con man I ever met." Two years later, Paul Gallico wrote about him in similar terms. "Utterly brazen, Barrie loves to dramatize himself and his nefarious work."

Mild-mannered and soft-spoken, "a merry twinkle darting from his dark grey eyes," the prisoner did not view his occupation as a crime. "I'm not beating anybody except some lousy bookmakers," Barrie insisted, "and they ought to be beat."

The Miami court seemed inclined to agree, since dyeing horses was not a criminal offense. The district attorney was reported to have remarked, "You can't charge a man with painting a horse. It's an unusual branch of artistry, but it doesn't appear to be criminal."

When it was suggested that cruelty might be involved, Barrie told the court that he gave horses carrots while he painted them. "Supposing you were to dye my hair," said the magistrate, "what would you give me?" "A large Scotch and a small soda, your Honor," Barrie replied.

The police stood aside, and the immigration authorities stepped in to start deportation proceedings, but it would be 60 days before the case could be heard. On March 13 Barrie was released on $500 bail. It would be two and a half years before the Pinkertons caught up with him.

"I wouldn't be surprised to see him bob up serenely with another ringer," wrote the enchanted Howard. Nor would Barrie. "It's the softest thing in the world to ring a horse," he bragged.

Several months earlier, in the wake of the Shem case, defensive action had been discussed. The *Daily Racing Form* noted that, "No man of good reputation has been guilty of 'ringing,' and when there is proper care taken in licensing trainers and proper control of the men who race horses is exercised, there can be no cases like that of Shem." Unfortunately, proper control was not always exercised.

It was suggested that, to qualify for racing, a horse should be with a recognized trainer for 30 days and that, if there was a query about its identity, the horse should not be allowed to run until the matter was resolved. Rather complacently, the article concluded, "The 'ringing' of horses is so rare now that it cannot be considered a serious menace to racing."[27]

The menace seemed more serious after Aknahton's latest escapades, and with doping also in mind, in March of 1932, New York introduced a law that made it a felony, punishable by up to three years in prison, to willfully tamper with a racehorse.

Barrie was undeterred. Fixing races was his job. He liked doing it, and the gangsters who controlled him liked him doing it. In fact, they probably insisted. To them, Barrie was merely another string to their gambling rackets.

The "King of the Ringers" set off for New York, and from a stable based — in as far as it was based anywhere — at Red Bank, New Jersey, proceeded to prove that his title was justified. Barrie launched himself on a bewildering ringing spree. The full torrent would be too much to bear; what follows is a sample.

On June 16, 1932, Harry and Ethel Williams booked into the Place Viger Hotel at the Canadian Pacific railway station in Montreal. Ethel was a slim, well-dressed, strikingly attractive blonde in her twenties. So was Ethel Patricia von Gerichten, and Mrs. E.P. Bell, and Jean Browning, and Helen Lewis, for they were one and the same.

Harry, who was not her husband, was not Harry either. At 44, he was almost twice as old as Ethel, a couple of inches shorter, with a dark complexion. His real name, of course, although he rarely used it, was Peter Christian Barrie.

Ethel's real name may once have been Patricia Moloney, an Irish girl Barrie met in Paris before moving to America, "the sweetest and cleverest and most daring little colleen that ever drew a crowd to a Paris beauty parlor." In 1935 he stated that "Patricia followed me out to America, and we've been 'ringing' together ever since."[28]

Mr. Ribey, Pinkerton's Canadian representative, discovered that the couple had stayed at the hotel until July 26. It was convenient for Blue Bonnets racetrack, where Barrie and his backers allegedly won almost £20,000 when Sun Memory won in the name of Hostage.

The same month, a four-year-old filly called Voltagreen was claimed at Arlington by T. Carro for $3,000 and then, according to Carro, sold to a stranger for $3,500. On July 23 Voltagreen ran in Montreal in the ownership of Mrs. E.P. Bell.

The trainer, Charles Garrigan, was suspicious of the Bells and suggested that they find another trainer. Barrie chose

Tommy Webber, whose string included a horse called Janie G, a three-year-old who had run poorly in her previous start, at Hamilton, and whom Webber had entered for a race at Fort Erie on August 6.

Converting Voltagreen into Janie G was only a minor obstacle. A more serious one was Janie G's owner-trainer who, according to Barrie, was not part of the conspiracy. Conveniently, Webber was temporarily hospitalized by a car accident. On August 6 Webber was still listed as Janie G's owner, but the trainer was now a J.S. Flynn.

Janie G won by four lengths and paid a welcome $28.20 for $2 staked. One of Barrie's followers, whom he called "Flash Harry" Kestering, but was generally named as George Kestering, Kesterling or Kesteringer, bought $800 of tickets on Janie G, not all to win, and collected $7,600. His insistence on being paid in cash increased suspicion. Racetrack officials seized the winner. Barrie, who claimed that the gang had won over $60,000, disappeared across the border, with Pinkerton's Captain Duhain in determined pursuit.

The Niagara Jockey Club and Canadian Racing Association launched an investigation. On August 11 Webber emerged from the hospital and told the stewards that the winning horse was not Janie G.

Janie G had been branded with the figure 16, but the brand did not appear on the winner. When the horse was washed with benzine, dye came off, and a white blaze appeared. By August 15 the stewards were satisfied that the winner was Voltagreen. On August 22 Garrigan inspected the horse and agreed with them.

The guilty parties were to be punished, but, not for the first time, it proved harder to put names to the ringer's connections than to the ringer. Various individuals had appeared and disappeared under various identities.

On September 10, acting on the stewards' recommendations, the Canadian Racing Association suspended H. Williams — aliases P. Christie, E.P. Bell — and George

Kestering, making two people in all. The stewards had discovered three versions of Peter Barrie, but not Barrie himself. Webber and Flynn were also suspended, the stewards declining to believe that they were innocent tools.

In mid-August, Captain Duhain caught up with the gang near Saratoga Lake, with Barrie in the guise of Howard Elkins. The gang and the two horses they had with them quickly disappeared.

Barrie's own reputation drove him on. "Men living the kind of life I was leading can't keep out of the gangs easily, even if they want to," he wrote later. "They are tied by the leg to their own bad record, and the boys had spotted and fastened on to me before I had been in Saratoga half a day."[29]

The boys, as ever, wanted another payday, and so did Barrie. They bought the appropriately named Regula Baddun, a reasonable three-year-old sprinter trained by James "Sunny Jim" Fitzsimmons, who had already trained one Triple Crown winner, Gallant Fox, and would soon train another, Omaha. Barrie then bought a two-year-old called Saintlite from George Widener. Their new owner was Mrs. Jean Browning, alias Barrie's lover.

The new acquisitions were similar in build but dissimilar in color and markings, with Saintlite conspicuous by virtue of a gray hind leg and a star on his forehead. Barrie spent two days making the dissimilar, similar. "I spent longer on the job than I ever had before," he wrote, inevitably adding, "I turned out a masterpiece.

"First, I plucked Regula Baddun's mane and tail to match those of the two-year-old, and then I attended to his teeth. After that I had to bleach him almost white before I could dye him Saintlite's exact shade of light brown. The star on the forehead was an easy matter. There remained only the leg.

"This peculiar 'stocking' was not just a plain gray. It was really rather like the pelt of a silver fox, and to get a perfect effect I had to work on Regula Baddun's leg with teasels, almost bleaching hair for hair. It was the most difficult piece of 'painting' I have ever done in my life, but when I had finished, I stood back and stared delightedly at my work. I think I know what an artist must feel when he goes to look at his picture hanging on the line at the Academy."[30]

The finished picture was sent to New York trainer Elmer Fred, who was under the impression that Mrs. Browning was a wealthy owner. After proving himself in a workout, Saintlite was entered for a two-year-old maiden race at Jamaica racetrack on Long Island, with jockey Frank Coltiletti booked.

It was October 3, 1932, exactly a year since Shem had ensured Barrie's place in American history, but the outcome was less successful. Saintlite opened at 30-1 and closed at 10-1, with the gang allegedly standing to win $110,000, but there was a problem with the ringer; he had a suspect ankle. Saintlite held second place into the straight, then broke down.

While officials pondered the betting patterns, Barrie swiftly removed Saintlite and handed him to a member of the gang.

On October 19 Mrs. Jean Browning was ruled off by the New York Jockey Club, and Elmer's license suspended. The *New York World-Telegram* reported, "Barrie probably will be ruled off the turf in New York as a result of the job. This would not be a novelty to him, however, as he has been banned by the tracks of England, Canada, Maryland, and Miami."[31]

While Pinkerton's detectives continued their unavailing search, Barrie, predictably broke, sold his story to the *New York Daily News*. The first of a dozen slender installments appeared on November 21, under the banner, "$6,000,000 Race Horse Ringer." The final zero might have been a mistake.

"Herewith begins the most amazing race track serial ever printed," declared the *Daily News*, "the story of Paddy Barrie, Ringer of Horses and Master Horse Faker."

Barrie was said to have left the country three days earlier, for an unknown destination, leaving behind him "a trail of the most sensational swindles in the annals of racing."

"I never had any compunction about ringing a horse," Barrie revealed. "Certainly it was crooked, but all racing was crooked. The game is full of thieves. I was cheating cheaters."

Readers were offered a spritely dash through Barrie's stateside career, syndicated to other newspapers for delayed publication in December.

Barrie was presented, not merely as the "master equine make-up man" but also as an expert doper, his favorite prescription being "heroin mixed with digitalis, cola nut, glycerine, and strychnine. A few shots of this and the horse wants to take off." Barrie always doped his ringers, he said, "to make assurance doubly sure."

It hadn't always worked, which was why he was now "broke and a fugitive. The gangsters who employed him took the lion's share of the loot."

The Pinkerton's Detective Agency was assured that it could suspend its manhunt, but if Barrie had left the country, he hadn't left it for long. "I was in England only a month," he said later, "and I came back to Canada and so back into the states."

That brief interlude may have been earlier in the year, if at all, for, on December 14, Steve Mabey questioned the suggestion that Barrie was out of the country, insisting that, a few days earlier, he was at Laurel, in Maryland. It no doubt suited Barrie to have people, especially Pinkerton's people, believe that he had gone.[32]

Barrie was active during 1933, and so in October was "the million dollar ringer," Aknahton, still only a five-year-old, but unsound. After breaking down at Hialeah, Aknahton was reported to have been sold to William Gallagher of New York, who later claimed to have allowed a Mr. M. Searborough to take Aknahton to race at horse fairs in Pennsylvania.

On October 5, at a fair at York, Pennsylvania, Aknahton, racing in the name of Chinese Puzzle, finished second to Justa Flapper. He would have won if one of the best local jockeys had not turned the ride down, forcing Chinese Puzzle's connections to put up an apprentice, who gave the horse a poor ride.

Two men from Baltimore recognized Aknahton and, a few days later, the York Fair Association ruled that, "For the lack of proper identification, and pending further investigation, the horse Chinese Puzzle is suspended, as is also Mickey Limerio, his owner and trainer."[33] Aknahton had disappeared; so had Mr. Searborough.

Two months later, a man called Michael Krock was suspended by the stewards of the Shenandoah Valley Jockey Club after a horse called Hustle Over was found in a "painted" condition, apparently being prepared for a race at the newly opened track at Charles Town, West Virginia.

Krock was an associate of Waxey Gordon, real name Irving Wexler, a former partner of Arnold Rothstein. Gordon was a leading bootlegger and racketeer who was currently being tried for tax evasion.

Krock was uncooperative and, while the black dye faded to brown, there was speculation over the horse's identity. Was it Hustle Over, or Two Brooms, or Aknahton?

On December 30, 1933, *The New York Press* asked its readers, "Can You Tell Us Where Aknahton Is?" with the offer of a year's free subscription for information leading to his discovery. Aknahton had not been seen since the Chinese Puzzle incident.

Barrie was ideally placed to claim the prize, since he had purchased Hustle Over, Two Brooms, and Aknahton, but he didn't claim it. When the Charles Town stewards' arrested the mystery horse, Barrie, in his latest disguise as Mr. Smithson, disappeared.

In January 1934, the horse also disappeared. Krock and an associate had seized him and handed him to Barrie, who converted himself into Mr. Garvan and moved on to Carolina. His had become a life constantly on the move, driving the roads of New Deal America, changing addresses as often as he changed names

Pinkerton's detectives were still fitfully on the ringer's trail. In February 1933, they traced Ethel Patricia von Gerichten and her mother Mae Enright to an apartment block in Astoria, New York. That July, they received information that Barrie had been seen in a Brooklyn saloon with Ernest Vought, a racehorse owner and ex-jockey.

In December, at Charles Town, a Dick Hohlman had been seen at a hotel with Barrie's girlfriend. Pinkertons men couldn't find Hohlman nor a car registered in the name of George von Gerichten, believed to be Barrie's driver, Phil Olwell.

In April 1934, the disaffected Mabey told a Pinkerton's detective that Barrie was in New York and regularly visited certain newsstands and a particular tobacco store. They still couldn't find him.

Barrie's downfall, inevitable sooner or later, stemmed from another ill-advised association, this time with John Galvin, whom Barrie met at a gambling joint in New York. They became partners in a horse called Easy Sailing but fell out.

In August of 1934, Easy Sailing was at Galvin's stable at Saratoga. Francis Ginley, a stable hand there, was approached by two women and a man. The younger woman, "a flashy individual of considerable beauty," in her twenties, told Ginley that Easy Sailing was her horse, and she had come to take it away.[34]

The woman, who called herself Ethel, took the horse to Patrick Malone's nearby barn, accompanied by Mae Enright and John Bottnick. Ginley followed them, then tipped off Captain Duhain.

When the Pinkerton's man and the police arrived at Malone's barn, they found Barrie spectating and arrested all four. A note written by the younger woman was in the same handwriting as that of Jean Browning, warned off after the Regula Baddun case. It was August 14, 1934, and Duhain confessed that he took great pleasure in Barrie's arrest. It had been a long chase.

The Blood-Horse remarked, "His arrest marks the end of two years of work on the trail of the little Englishman who has been blatant in advertising his skill in disguising one horse to run as another."

Barrie was taken to Saratoga County Jail, where he gave his birthplace, wrongly, as London, just as when he had applied for a passport, he had given a false date of birth. Typically, he appeared unconcerned. "He was boastful and very proud of his feats, even though he was broke," David Alexander remembered.[35]

Barrie was charged with having attempted to steal Easy Sailing, but Galvin failed to appear at the court hearing and Barrie, who claimed to own the horse, had not taken an active part in its seizure. The jury declined to indict him either on that charge or on a charge of issuing a worthless check.

The con man had won a small battle but still lost the war. He was promptly rearrested by the immigration authorities. Barrie had given his pursuers a good run, a very good one, from north to south and east to west, but the game was finally up.

In October 1934, at Ellis Island, Peter Christian Barrie was ordered to be deported for having entered the United States illegally and having a prison record. On November 3 a Pinkerton's operative submitted his final report. "Today, I went to the Cunard-White Star Line pier, foot of West 14th Street, New York, for the purpose of boarding the *SS Caledonia* to observe Patrick C. Barrie." At noon, he observed him sail for Glasgow.

A recent history of racing at Saratoga, recalling Barrie's arrest, noted, "The last of the great artists was deported to Scotland and died six months later." Barrie was always good at fooling people. The "King of the Ringers" wasn't finished yet.

"The clever Turf rogue has a marvellous chance in England," Barrie himself remarked, doughtily, a few months later.[36]

Simmering Down 3

"Ringer" Barrie returned to London and set about selling his story. It was a good story, the story of a man who had once been notorious in Britain and for the past twelve years had been "ringing the changes with racehorses in the United States, cleaning up millions of dollars as fake winner after winner, cleverly dyed by Barrie, came romping home."

It was a story, not merely embroidered, but without a happy ending. Barrie had sailed for America, "pretty well down to loose change." Now he had returned, age 46, "more or less broke." Barrie enjoyed telling his story, but the main reason he told it was because he needed the money.[1]

That, and vanity, was why he had sold his story to *John Bull* in 1923, why he sold it to the *New York Daily News* in 1932, and why he was selling it again, this time to *The People*. It would not be the last time that Barrie sold his story. "You can't hold on to crooked money," he wrote, to excuse himself. "It's as slippery as a fish and, like a fish, it won't keep."[2]

His latest offering was the most substantial. The first weekly installment appeared on January 25, 1935, to be followed by twenty more. The story Barrie told was fascinating, self-promoting, an infuriating mixture of accurate detail and pure invention, rarely interrupted by the mention of dates or chronological sequence. It portrayed a whirlwind of activity, most of it fraudulent.

After the final episode on June 9, Barrie immediately launched a new series, lasting six weeks, called "What Punters Don't Know." They didn't know that the stewards rarely exercised their power to order saliva tests; that you could stop horses by putting lead discs in their bandages; that trainers put extra weights in weight cloths, knowing that only the first four jockeys home had to weigh in.

Based on his experiences in the United States, Barrie had some sensible suggestions to make, all of them, inevitably, ignored by the Jockey Club. He advocated starting stalls, called for the earlier declaration of horses and jockeys, urged the appointment of paid stipendiary stewards, and explained how the selling race system was open to abuse.

Form 178. 10-30-10m. ANSY

All Offices.

CRIMINAL RECORD

Number

Name PETER CHRISTIAN BARRIE.

Aliases Patrick Christian Barrie, Patrick Christy, Westley,
Patrick Williams, E.P. Bell, W.H.Browning, Patrick Christie.

Criminal Occupation Swindler (Horse Ringer) F. P. Class 11 R O / 21 . A 16 Ref. 11/2

Date Arrested March 1, 1932. Arrested at Miami, Fla.

Crime charged (Horse Ringing) XXXXXXXXX Held on small bond for deportation. Bond forfeited. Now XXXXXXXXX at large.

Date sentenced

Institution

CRIMINAL RECORD

3.20.1917. Liverpool, England, Police Court as Peter Christian Barrie; charged False Pretense (Scotland Yard No. 6199-17). Sentenced two months.

9.7.1920. London, England; False Pretense - 3 years Penal Servitude.

11.24.1927. Arrested Baltimore,Md.; charged Fugitive from Winnepeg, Canada. Was not extradited to Canada, but given hours. (Winnepeg charge Obtaining Money under False Pretense).

REMARKS: Said to be wanted by Mechanicsville, N.Y. Police on warrant charging him with obtaining $900.00. by means of false pretense.

WARRANT Under name of E.P.Ball issued for Peter Christian Barrie at Toronto, Canada, charging conspiracy and fraud in connection with the "ringing" of a horse at the Fort Erie,Canada, track (warrant issued about October, 1932) but the Toronto authorities will not extradite unless located and arrested in Canada.)

25-
11.1.32.

PINKERTON'S NATIONAL DETECTIVE AGENCY

Peter Barrie's criminal record, November 1932

Needless to say, he had abused it, by deliberately running a horse to be second, because half of the difference between the amount the winner was entered to be sold for and the winning bid went to the owner of the runner-up. There were some fierce battles for second place.

Barrie wrote to David Alexander, an American journalist, to ask him to try to get his story syndicated in the United States, but nothing seems to have come of it.

The People's blazing announcement of his return, " 'Ringer' Barrie Comes Back To Town," proved a mixed blessing. It was useful publicity for Barrie's career as a tipster — five years later he was still advertising himself as "The Man Who Wrote His Reminiscences In *The People*" — but it also put the racing authorities on their guard.[3]

Barrie needed money and, his story sold, he knew only one way to get it, crookedly. One of the things punters didn't know and Barrie didn't tell them, was how Rhum came to win the Westenhanger Selling Plate at Folkestone on Monday, June 24, 1935, while he was still writing for *The People*.

On June 25 *The Sporting Life*'s Meyrick Good reported, "Dr. S.A. Schuyler, a student at Charing Cross Hospital, gained his first success when Rhum got up on the line to snatch a short-head verdict from Diocles. His success was, indeed, a case of novice's luck, as Dr. Schuyler only recently purchased the gelding from Stanley Wootton."

The well-supported 7-2 joint second favorite aroused the stewards' suspicions, and the Jockey Club launched an investigation. They discovered that Dr. Schuyler was not a qualified doctor but an American student at Charing Cross Hospital with access to drugs. Schuyler shared an address with Barrie.

The student was addressing envelopes for Barrie's tipping service. "I was the Captain Christie who helped a Dr. Schuyler buy a horse called Rhum from Stanley Wootton," Barrie later confessed. "I was no captain and Schuyler was no doctor."

As a disqualified person, Barrie could not own horses himself. He had to borrow other people. Schuyler was one of his "owners for a day."[4]

According to Barrie, Rhum was collected from Wootton on the morning of the race, then given Barrie's special tonic, his "harmless dynamite," on the way to Folkestone. The Jockey Club's investigator reported a different sequence of events.[5]

On June 23 a telegram had arrived at Tattersalls's depot in Knightsbridge, where Rhum was already waiting. The telegram was from Schuyler, to inform them that his stableman would be accompanying Rhum on the journey to Folkestone.

Early the next morning an old man arrived at the depot. At 8:00 a.m. as they were about to set off, another man with an American accent approached the driver and said that he was acting for Dr. Schuyler and was traveling to the meeting by car. He tipped the driver five shillings and the horsebox set off, followed by the man in his car.

They stopped near Wrotham, the old stableman walked the horse, and another man joined them. The American left his car with the newcomer and rode with the horsebox driver until they had passed through Ashford, about 10 miles from the racecourse, where he told the driver that he would like to see how the horse was getting on. The American got into the back of the horsebox while the stableman sat with the driver.

About 100 yards from the racecourse, the American said that he wanted to get a shave, got out, and walked off. The American was believed to have been Barrie, and the reason he was in the horsebox was to dope the horse.

The stewards refused to allow the Folkestone winner to take up his next engagement, and on August 10, at Lewes races, Rhum was offered for sale. There was no bid, and Rhum was later registered as having been sold to Edward Emmanuel. Emmanuel was allegedly "head of a syndicate which included the infamous Barrie."

The Jockey Club reacted by refusing to allow trainers to

accept horses owned by Emmanuel or other suspected associates or aliases of Barrie, including a Captain J.E. Holliday. In the case of Silkstar, they were too late.

On July 9 Silkstar, owned and trained by Harry Cottrill, was due to run in the Open Selling Plate at Salisbury. Shortly before the race, Silkstar was sold and ran in the ownership of Captain Holliday.

The same horsebox driver who had taken Rhum to Folkestone drove Silkstar to Salisbury, and the same man joined him on the journey. Sent off the 5-2 favorite, in a field of 13, Silkstar finished fifth. *The Sporting Life* reported, "Silkstar, who changed hands before the race for the Open Selling Plate, performed indifferently." Barrie had either successfully administered a "stopper" or unsuccessfully administered a stimulant.

Four days later a four-year-old maiden called Brief won a three-runner race at Hamilton, at 6-4. Barrie, disguised as a gentleman farmer, had bought Brief at the Newmarket Sales, in the name of an American friend of Schuyler's, Mr. A. Bicchieri, another fleeting owner. Brief had been "treated" with Barrie's tonic.

In 1939 Brief's success was one of those listed on a circular issued by Barrie to promote his tipping business. The horses he listed had often been bought shortly before they raced and were raced in the name of innocent dupes.[6]

The other horses on the list included Racker and Foxdale. Barrie claimed that when Racker won a selling race at York on October 7, 1936, at 100-8, he had been delivered to his new owner that very day. Racker was trained by Willie Arrowsmith, the trainer of Brief, and an associate of Barrie's. The owner was a Mr. S. Childs.

Several months earlier Arrowsmith had inquired about using some stables at Bretby Park, near Burton-upon-Trent. The tenant, Clarence Bailey, agreed, and on October 24 three horses arrived, including Racker. On December 20 Foxdale joined them.

Arrowsmith went away for a few days over Christmas, and on Christmas Day Mr. Childs arrived. When Arrowsmith returned on December 28, Bailey told him to take his horses away. Bailey had not been paid any rent and had supplied the fodder himself.

Arrowsmith left, but Childs, who Bailey discovered was also known as Wilson, stayed on until the end of April of 1937, when Bailey locked the stables to prevent Childs gaining access. The landlord had still not received any money.

Meanwhile, on February 15, Foxdale won a selling hurdle at Derby, at 10-1, having been entered as trained privately and owned by Miss H. McAlpine, reputedly a friend of Barrie's.

After leaving Bretby Park, Childs, alias Wilson, alias Barrie, lived for a while in Southport, where he was involved with a trainer called William Bargh, a horse called Foxflair, and the application of dye on horses racing at "flapping" meetings, held outside the Jockey Club's jurisdiction. Like Foxdale, Foxflair was owned by Miss H. McAlpine, an owner for several days.

Brief had also been sent flapping. "He won more than fifty races that way, with 'help,' and we cleaned up a packet," claimed Barrie, who did not become more believable with age.

Shortly afterward he was reported to have been living at the County Hotel in Newcastle. In June of 1937, he allegedly obtained £70 by fraud from a Newcastle tipster, Harry Peart, in connection with the purchase of a horse called Witticism.

On January 3, 1938, Clarence Bailey went racing at Manchester. He was approached by Childs, alias Wilson, who asked if he had seen a trainer called "Snowy" Parker. When Bailey said that he had, Childs asked him to find Parker, as Parker had bought a horse called Inglesant from him after it had won a selling hurdle at Wolverhampton on December 28. Childs wanted to buy the horse back.

Bailey found Parker and passed on the message. He already suspected that Childs and Wilson were aliases for "Ringer" Barrie.[7]

Inglesant was another of the horses mentioned in Barrie's 1939 circular. When the nine-year-old won at Wolverhampton, ridden by Bruce Hobbs, at 100-8, he was listed as being trained privately and owned, not by Childs or Wilson, but by T.R. Patterson.

Patterson had given his address as 36 Athol Street, Douglas, Isle of Man. No one called Patterson lived there, but Patterson was the nephew of someone who did, Mrs. Fielding. Any mail addressed to Patterson was forwarded to another address, 1 Princes Avenue, Liverpool.

Patterson was not the only person who lived at 1 Princes Avenue. Rooms on the first floor were let to Peter Barrie. The situation was reminiscent of that of Dr. Schuyler, the young medical student. Patterson was a 21-year-old vet who had been persuaded to play the part of racehorse owner.

Inconveniently, at the auction following Inglesant's victory, Evan Parker, bidding on behalf of Victor Stout, a Lancashire bookmaker, had bought the winner for 105 guineas. Inglesant was taken to Parker's yard in Shropshire, where its new trainer was alarmed by the horse's behavior. A Jockey Club investigator reported, "According to Mr Parker, the animal was half mad and, in his opinion, undoubtedly had been doped."

Barrie was determined to get the horse back quickly. On New Year's Eve, Parker received a telephone call from Liverpool. The caller explained that he was phoning on Patterson's behalf. Patterson would like to buy Inglesant back for £130.

A deal was arranged, and even before the money was paid and the horse handed over, Barrie acted to remove Patterson from the scene and introduced another innocent, Miss Anna McCarthy.

On January 2, 1938, Patterson wrote to Weatherbys, informing them that all Inglesant's engagements, which included a selling hurdle at Haydock on January 5, were to be transferred to Miss McCarthy.

James McBeath, a diligent Jockey Club investigator, described McCarthy as "another of Barrie's dupes. She lives in a flat at 99 Bedford Street, Liverpool, quite close to Barrie's address. I understand she works in a Liverpool café and Barrie, with his usual cunning, one day asked her how she would like to own a racehorse." She liked the idea.

Parker later recalled that, on January 3, at Manchester racecourse, he was approached by Bailey, who said, " 'Ringer' Barrie is looking for you." Parker replied that he would wait for him at the back of the bar. Barrie appeared and suggested paying £30 on account for Inglesant, with the balance paid when the horse was moved.

Barrie then remarked, "Inglesant is entered for Haydock, but it will not win unless it is given a dose. He had brandy at Wolverhampton. On the other hand, you can make a bit by getting the bookmakers to lay it."

The next day the £100 arrived, soon followed by three men in an old cattlebox. One of them, called Dodd, said that he was taking the horse to his stables near Manchester. They were believed to be the same stables from which Inglesant had been sent to win at Wolverhampton on December 28.[8]

Inglesant duly appeared at Haydock on January 5, started the 7-2 favorite for the Wednesday Selling Hurdle, and having been badly left, finished last of the 12 finishers.

McBeath was told that a coup was planned for January 24, at Birmingham. The horse was entered in McCarthy's name, still trained privately, for the Stechford Selling Hurdle and on the morning of the race appeared among the probable runners, but Inglesant did not run.

By the time Inglesant appeared among the entries for another selling hurdle, at Leicester on February 1, Barrie had organized another game of musical chairs, and Inglesant was now owned by Mr. R. Dickens.

Richard Dickens was the 30-year-old managing director of Pureal Silks Limited, in Smethwick, near Birmingham. He was a prospective candidate for Birmingham City Council who knew nothing about racing but at the Queen's Hotel had got into conversation with an affable man called Captain Wilson who owned a string of racehorses.

Wilson told Dickens that he would be selling Inglesant cheaply at Birmingham races on January 24. Dickens agreed to buy the horse for £50 and was happy to leave all the arrangements to Wilson. He didn't even know precisely where Inglesant was stabled.

The owner of Dickens' company, Sidney Wharton, was better informed. Wharton was a substantial commission agent and racehorse owner, regarded by McBeath as "a very suspicious character." Wharton was also an associate of Barrie.

Satisfied that Dickens was the latest in a growing line of dupes, McBeath arranged to meet him. On January 28 he warned Dickens that Captain Wilson was really the notorious Peter Barrie and arranged to meet Dickens at Leicester races on February 1.

If McBeath was hoping to confront Barrie, he was disappointed. When the two men met at Leicester, Dickens told the Jockey Club investigator that Barrie had written to say that he was too busy to come. Dickens had already decided that Inglesant would not run, and the following day he wrote to Captain Wilson, at 1 Princes Avenue, informing him that he had a buyer for Inglesant and would like to bring him to see the horse. The horse was nowhere to be seen.

Two months earlier an informant had told the Jockey Club that horses appearing as owned and trained by M.J. Dawson were actually owned by Barrie. The informant was not regarded as reliable, and no action seems to have been taken.[9]

On February 10, 1938, Unlimited, ridden by D. Beeforth and trained by M.J. Dawson, won a selling hurdle at Derby. A year later, on February 14, 1939, Dawson was the rider and Beeforth the trainer when Unlimited, owned by Mrs. E. Spalding, won the Stayers' Handicap Hurdle at Nottingham after being backed down to 9-2 second favorite.

The Nottingham stewards were unhappy, asked Dawson to explain the horse's running compared to a previous outing three days earlier, were not satisfied with his explanation and referred the matter to the stewards of the National Hunt Committee.

On February 23 the *Racing Calendar* reported, "The National Hunt stewards, not being satisfied with Mr. Dawson's explanation, warned him off all courses where National Hunt Rules are in force. The stewards also withdrew the licenses to train and ride of D.A. Beeforth, trainer of the horse."

No further explanation was given, but there was more to the stewards' action than Dawson's riding.

Barrie was operating a tipping service from 20 Orange Street, near Trafalgar Square. McBeath reported that Barrie had tipped Unlimited when it won at Birmingham on January 24, at 10-1.[10]

When Barrie tipped a horse, the Jockey Club, understandably, were suspicious. They may have suspected that Mrs. E. Spalding, like Dr. S.A. Schuyler, T.R. Patterson, Anna McCarthy, and Richard Dickens, was being used as a cloak. Whatever Mrs. Spalding's status, before long there was evidence that Barrie had recruited another dupe. This time the dupe fought back.

In May 1939, Mrs. Dolores Hunter met a man called Captain Christie in Jack's Club, two doors away from Barrie's office in Orange Street. "Do you want to buy a horse to win a race?" the Captain asked. When Mrs. Hunter showed interest, Christie encouraged her to buy St. Botolph.

St. Botolph's owner, A.B. Tully, a Kelso vet, received a phone call from a Major Christie, who said he was acting for Dolores Hunter, who was interested in buying the horse. Tully said he would accept £100, and they finally agreed on £80, plus another £20 if the seven-year-old won a race.

Hunter supplied a check for £80, and Christie sent a man called Martin to collect St. Botolph, who was driven straight to Cartmel, where he had already been entered for the Grange Selling Handicap Hurdle.

At about 11:30 a.m. that Whit Monday morning, May 29, Cartmel's clerk of the course, Horace Pain, received an anonymous telegram from Southend-on-Sea. It read, "Ringer Barrie owns St. Botolph and is attending to it at 12:25."

While the stewards were pondering this puzzling message, Mrs. Hunter informed them that she had recently bought St. Botolph, together with its engagements, and produced the necessary documentation. The stewards decided that the horse was qualified to run. Ridden by G. Spann, St. Botolph proceeded to win but was not auctioned afterward, as the horse could not be found.

On June 1 Tully received another call from Major Christie, asking him if he would buy St. Botolph back for £80, a sum doubtless intended for Barrie's pocket rather than Mrs. Hunter's, but no agreement was reached.

Hunter had also received a phone call, from a man who said, "You don't know who I am but I am Ringer Barrie, and unless you send me £20 or £25, I shall do the horse in." If true, Barrie must have been desperate, because intimidation was not a standard part of his repertoire.

Hunter promptly instructed Cartmel's clerk of the course to send St. Botolph, who had resurfaced, to London and sent a man called Tunley to collect the horse at Euston Station. When St. Botolph arrived, the horse was accompanied by Martin.

Tunley went to the office to make the necessary payment and was told that there was nothing to pay, since a check had already been received, signed by Barrie. When Tunley returned to the horse, it had disappeared.

Hunter contacted the police, and the horse and Martin were tracked down. Tunley took Martin to a police station with a view to charging him with stealing his bridle. While there, Martin told Hunter about several horses that belonged to Barrie but were registered in other people's names.

Barrie allegedly sent Hunter several threatening letters and cheekily joined her in resorting to a solicitor, putting Messrs. A. Wood & Co. into brief battle with Addis, Edwards & Co. On June 9 Hunter's solicitor wrote to Cartmel, which had withheld payment of the prize money. "We are instructed to say that Mr. Barrie's statement that the ownership of the horse is in dispute is sheer impudence."[11]

Barrie's secret ownership or control of horses may have been behind a cryptic announcement in the *Racing Calendar* for July 13, 1939, which reported, with characteristic lack of elaboration, that "The stewards of the National Hunt Committee continued on Thursday last an inquiry into the ownership and management and training of the following horses, viz: Mrs. E. Spalding's Unlimited, Miss Doris Brake's Ellanberg and Hair Shirt, and Mr. F. Barber's Belladore, Luron, Pikanti, and Willowmead.

"They declared the above mentioned horses to be perpetually disqualified for all races to which National Hunt Rules apply, that F. Barber be warned off all courses where National Hunt Rules are in force, and that no further entries be accepted from Miss D. Brakes and Mrs. E. Spalding."

Most of these horses were not good enough to win, and Barrie's chronic problem was lack of funds. He needed a supply of innocents, not merely to disguise his ownership of horses but also to pay for them. Schuyler, Patterson, and McCarthy may have supplied only their names, but Dickens and Hunter paid for horses that Barrie sought to control.

In November 1938 McBeath had reported, "Barry (sic) has lately been in straitened circumstances and has gone to prison on two occasions for two months at a time, for debt."

In 1940 Barrie was still running his tipping service from Orange Street. "Sorry Pedigree did not run," he told his clients on March 12, "for reasons which I hope you will appreciate, need not be mentioned here. However, Pedigree will run under new ownership and should win next time out."

On March 3 Robert Gore, who trained Pedigree at Findon, in Sussex, had received a phone call from a Captain Jones. Jones was anxious to buy a cheap horse for his son to ride at Fontwell. Pedigree had an engagement in a selling hurdle at Fontwell on March 5, and Gore agreed to sell the nine-year-old for £60.

Jones, who gave his address as Irving House, Irving Street, London, sent Gore £20 as a deposit, but the trainer heard nothing more. He sent a telegram to Jones on March 12 and a registered letter the day after. On March 15, puzzled, he wrote to Weatherbys, asking if they knew of Captain Jones.[12]

Perhaps Barrie simply couldn't come up with the other $40. When Pedigree next appeared, on April 24, he was still owned by Gore.

Mr. Childs, Captain Wilson, Major Christie, Captain Jones; a second identity was second nature to Barrie, now 52 and struggling. With the racing program heavily curtailed during the Second World War, and suspended altogether for several months in 1940, the demand for tipsters fell, and there were fewer opportunities for race-fixing.

Barrie had worked with horses in his own, perverse way all his adult life; horse racing was all he knew. Unless he found a new medium for his talents, the war years must have been difficult ones.

In 1945 the Jockey Club's William Bebbington spotted Barrie at a race meeting. "I met him and told him he must go," Bebbington recalled. "He did so quietly. It is a pity he should have decided that swindling on the Turf was the career for which he was mapped out. He was so capable that he might have made a fortune if he had gone straight."[13]

That was never likely. As Steve Mabey had observed, Barrie had "so much larceny in him," but his criminal cleverness was flawed. He had charm and audacity, perseverance and resilience. Barrie could persuade complete strangers to buy horses, win over journalists, and present himself, convincingly, as a cheeky rascal, dangerous only to bookmakers.

What he could never do was keep the money. He left the gambling largely to others, to Gilbert Marsh, Murray Marks, "Nate" Raymond and other criminals, and relied on them to give him his share or on clients to pay for his tips. They regularly let him down and so did the horses. Without money himself, Barrie was forced to rely on others to fund his frauds. Involving other people increased the risk of exposure.

In the past, when he had money, Barrie had lived well, in city hotels, with his red-wheeled Lincoln, a tall blonde on his arm, proud of his unique place in horse racing, the King of the Ringers but, for a long time it had been a life on the move, on the run. He had no home, no contact with relatives, no obviously lasting friends. He was a man without an address, at least, not in his own name.

Maybe he kept in touch with Patricia von Gerichten. In September 1937, the U.S. Immigration Service received an anonymous phone call claiming that Barrie had been at Belmont Park. In November 1939 he was reported to have returned to the United States and to have been in contact with von Gerichten, who was living with her mother, Mae Enright, and with Phil Olwell and another man in Flushing, Long Island. Perhaps, although it seems doubtful whether Barrie could have afforded the trip, even if he could have talked his way in on arrival.[14]

Although Barrie had left America virtually penniless, there had always been criminals willing and able to back his "ringing." In Britain, partly as a result of advertising his return in *The People*, Barrie was a marked man.

He had no wealthy backers; he could not seek fresh anonymity in a distant state; he could rarely afford to buy horses himself, and the ones he periodically controlled were barely capable of winning a selling race, doped or not. "Ringer" Barrie was on the slide.

Barrie himself had nothing to fear from the Jockey Club's superficially hard line on doping since he was already a disqualified person, but licensed trainers did. The relevant rule warned uncompromisingly that, "If in any case it shall be found that any drug or stimulant has been administered to a horse for the purpose of affecting its speed in a race, the license of the trainer of the horse shall be withdrawn, and he shall be declared a disqualified person."

The odds against detection were long because few samples were tested. In flat racing, between 1946 and 1951, a grand total of 28 sweat and saliva samples were tested by the Jockey Club, 13 of which proved positive. Under National Hunt

Rules, between 1948 and 1951, 11 samples were tested, seven of which were positive.

The few trainers whose horses tested positive faced the inflexible rigor of the rules. In 1947 James Russell's license was withdrawn after Boston Boro, the winner of the John O'Gaunt Plate at Lincoln on March 26, tested positive. Russell sued the Jockey Club stewards, ultimately unsuccessfully.

In 1949 George Allden's license was withdrawn after Luxuriant tested positive after winning at Pontefract. "I consider the verdict most unjust," the Newmarket trainer complained. "Although I am innocent, I am deprived of earning my livelihood through circumstances over which I have no control. I believe that doping is being carried out by doping gangs on a large scale in both Newmarket, Epsom, and possibly other training centers, and that the racing world would have a shock if every case could be brought to light."

In 1950 the stewards withdrew John Beary's license after La Joyeuse was found to have been doped with cocaine. His brother Michael protested, "John can only regain his livelihood and honor by finding the man who doped La Joyeuse, which is like looking for a needle in a haystack. My brother John is ruined financially and socially, although innocent."[15]

His protests, like others before and after them, fell on deaf ears. In every case the trainer was held wholly responsible for the horses in his care. Then Barrie stepped forward.

On January 7, 1951, the front page of *The People* proudly announced, "Ringer Barrie in Racing Sensation: 'I've been doping.' "[16]

Barrie, sportswriter Maurice Smith noted, was "thought by most racing people to have died twenty years ago. It was known that he went to America. He seemed to have disappeared from the Turf for good. And as the years went by, the exploits of Ringer Barrie became just a legend."

Now, thanks to "the most amazing confession ever made to me by anyone in sport," Smith was able to reveal that "the brain behind some of the most audacious swindles in racing history is operating again on the English Turf, and has been for years, in spite of the Jockey Club ban against him."

Claiming to be motivated by a sense of injustice at the disqualification of innocent trainers, Barrie confessed to having doped more than 100 horses, as well as having administered his "harmless dynamite," the "Barrie Tonic."

"The dope usually given to stayers is called the 'long-hop,' " he explained. "It consists of a mixture of heroin, strychnine, digitalis, and liquid kola-nut, in a half-pint of distilled water. The 'short-hop,' used on sprinters, consists of pure cocaine, and is generally given by means of the needle."

Barrie was still doping horses but by invitation only, at 200 guineas a time, and preferred to use his own tonic, which he insisted did not contain dope. "It took me 13 years of experiment to develop the Barrie Tonic, and I am satisfied that in it I now have the perfect means of producing winners. I maintain that it is not doping, as defined by the authorities, but, believe me, it's just as certain. Surely there is nothing wrong in turning a bad horse into a good one?"

So far, 48 horses had won after receiving Barrie's wonder mixture. "There will be many more such winners yet," he boasted.

James Russell, the disqualified trainer of Boston Boro, was "entirely innocent. He knew nothing of what was happening. I know who doped that horse, because it was done under my guidance. How unfair it is for a trainer to have his license and his livelihood taken away from him on the strength of an alleged doping, whether he knows anything about it or not."

Barrie was not normally given to outbursts of moral indignation, and the real motive behind his confessions was financial desperation. The truth was that Barrie had much less to confess than he would have wished. As his 63rd birthday approached, Barrie was an echo from the past, rung-in as a real player.

In Barrie's latest offering, names were scarce and dates nowhere to be found. If he had included them, they would have revealed that the horses Barrie claimed to have owned in defiance of the Jockey Club's ban dated from the 1930s. His "owners for a day," were Dr. Schuyler and T.R. Patterson; his horses, Rhum, Inglesant, and Brief. Barrie was living eleven years and more in the past and presenting it as the present.

He had little to confess, but he had the Barrie Tonic to market, at 25 shillings a bottle, and a tipping business to promote. The label read, "Barrie Tonic. Shake bottle well 3 and a half hours before race, and you will have a winner." He had become a quack.

"I am looking to this tonic to give me the fortune I intend to have before I retire to a life of ease in Australia," Barrie admitted. Judging by the number of letters from trainers Smith had seen at Barrie's South London flat, as well as false moustaches, he was already well on his way.

The equine "artist" had abandoned his art, although he offered no explanation. "I am acknowledged to be a past master of it," he said, with his old conceit. "I don't go in for ringing horses now; there's very little of it done, anyway." Yet the Carmeen case had recently passed through the courts and that of Liffey Valley was being heard.

Maybe ringing horses had lost its appeal, or maybe Barrie simply didn't have the money to buy a suitable horse, nor a backer to buy one for him.

He provided *The People* with one nice story when, early in February 1951, he entered Warwick racecourse in disguise, complete with false moustache, chatted with a policeman, placed bets, and posed, unchallenged, next to a horse, but Maurice Smith's attitude to Barrie hardened, perhaps because Barrie's confessions proved disappointing.

On February 2, three days before his appearance at Warwick, Barrie appeared at the London Sessions, accused of fraudulently converting to his own use a sum of £75 received from Dilton Bershaw, with whom he had shared a room. Bershaw had allegedly given the money to Barrie to buy savings certificates.

At a subsequent hearing Bershaw delivered long, rambling statements from the witness box and was eventually ruled unfit to give evidence. Barrie, who gave his address as Albury Street, Deptford, London, was acquitted, although the judge emphasized that there was ample evidence to justify the charge.[17]

By mid-February, instead of relaying Barrie's confessions, *The People* was exposing him. A front-page story reported that he was involved with a tipping agency called The Barrie Ring. For a membership fee of £1 and a promise to pay Barrie the odds to 10 shillings on each winner, subscribers were offered a "golden opportunity to beat the bookmaker."

Recent tips had fared badly, while dozens of disgruntled subscribers had written to Smith complaining that they had sent their £1 to Barrie weeks ago and had heard nothing.

A week later, the headline read, "Ringer Barrie's 'Harmless Tonic' is Dangerous Dope." Smith had obtained a bottle of the Barrie Tonic, containing a dark brown, salty-tasting liquid, and had it analyzed. It contained large quantities of potassium bromide, caffeine, and alcohol.

Expert opinion was that it was "a cunningly devised dope," with the potassium bromide producing a temporary sedative effect, followed by stimulation from the alcohol and caffeine.

Smith reminded his readers that several weeks earlier Barrie had circulated details of his "harmless dynamite" to all registered trainers and owners and that Smith had seen orders placed by trainers. Barrie was "a menace to the Turf if ever there was one."

Several months later Lord Rosebery, a leading owner and former senior steward, offered a £1,000 reward for information about the doping of one of his own horses, Snap. Rosebery had arranged a private dope test after Snap had run badly when favorite for the Dalham Stakes at Newmarket on October 31.

Snap had been given a "stopper." If the test had been conducted by the Jockey Club, Jack Jarvis, the horse's trainer, would automatically have lost his license.

Racecourses promptly tightened their security. The stables at Hurst Park were to be guarded "night and day, to prevent any attempts at nobbling," with similar arrangements at Windsor and Wincanton.

From June 1952 passports were issued to all persons authorized to enter racecourse stables, and that December the Jockey Club met to discuss the findings of the stewards' review of the doping situation. They found no evidence of the existence of doping gangs, and it was decided not to change either the rules or the Jockey Club's policy.

In 1960 the rules were belatedly reviewed again by a committee chaired by the Duke of Norfolk. It was proposed that routine testing be introduced and, with effect from February 1962, the draconian treatment of trainers was finally eased. The amended rule stated, "Provided that, if it be established to the satisfaction of the Stewards of the Jockey Club that the trainer used all due diligence to prevent the occurrence and that the said substance was administered without his consent, connivance or default, his license shall not be withdrawn and he shall not be declared a disqualified person."[18]

By then, the King of the Ringers had vanished from view. His latest public confessions probably damaged rather than boosted his business. In 1972 an article in *The Blood-Horse* suggested that Barrie "finally settled down and lived quietly in Ireland, putting out a tipsheet." It's a nice thought; perhaps it was even true.

Ten years earlier Barrie was in London, at Australia House, in the Strand. He told an official that he had never applied for his First World War medals and would like to. The Army Records Office in Melbourne was contacted and on March 16, 1962, the 1914/15 Star, British War Medal and Victory Medal were dispatched to Barrie, c/o Australian Army Staff, Australia House.[19]

On April 30 Barrie signed to acknowledge his receipt of the medals. He was 74, an old man thinking of the past. Yet he had another eleven years to live. How he lived them is a mystery, but his admission to Carrington House, the lodging house for single men run by Lewisham Council, was evidence of his final poverty.

When Peter Christian Barrie died on July 6, 1973, he didn't leave a will. There was nothing to leave, except his remarkable story.

part 2

FOLLOWERS

4 Possums

"The evidence the Crown will present reveals a case that would have done credit to Nat Gould at his best."

— W.C. Gillespie, Counsel for the Crown, Adelaide Police Court, September 13, 1934.

While "Ringer" Barrie exercised his special skills in North America, the skulduggery he had doubtless engaged in as a young man in Australia flourished.

Ring-ins or "possums" were a well-established feature of a colorful antipodean racing scene. By the early 1930s, with the depression supplying an extra inducement to crime, racing's fragile integrity faced attacks on several fronts, some chemical, some electrical.

Dope and batteries figured regularly in newspaper coverage of the Turf. In January of 1932, a jockey by the name of W. Donaldson was disqualified for life after the stewards at a Rosebery Racing Club meeting in Sydney sought an explanation for the sharp burst of speed shown by Donaldson's mount, Fidele. They found it in the shape of a battery.

A few days later a jockey named R. Fuller reported that he had been approached by a man offering to go one better and sell him an electric saddle, "one in which he would never be defeated." Fuller accompanied the man for a demonstration, but when the jockey sat on the saddle, he was almost unseated by the shock.[1]

Whips, weights, and scales were all tampered with, while drugged horses staggered on the track, where bars with needles in them presented an occasional hazard and good horses were substituted for bad.

On June 8, 1931, at Flemington, the home of the Melbourne Cup, 17 horses lined up for the Rothsay Trial Stakes over seven furlongs. None of them were darker than Gagoola, unheard of and apparently unraced but vigorously backed down to 7-4 favorite.

One of Melbourne's daily papers, *The Argus*, reported, "When betting opened on the Rothsay Trial Stakes, Gagoola was quoted at about 20-1. 'Who is Gagoola?' many people asked, but no one seemed able to supply an answer. When it was seen that backers were literally falling over each other to back this unknown horse, curiosity increased, and there were expressions of astonishment when it was seen that many bookmakers would not lay a longer price than 6-4 about him. At barrier rise, 7-4 was obtainable.

"Two furlongs from home, Gagoola had taken charge. It appeared as if the 'good thing' would succeed, when the outsider Stephanite came with a fast run and soon placed the issue beyond doubt. Had Gagoola won, a great coup would have succeeded."

When the Victoria Racing Club examined bookmakers' books, they discovered that victory for Gagoola would have involved a racecourse payout of about £22,000.

Defeat did not end curiosity. Gagoola's owner-trainer presented himself as Mr. H. Graham. He told *The Argus*'s reporter that the unraced three-year-old had been trained at a farm at Cabramatta, west of Sydney. "His galloping ability impressed Mr. Graham so much that he decided to try his luck with him in Melbourne. Mr. Graham, who invested £200 on Gagoola, was rather disappointed at the result, but he has entered the horse for the Totalisator Handicap at Epsom on Wednesday June 17."[2]

The day before the Epsom race, Graham put Gagoola on a train to Sydney and was never seen again. Nor was Gagoola.

The Argus remarked, "It is curious that the reported owner of Gagoola has not made any demand for the stake of £60, which was won by the colt, although he remained in Melbourne for several days."

Suspicious racing officials set off in pursuit of the mysterious Gagoola. On June 22 Mr. A. Loddon Yuille, keeper of the *Australian Stud Book*, visited a farm at Cabramatta, where a man escorted him to a pile of ashes. "Gagoola broke a leg," he told Yuille, "and I had to shoot and burn him."[3]

The mystery of Gagoola soon merged with the mystery of Simba. On May 5 Joe Smith, a trainer at Kensington racetrack in Sydney, received a telephone call informing him that a horse consigned to Joe Smith had arrived at the docks from New Zealand. It was a surprise to Smith, who was not expecting a horse and did not receive one.

The horse was Simba, a three-year-old who had been trained by J.T. Jamieson to win three times in New Zealand. Jamieson, acting on behalf of a Mr. Smith of Kensington, had bought Simba from his owner, J.S. McLeod, for £1,000 and dispatched the horse to Sydney.

On May 4, the day before Simba's arrival on the *Ulimaroa*, a man calling himself James Smith contacted William Calnan, a livestock transporter, to discuss transport arrangements. When the horse arrived in Sydney, Smith drove it away himself. Calnan knew Joe Smith, the trainer, and the two Smiths were not the same. Like Mr. Graham, Mr. Smith vanished without trace.

Horses exported from New Zealand to Australia were issued with a certificate giving details of their age, breeding, brands, and distinguishing marks. To race in New South Wales, horses had to be registered, and to be registered, imported horses had to be inspected by an approved veterinary surgeon, who checked that the horse matched the details on the certificate.

Curiously for a £1,000 racehorse, Simba was neither presented for examination, nor registered, nor entered for any races. Along with James Smith, Simba simply disappeared. In the wake of Gagoola's appearance and disappearance, racing officials wanted to know where Simba was.

On July 8 *The Sydney Morning Herald* reported that a man called George Guest had acknowledged ownership. Asked why, given the publicity, he had not come forward before, Guest replied unconvincingly that he had been waiting for someone to ask.

"Mr. Guest did not seem disposed to discuss Simba's movements," the paper reported. When asked where Simba was, he replied, tersely, "He is in my care." In explanation of his failure to register the racehorse, Guest said that Simba had been gelded and was being given time to recover.

Simba's owner was no more forthcoming when he appeared before the Australian Jockey Club on July 17. On the advice of his solicitor, he refused to supply any information as to Simba's whereabouts. Simba himself remained unregistered and unraced.

The curious tale became more curious. In late November Simba was allegedly stolen from his stable in Alexandria, although the theft was not reported until early the next month. All attempts to find him failed, until March of 1932 when Sergeant Small, walking home in the Enfield district of Sydney, noticed a horse with a fine head standing in a backyard.

Guest, who had offered a reward for information leading to Simba's recovery, was contacted, and at two o'clock in the morning he and Sergeant Small went to inspect the horse, which was clearly Simba, although he had been branded and an attempt made to whiten one of his fetlocks.

A 41-year-old man, Albert Norman McCoy, was roused from his nearby bed, taken to Burwood police station, and charged with theft.

On April 1, when the case was heard at Redfern Police Court, the solicitor acting for Guest declared, to the police's amazement, that his client was satisfied that McCoy was innocent and that he did not propose to offer any evidence against him. McCoy was released, and Simba took up residence at a stable in Randwick.

In June of 1932, an application for Simba's registration was finally submitted and Simba entered for races at Victoria Park. This was the Victoria Racing Club's chance. It refused to register Simba and asked Guest to appear before it.

The invitation did not have the desired result. On July 2 the unfortunate Simba was reported to have tripped over an obstacle in his paddock at Randwick, broken a leg, and been destroyed.

The police and racing officials visited the boiling down works where Simba's carcass had been taken and managed to establish that certain markings corresponded with those of Simba, although detailed identification was not possible.

All the VRC's efforts to trace Mr. Graham, Gagoola's owner, failed, and on July 21 a special meeting was held that concluded that, "After having heard evidence, the committee decided that the horse entered and run under the name of Gagoola was, in fact, the New Zealand-bred horse, Simba."

George Guest was disqualified for five years, and Simba, in case he returned from the alleged dead, was disqualified for life.

The VRC suspected that Guest was not the guiding mind behind the ring-in for, at its annual meeting the following month, chairman Lachlan Mackinnon suggested that it was more than likely that the "arch-offender" had not been reached; the elusive Mr. Graham, alias, perhaps, the equally elusive Mr. Smith.

The case of Gagoola and Simba must have been in the minds of delegates to a conference of Australia's principal racing clubs, held in November 1931. Their deliberations led to an amendment to the Rules of Racing. From March 1, 1932, no horse was to be entered at any registered meeting unless its name had been registered, and "no horse shall be so registered unless it shall have been previously branded for identification purposes."[4]

Branding was a help but not a complete solution, as the racing clubs were soon to discover.

~

When people don't use their own names, it can get very confusing. In 1929, at Ballarat, 70 miles west of Melbourne, a trainer called James Henry O'Connor registered a horse called Comedy Jim. In 1930 Alfred Miller, also of Ballarat, applied to register a horse called Borapine. Miller did not exist.

It was O'Connor, in the name of Miller, who had registered

Borapine, but O'Connor didn't exist either. His real name was James Donovan.

Donovan had links with Roy Francis, also known as Alf Anderson. When Francis arrived in England in September of 1934, the police arrested him under the name of Mr. Stedworthy, which may even have been his real name.

If Stedworthy had been taken back to Australia to face trial, he might have been named as the leader of a criminal conspiracy, but he wasn't taken back. A police officer explained, "bringing him back was a matter of expense."

So it was left to Charles Prince, who at least had the decency to use his own name, to pay the price, which was two years with hard labor.[5]

On November 28, 1933, almost a year before Stedworthy landed in England, a horse called Chrybean, backed from 4-1 to 6-4, won a maiden race at Kilmore, about 40 miles north of Melbourne.

Curious observers questioned the identity not only of the horse but also of its owner and trainer, who appeared in the race book as S. Stenning and T.C. Granfield, respectively. The Victoria Racing Club asked the Kilmore Turf Club to send the nomination form for Chrybean for inspection. The form gave the owner as R. Stenning of Ripon Street, Ballarat, and the trainer as T.E. Granland. Inquiries located Ripon Street but not Mr. Stenning, who did not exist.

Granland, who did exist, insisted that he knew nothing about Chrybean's entry at Kilmore, nor about Chrybean, although he had trained a horse called Chrysbeau, who had been removed from his Ballarat stables on November 25.

Officials wanted to examine the winner, but the winner had disappeared and no one came forward to claim the prize money.

The VRC was also concerned about the credentials of Duke Bombita, who had finished second in a race at Ballarat on September 20 and again at Seymour on October 6 before winning at Chiltern on October 28.

Across the state border, in New South Wales, Duke

Bombita's success at Holbrook on October 14 was being investigated by the Southern Districts Racing Association. In January 1934 the SDRA announced that it was satisfied that Duke Bombita's real name was Erbie, a prolific winner in Sydney and at country tracks in New South Wales.

Erbie was disqualified for life, along with trainer Stanley Wilfred Biggins, nominator Rupert Coughlan, co-lessee Thomas McMahon, and John Herbert Nathan, although Biggins and Nathan were cleared on appeal. Rupert Coughlan, in the minor variation of Rupert Coughlin, was soon active again.

So was Charles Prince, a former jump jockey who had recently obtained a trainer's license in Victoria. According to Prince, in April 1934 he met a man called Alf Anderson in the bar of the Pastoral Hotel in Melbourne, "a flashy sort of chap, always well dressed, with a smart manner about him."

Anderson told the new trainer that he owned a smart horse called Redlock, which Prince obligingly agreed to buy, unseen. A few months later Prince showed the stewards of the South Australian Jockey Club a receipt written in pencil on a piece of notepaper. It read, in part, "Received from Charles Prince the sum of £30, being payment in full for my horse Redlock." The receipt was signed "L. Anderson" and dated April 8, 1934.[6]

Anderson later told Prince that his name was actually Roy Francis, that he had rented some stables at Sunbury near Melbourne and wanted Prince to train a horse called Erbie, as well as Redlock.

Coughlin told the police that he also met Francis in a Melbourne hotel in March or April of 1934, and was also asked to work at the stables at Sunbury, where Francis subsequently appeared with Duke Bombita, alias Erbie. Later, Prince arrived with Redlock.

In court Coughlin told a different story, according to which Francis had told him that the two horses were Redlock and Melthos. To complicate the already complicated, Coughlin was known to Prince as Mr. Clark. No wonder officials were confused.

When Prince worked Redlock with Erbie, alias Duke Bombita, alias Chrybean, alias Melthos, he discovered that "Erbie could 'eat' Redlock and was a first class galloper."

Francis confided that he intended to ring-in Erbie as Redlock, and Prince didn't object. Both horses were dark bay, but Erbie had a white blaze and was branded with an inverted T above a Y on his near shoulder, whereas Redlock's brand was an H within the angle of a larger L. It was agreed that Francis would deal with the blaze, while Prince tampered with the brands.

After Francis had finished with his dye, Prince, by his own account, "got to work on the brand with a pair of eyebrow tweezers. It took about three hours to change it to look like Redlock's."[7]

Disguised as Redlock, Erbie was ready for the Trial Stakes at Murray Bridge, near Adelaide in South Australia, to be run on July 28, 1934. Prince took Erbie to Murray Bridge, while Coughlin hid Redlock in Malmsbury, a small township 60 miles northwest of Melbourne.

Coughlin then made his way to Murray Bridge, where Francis did his best to drive the bookmakers out of business, forcing Redlock down from 10-1 to 6-4, with more money placed off-course, in Adelaide.

Prince had booked Pat Slattery, a local jockey. As he legged him up, he said, "You might win this, Pat. This fellow can gallop a bit." He did, to win by six lengths.

Back in Melbourne, Bert Wolfe, who wrote for *The Herald* as "Cardigan," was incredulous. Wolfe knew his horses and couldn't believe the result. The race was on a Saturday. Monday's *Herald* bore the skeptical headline, "Redlock Won At His 19th Start."[8]

"It was a clear cut win," the paper reported, "and caused a buzz of excitement on the course, as the second horse, Jalisco, is a smart sprinter." Redlock wasn't, having run 18 times in and around Sydney and Melbourne without success.

Prince claimed not to have backed Redlock himself but had

agreed with Francis that he would be given half the winnings. His version of events, related twenty years later, was not wholly convincing. Prince stated that Francis gave him his share, £1,500, on the evening of the race day but immediately persuaded him to hand it back and collect it about a week later, from Hosie's Hotel in Melbourne.

It was at least two weeks later that he telephoned Hosie's Hotel and discovered that Francis was not known to them. By then, "Redlock" had raced again.

If the conspirators had settled for their Murray Bridge winnings, they might have escaped detection, but on Saturday, August 11, Redlock was sent to Kadina, 90 miles northwest of Adelaide, to contest the seven-furlong Trial Stakes.

Ironically, the decision to run the ringer again was probably encouraged by the official attention the horse received. On August 8 Matt Hogan, the South Australian Jockey Club's chief steward, visited Prince and examined the winner's markings. He found that they corresponded with those recorded when Redlock was a yearling.

Two days later Hogan returned with a veterinary surgeon, Mr. W.R.B. Wakeham. Wakeham washed the horse's face with methylated spirits but failed to expose Erbie's blaze. *The Argus* reported, "The officials are satisfied that Redlock is the horse who won the Trial Stakes at Murray Bridge on July 28. They see no reason for any further action and will allow Redlock to start in the Kadina Trial Stakes."

Bookmakers were wary and made Redlock a 6-4 on chance. With Pat Slattery again on board, Redlock won by 12 lengths.

There was a large crowd, boosted by Redlock's attendance, and it included Bert Wolfe, who had traveled from Melbourne. While Wolfe scrutinized the winner, *The Herald*'s sports editor, Fred Laby, was examining the real Redlock, tracked down by the paper to his paddock near Malmsbury.

Laby was satisfied that the owners of the paddock were ignorant of the horse's identity. One day a man who introduced himself as Mr. Stedworthy had arrived in a car and asked to see the horse. The horse wasn't there but arrived shortly afterward.

Laby contacted the VRC, and the next day, Sunday, August 12, he accompanied officials to Malmsbury, where they identified the horse as Redlock.

Monday's edition of *The Herald* blazed the front page headline, "Murray Bridge Redlock a 'Ring-In' — Audacious Fraud Exposed — 'Cardigan' Says Ring-In Is Erbie."

Wolfe had wired from Adelaide, "I am satisfied that the gelding which raced at Kadina on Saturday is not Redlock, but is Erbie."

Under his nom de plume of "Cardigan," Wolfe wrote, "I have no hesitation in asserting that the gelding which raced at Kadina on Saturday is our old friend Erbie in a new guise. I know Erbie well. I have watched him race and win on numerous occasions in Sydney and on the provincial tracks. I have watched Erbie work at Randwick and have timed his gallops frequently. I know his markings and his characteristics and, after seeing 'Redlock' win the Trial handicap at the Kadina and Wallaroo meeting on Saturday, I say definitely that 'Redlock' is Erbie.

"He still has his heavy tail and the half white sock on his near hind leg, with exactly the same jagged edges where the white hairs meet the brown. But this time he hasn't a blaze down his face, and his brands are different."[9]

After the race the winner had been taken to stables at Morphettville racecourse in Adelaide. On Monday,. August 13, the day of Wolfe's expose, the SAJC placed the horse under stable arrest. The next day Matt Hogan led another team of officials, including John Dow, an expert on brands, to reexamine the horse.

In Dow's opinion the brand on its near shoulder, an H within the angle of a larger L, had been superimposed on a different brand, an inverted T above a Y, Erbie's brand. Wolfe's accusation was vindicated. At an inquiry on August 16, 1934, the SAJC disqualified Prince and Redlock for life.

When Prince left the SAJC's offices, he was immediately arrested by the police and charged with having obtained £15, the prize money, from the Murray Bridge Race Club by falsely pretending that the horse entered for the Trial Stakes was Redlock.

At Adelaide Police Court on August 17, the prosecution alleged that Prince must have known that the winner was really Erbie because, if the horse's white blaze had been dyed before he bought it, white hairs would have emerged over the next few months. The defense responded that the stewards had washed the horse's face and failed to expose any white hairs and had cleared Redlock to run at Kadina.

Prince was remanded on bail until September 13 when W.C. Gillespie, prosecuting, told the Court, "The evidence the Crown will present reveals a case that would have done credit to Nat Gould at his best."[10]

Despite Gillespie's promise there were few surprises and on October 4 the jury took just over an hour to agree that Prince, aged 40, was guilty. Later that month Mr. Justice Napier sentenced him to two years with hard labor, observing that it was apparent that the Redlock case "was no more than an incident in a carefully planned fraud" and that Prince was "a cat's paw of others."

Other cat's paws were being tried elsewhere. In Melbourne City Court, Rupert Coughlin, described as a 38-year-old laborer, was charged with conspiracy to defraud the Murray Bridge Race Club by representing a horse entered for the Trial Stakes as being Redlock.

Coughlin's counsel, Mr. R.T. Cahir, insisted that, until he watched the race at Murray Bridge, his client was unaware that Redlock was really Erbie. "When Coughlin saw the race run," Cahir said, "he knew for the first time that he had been made a cat's paw. The horse that ran was the horse that he knew as Melthos."

The jury was not persuaded. On November 20 Coughlin was found guilty and sentenced to nine months in prison.

Coughlin provided a link with another set of ringers. He had registered a filly called Lady Primero, who had allegedly run in the name of Miss Carolin. The filly was a stablemate of Comedy Jim, seized by the police on September 11, along with his trainer, James O'Connor.

Comedy Jim, alias Borapine, had run at Grafton, in northern New South Wales, on July 23 and August 4, winning on the latter occasion. He then raced and won at nearby Casino.

By the time O'Connor appeared at Grafton Police Court, on September 17, he had already been disqualified for life by the Northern Rivers Racing Association and Downs Racing Association, a fate soon shared by Sydney Spencer Davis, Comedy Jim's owner.

The jury in O'Connor's case could not agree, and a new trial was ordered. On March 4, 1935, O'Connor, in his mid-fifties, finally heard the same verdict as Prince and Coughlin, and was bound over to be of good behavior for 12 months.[11]

O'Connor escaped lightly but not as lightly as the guiding hand behind the conspiracy, Messrs. Francis, Anderson, and Stedworthy, one and the same.

Prince served only five months of his two-year sentence, thanks to remission to mark a visit by the Duke of Gloucester. In 1954, when he was 60, he had further cause to be a royalist. To mark a visit by the newly crowned Queen Elizabeth, the South Australian Jockey Club lifted Prince's life disqualification.

The mischievous looking Prince told *The Sun*, a Melbourne paper, that he was happy in his job, working in the bar of a hotel in Violet Town and growing vegetables.

"I made a stupid mistake in helping to ring in Erbie as Redlock," he confessed. "I hope that nobody else will be as silly as I was and try to get away with it."[12]

It was a vain hope.

The Frantic Forties 5

"No thoroughbred shall be permitted to start at a member track unless the Jockey Club registration certificate number has been officially tattooed by the Thoroughbred Racing Protective Bureau beneath the upper lip of the horse, for identification purposes."

—Thoroughbred Racing Associations' code of standards, 1950.

"We do not consider it practicable to institute a marking procedure. There is, in practice, very little trouble in establishing the identity of a British racehorse running at home."

—Report of British Jockey Club committee, 1951.

In 1935 "Ringer" Barrie declared, "People in England haven't got the foggiest notion of what really crooked racing means. Out in the States, the 'Sport of Kings' is just another racket, with the gangsters and the gunmen pulling most of the strings."

Barrie's depiction of horse racing in the United States was colored by his own peculiar experiences, but the claim was untrue only in degree. Racing attracted criminals like wasps to raspberry jam, and the racetracks had no effective system for dealing with the wasps.

In 1945 the Thoroughbred Racing Associations, representing the major tracks, approached J. Edgar Hoover, head of the Federal Bureau of Investigation, for advice on setting up racing's own specialist investigative agency.

At Hoover's suggestion the TRA approached his former assistant, Spencer Drayton. In January of 1946, the Thoroughbred Racing Protective Bureau was established, with Drayton as its president and several former FBI agents on its staff.

Drayton later recalled, "There were three main problems confronting racing at the time. There was the stimulation, that is, doping, of horses; there were quite a few ringers; and there were a lot of undesirables with criminal records who owned horses."

Barrie's deportation at the end of 1934, had brought a uniquely colorful episode in the history of ringing in North America to an end, but it had not ended the practice. The problem, according to Drayton, was that "There was no real way of identifying horses. The tracks used 'identifiers' who were supposed to know all the horses, but they didn't. It was impossible to recognize them all. We found that some trainers couldn't even distinguish some of the horses in their own stable."

On January 29, 1946, exactly two weeks after the TRPB's creation, Willow Run landed an almighty gamble when winning a six-furlong claiming race at Fair Grounds, New Orleans, having been backed from 20-1 to 7-4.[1]

Officials were sufficiently suspicious to suspend Willow Run's trainer, Roland Sanner, and place a bar on any further entries submitted by either Mr. or Mrs. Clyde Inscoe, the horse's owners, pending investigation.

The Inscoes also owned, and Sanner trained, a horse called Flying Kilts. On March 18, at a hearing before the Louisiana Racing Commission, all three suspects were charged with having "deliberately planned and substituted Flying Kilts for Willow Run on January 29, with the avowed purpose of misleading the public and track officials."[2]

Significantly, evidence was presented by Richard Johnson, an agent of the new TRPB. None of the defendants made a personal appearance, and all three were banned for life while the winning jockey, Charles Bowers, was suspended for a year.

It soon emerged that although Mr. and Mrs. Inscoe had bought Flying Kilts as recently as the previous December, the horse was already an experienced ringer. In January of 1947 Sanner and James O'Donnell, Flying Kilts' previous owner, were sent to prison for 18 months and two years, respectively, for having twice run Flying Kilts in the guise of Rounco at Pimlico in November of 1945.

In Drayton's first major public address, delivered to the Kentucky Thoroughbred Breeders' Association on May 14, 1946, the president of the TRPB highlighted the new agency's role in the investigation of the Willow Run case.

"It is not sufficient," he warned, "to investigate a ringer case after a race has been run and attempt to bring the guilty to justice. The betting public has already been defrauded.

"We believe that if an adequate system of horse identification can be developed and properly administered, the problem of horse substitutions or 'ringer' cases can be eliminated. In this connection, we are studying all the present systems of horse identification employed by the tracks in this country. We are also studying the possibility of utilizing the system of tattooing horses as developed by the Army Remount Service.

"The Army Remount Service at Pomona, California, for three years has been tattooing horses under the upper lip. I understand the Remount Service has been so successful with this means of identification, it has officially adopted this method throughout the service."

Drayton did not have to wait long for further ammunition in his campaign. At the end of July, he announced the conclusion of an investigation that had taken his agents to eight states.[3]

In June of 1945, a man acting for William Mink of Wilmington, Delaware, paid a humble $210 for a four-year-old called Allpulch, allegedly sold a few months later, "sight unseen," to a Mr. Creal for $500.

At about the same time, Robert Drummonds claimed another, better four-year-old called Sea Command out of a race at Pimlico for $3,750. Drummonds trained for Mink and had bought Sea Command for him but in the name of Paul Middleton, who also came from Wilmington.

Acting on Mink's instructions, Drummonds shipped Sea Command to Middleton's farm. Sea Command promptly disappeared from public view, but shortly afterward a horse with

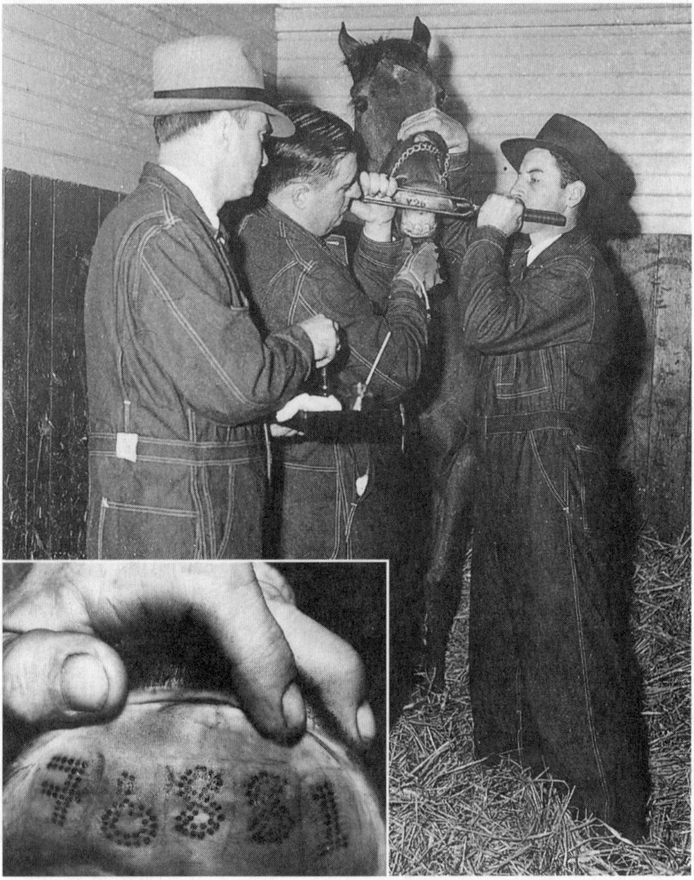
THE BLOOD-HORSE

In 1947 the TRA instituted lip tattooing to identify racehorses better.

a registration certificate in the name of Allpulch was shipped from Middleton's farm to Rockingham racetrack in New Hampshire.

On November 13 an apparently much improved Allpulch caused an upset when winning a $1,250 claiming race, paying clairvoyant punters a win dividend of $26.40. One unidentified individual cashed over $30,000 in winning tickets. Investigators suspected that the individual was Mr. Mink.

Three days later Allpulch appeared in a $2,000 claiming race at Narragansett, Rhode Island, 100 miles south of

Rockingham, winning by an easy five lengths. Allpulch was then claimed by the Frances Stable and went on to win three more races before being exposed as Sea Command.

The case provided further grounds for action. In February of 1947, with The Jockey Club's approval, the TRA gave its backing to Drayton's recommendation that a system of lip tattooing be introduced. From 1948 all runners at TRA tracks were to be tattooed.

In 1950 a new section of the TRA's code of standards read: "No thoroughbred shall be permitted to start at a member track unless the Jockey Club registration certificate number has been officially tattooed by the TRPB beneath the upper lip of the horse, for identification purposes."

The TRA declared its belief that this system would provide "the final answer in protecting racing against horse substitution or 'ringer' cases."[4]

Tattooing was not a foolproof system, but it was a powerful deterrent, particularly when combined with the TRPB's simultaneous drive to tighten up the system of licensing trainers and owners.

For 25 years the sound of ringing was rarely heard in the United States, although the bells rang for a little longer on the other side of the Atlantic, in tattooless Britain; three times in 1949.

~

With food still rationed, some working class families in post-war Britain queued to eat horses rather than back them. They queued in drab clothes because, until March 1949, clothes were also rationed.

In a climate of constrained jollity, sports fans gloried in the cavalier displays of soccer and cricket heroes Stanley Matthews and Denis Compton, and of Gordon Richards, who remained champion jockey throughout most of a restricted wartime program.

Liffey Valley was also a sportsman but with no pretensions to greatness. The nine-year-old bay gelding arrived at John Roberts's Prestbury Court Stables, near Cheltenham, in October of 1948, trailing a winless record in Ireland behind him.

Roberts is now remembered, if at all, for having trained Four Ten to win the 1954 Cheltenham Gold Cup. Liffey Valley was to provide him with another unwanted claim to fame.

An acquaintance of Roberts, called John Connolly, had asked him to train the horse for John Duggan, from Limerick. Both men were bookmakers.

Connolly had bought Liffey Valley in Ireland the previous month for £200. Even that seemed too much when, on its English debut at Worcester on December 3, Liffey Valley finished unplaced in a novices' hurdle at 33-1. He repeated the performance at Leicester on January 10, 1949, at 25-1, after which his form and connections' confidence suddenly improved.

A week later in a maiden hurdle at Birmingham, Liffey Valley, described by *The Sporting Life* as "a lively springer from long odds," was returned 7-1 co-favorite in a field of 19. He finished third to Benedictine, who had won the Free Handicap in 1947, was making his debut over hurdles, and subsequently finished sixth in the Champion Hurdle.

If the horse's connections had lost their money, they probably lost more at Nottingham on January 31 when Liffey Valley, at 6-1, beat 25 rivals but failed to beat the 26th, Fulke Walwyn's Roselite, who had recently finished runner-up to the useful Usher.

The Sporting Life reported that Liffey Valley "was travelling like a winner when he hit the last hurdle hard. Even then, Bryan Marshall had to ride his hardest to beat him, all out, by a length."

There was more frustration to come. On February 21 Liffey Valley returned to Birmingham for another maiden hurdle, with jockey Tommy Cusack taking over from P. Murray. Hal o' the Wynd, making his debut, came with a late run to beat Liffey Valley, the 7-2 favorite, by a short head. On his next outing, Hal o' the Wynd finished fourth in the Gloucestershire Hurdle at Cheltenham.

Liffey Valley's connections were plagued by either poor placing or poor fortune but found an easier opportunity at Worcester on March 5, by which time their horse's form was there for all to see.

"Everyone had been waiting for Liffey Valley after his last two good races," *The Sporting Life*'s reporter remarked, "so that, when plenty of even money was available about him, backers were able to congratulate themselves, even if he had 23 opponents."[5]

The biggest danger was the weather, which was miserable. Snow fell steadily, visibility was poor, and racing was eventually abandoned, but not before Ken Mullins had steered the 11-10 favorite to an easy eight-length victory. It was, it seemed, no more than the horse and his connections deserved.

After an unsuccessful expedition in a handicap hurdle at Wolverhampton on March 14, Liffey Valley continued his career in different colors, those of Mrs. Kathleen Manship.

Mrs. Manship was employed by Gomer Charles, a Welsh bookmaker who was later sent to prison for his part in the Francasal affair (See Chapter 6). According to Charles, Connolly was one of his clients and owed him £3,000. Charles agreed to accept Liffey Valley in lieu of £1,000 of the debt, although Liffey Valley was officially owned by Duggan. Charles then presented the horse to Mrs. Manship as a gift.

The 10-year-old was a late-flowering success, winning four races for his new owner between April and July of 1949. His form subsequently deteriorated, and when Charles watched Liffey Valley at Stratford in April 1950 he formed the opinion that the horse was not fit to race again. Later that year Liffey Valley was destroyed, suffering from cancer.

It was the second time Liffey Valley had been killed, for the real Liffey Valley had disappeared and probably been destroyed shortly after Connolly bought it, in September of 1948. The horse had served its purpose, which was to exist, registered, named, a bay gelding.

The same month that Connolly bought Liffey Valley, a man

called Thomas Ryan, from Dublin, visited William Dwan at Thurles, County Tipperary. Dwan was a member of the Irish Racing Board and the owner of a decent hurdler called Newtown Rock. A 10-year-old bay gelding, Newtown Rock had won 12 races.

On a second visit Ryan was accompanied by Connolly, who provided a check for the purchase price of £1,250. On October 4 Ryan phoned R.J. Goff and Co., in Dublin and arranged for Newtown Rock to be collected from Dwan and shipped to a Mr. Duggan of Stratford Road, Hall Green, Birmingham. That was Connolly's address, where Duggan stayed when he visited England.

Newtown Rock was shipped on October 11, the day before Liffey Valley was said to have arrived at John Roberts's yard. Between Birmingham and Cheltenham, the talented Newtown Rock became the talentless Liffey Valley, conveniently eligible for all the maiden and novice hurdles from which Newtown Rock's successes excluded him.

It is not clear exactly when or why suspicions were aroused, although Liffey Valley's much improved form may have prompted questions from those familiar with Irish racing.

In June of 1950 Martin Byrne, a Dublin vet who had treated Newtown Rock when he was with his previous owner and issued a certificate of soundness when the horse was sold to Ryan, visited Roberts's stables, presumably at the request of the police. Byrne was certain that the horse he examined was Newtown Rock.

In July, Detective Inspector Eric Oliver visited the Connollys, who had moved from Birmingham to Nottingham, and, a few days later, confronted Duggan in Ireland. Duggan denied ever having owned either Liffey Valley or Newtown Rock and refused to make a statement.

In October the Connollys and Duggan were arrested and charged with having obtained £105 by false pretenses, the prize money won by Liffey Valley at Worcester.

Duggan applied to the High Court in Dublin to prevent the

Irish police from sending him to Britain, but the Supreme Court ultimately dismissed his appeal and on December 18 he joined Mr. and Mrs. Connolly at Bow Street Court, in London, before moving on to Marylebone Magistrates Court.

The identification evidence was compelling, although the Connollys' solicitor managed to embarrass Michael Byrne by forcing the vet to concede that he had once been asked to destroy a horse and had shot the wrong one, a mistake that cost him £1,600.

Byrne was not the only witness to have identified the horse in Roberts's yard. William Dwan had owned Newtown Rock for many years. Not only did he recognize the horse, he claimed that the horse recognized him.

"I used to call it Rocky and it would wag its head," Dwan testified. "When I saw it in Mr. Roberts's stables, I called Rocky and it wagged its head again."[6]

On February 12, 1951, John Connolly, aged 50, Dorothy Connolly, aged 48, and John Duggan, aged 37, graduated to the Old Bailey.

Duggan had some grounds for optimism, since Mrs. Connolly was alleged to have filled in the necessary forms for Liffey Valley in his name, while Mr. Connolly paid the trainer's bills. Duggan's involvement in the conspiracy remained to be proved.

On the third day of the trial, recognizing that his was a lost cause, John Connolly changed his plea to guilty and was sentenced to 20 months in prison. The prosecution then dropped the charges against Mrs. Connolly, and on Judge Beazley's instructions, the jury returned a verdict of not guilty on Duggan, there being insufficient evidence to proceed.

What was striking about the ring-in was Newtown Rock's failure to achieve what was required of him — win a humble novice hurdle race when the money was down.

It was never suggested either that Roberts was privy to the conspiracy or that the real Liffey Valley ever appeared in Britain. When Newtown Rock was unplaced and apparently unbacked on his first two outings, at Worcester in December

1948 and at Leicester the following month, he was presumably either unfit or a non-trier.

When he was backed, the conspirators were unlucky to bump into some distinctly useful novices, Benedictine, Roselite, and Hal o' the Wynd. Maybe they were not careful enough in their choice of race.

Another curious feature was the role of Gomer Charles. How much did the future Francasal conspirator know about the horse he accepted in part-payment of Connolly's debt?

Before "Liffey Valley" had finished winning for Kathleen Manship, another Irish ringer was already gracing Britain's racecourses.

Perhaps Jack Morris just had time to watch Pan II spoil Winston Churchill's hopes of winning the Ascot Gold Cup with Colonist II before Detective Superintendent John Black arrested him. Earlier the same day, June 14, 1951, Black had driven to Kennett House at East Ilsley, near Newbury, and arrested Edward Hill.

That evening both men were charged with "unlawfully conspiring together to cheat and defraud such persons as might own horses running in races in which a horse called Stellar City was entered in the name of Peaceful William."

The two men were close friends. Morris was a 50-year-old gambler with a house in Epsom and a flat in Mayfair, while Hill was a 45-year-old former jump jockey turned trainer. Hill was also a gambler and freely admitted using Morris to place his bets. "If you have a person in the stable who can get your bet on without the bookmakers knowing," he explained, "he might return very fair odds."[7]

If you can arrange for a good horse to run in the name of a bad one, you might fare even better.

In May 1949 Hill and Morris had traveled to Ireland. They visited Edward Martin Quirk's yard and bought his wife's promising two-year-old, Stellar City, for £1,400. In three outings Stellar City had won twice, at Baldoyle and Phoenix Park, and finished third at the Curragh.

A week later they met Edward Callaghan, a horse owner and dealer, at the Gresham Hotel in Dublin and agreed to buy another two-year-old called Peaceful William for £325.

Peaceful William's prospects were less rosy. He had raced just once, when out of the first 10 in a 20-runner maiden race at the Curragh. In poor condition, he had since been moved to trainer Michael Connolly, who testified that the colt was not fit enough to be given a hard gallop, let alone race.

His head lad, Thomas Doyle, was later asked, "Are you prepared to say that if this horse was fed up by giving it eggs and stout and things a racehorse is given in England, it would not be ready to race in six weeks?" "It would not," Doyle replied.[8]

One obvious physical difference between the two horses was that Stellar City had a white star on its face, whereas Peaceful William did not.

The newly acquired horses were shipped from Dublin on May 23 and arrived at Hill's yard the next day. As with Liffey Valley and Newtown Rock, the journey from Ireland had a miraculous effect on the horses' identities. When they arrived at East Ilsley, Stellar City had lost both his white star and his ability, both of which had suddenly been acquired by Peaceful William.

Early in June, long before his former stable considered he would have been fit to gallop, Peaceful William was taken to the gallops and given a severe five-furlong test. Its seriousness was indicated by the trainer's choice of riders.

Peaceful William was ridden by Harry Sprague, who won the 1956 Champion Hurdle on Doorknocker. His rivals were ridden by Ken Gethin and Arthur Wragg. Wragg was one of a famous collection of brothers, completed by Sam and Harry, while Gethin had won the previous year's Eclipse Stakes on Petition and, in the early 1950s, rode winners of the One Thousand Guineas, Eclipse Stakes, Coronation Stakes, Cambridgeshire, and Cesarewitch.

What mattered more was their weight. Sprague was much heavier than either Wragg or Gethin. While their mounts were each carrying about 8 stone 6 pounds (118 pounds), Peaceful William was burdened with 9 stone 12 pounds (138 pounds).

Sprague, now a spritely 82, remembers it well, because it was his first contact with Hill and Morris. "I'd ridden for gambling stables all my life," he told me. "They knew I could keep my mouth shut. Morris rang to say they were thinking of running a decent two-year-old and wanted to have a gallop. At the gallops he said, 'That one's yours.' I thought, 'God, that's a nice two-year-old.' I just won the gallop, by about three-quarters of a length."

There was one other matter to attend to. Hill made a mark on the noseband of a bridle and told his head lad, Lincoln Close, to take it to the saddler and have a leather disc sewn on to it. In 30 years working with horses, Close had never seen a bridle changed in that way. The disc, sewn on to an Australian bridle, covered the white star on the face of the horse the stable staff knew as Peaceful William.

The stable's new star was unleashed at the humblest of levels, the five-furlong Trial Selling Plate at Carlisle on June 29, 1949. Sprague was riding at the meeting for Jack Reardon, another Epsom trainer. "Morris said to me, 'I'll put you down for Peaceful William, because you're a jump jockey. When we get there, you say you're ill, and we'll put Gethin up.' "[9]

Backed from 3-1 to even favorite in a seven-runner field, with Gethin in the saddle, Peaceful William won by a cozy length.

The reward in prize money was £180 and a normal present to the jockey would have been about 10 percent of this, but Hill gave Gethin £100. The trainer could easily afford it, as he admitted having arranged for Morris to put £600 on Peaceful William for him, and Morris stated that he had put another £500 on for himself, getting 5-2 for Hill and 2-1 for himself. The true sums were likely to have been much bigger.

Hill bought the winner back at the subsequent auction for 610 guineas and then ran him in another selling race at Yarmouth on July 6, when Arthur Wragg was given the ride. Backed from 6-1 to 5-2, Peaceful William surprisingly was beaten into third place, a defeat that Hill and Morris claimed had cost them £400 each in lost bets.

When Edgar Britt, a top Australian jockey, was given his turn on Peaceful William, again in a selling race, at Lanark on July 21, he won by an easy five lengths, having been backed from 6-1 to 2-1. Hill bought the winner in for 1,200 guineas, a record price for a selling race in Scotland, and gave Britt a present of £100.

Wragg had been promised a very good present if he won at Yarmouth and was understandably keen to ride Peaceful William in its next race, at Alexandra Park on August 22.

When Hill told him that Peaceful William would not be running, Wragg accepted another ride. When he discovered that the horse was a runner after all, he offered to abandon his ride in order to partner Peaceful William. Hill, fearful that the move would advertise the stable's confidence in the horse's chance, promised to give Wragg £200 as compensation if Peaceful William won, and when that wasn't sufficiently tempting, allegedly increased the offer to £400.

Britt kept the ride, won the selling race by three lengths, at 3-1, and was given another £100 present, while Wragg was given £200. With Hill admitting to a bet of £600 and Morris £500, both probably having bet much more, there was plenty to spare.

Peaceful William was clearly no ordinary selling plater. *The Sporting Life*'s reporter remarked, "Peaceful William must be a good plater, for he thoroughly outpaced the much fancied Model Link," giving Britt "an armchair ride." Hill had to go to 1,050 guineas to buy the winner in.

The entertainment ended at Bath on September 1 when, facing stiffer competition and unfancied at 100-9, Peaceful William finished a well-beaten third.

Michael Connolly, who had briefly trained Peaceful William in Ireland, confessed to being "a wee bit surprised" when told that the former weakling had won at Carlisle but not as surprised as Lilian Gertrude Quirk at the non-appearance of Stellar City.[10]

When she saw Hill, she asked him why Stellar City hadn't run. Hill told her that the horse had pulled a muscle. Mrs. Quirk wasn't convinced, and it may have been her skepticism that eventually triggered an investigation.

The horses' subsequent movements were difficult to untangle. According to Hill, in October of 1949, Peaceful William was sent to Alfred Worsley, a breeder based in Chepstow, to be prepared for another season's racing. He was returned to Hill at the end of April of 1950 but, according to the trainer, "turned sour, and turned a pig, and would not go on the Downs."[11]

Hill eventually sold the horse to the meatman, Albert Passey, but it was not until February 21, 1951, that Passey bought Peaceful William from Hill, for £20.

At about the same time that Peaceful William was sent to Worsley, Hill sold Stellar City to Morris for £1,200, a generous price for a horse that had been unable to race. Hill never saw the horse again. Morris sent Stellar City to Les Hall, who later established a reputation as a gambling trainer under Jockey Club Rules but was then training under Pony Turf Club Rules.

During his time with Hall, Stellar City raced several times without success. Morris claimed, "I put sums varying from £600, £200, and £50 on him, but he lost."[12]

According to Morris, in January 1951, he moved Stellar City to some stables at Tadworth, near Epsom, where a Mr. Lock also trained under Pony Turf Club Rules. Other evidence suggested that Stellar City did not leave Hall until February 8 and did not arrive at Tadworth until March.

One horse was dead and one alive; but which was which? Hill, supported by Morris, claimed that the horse that had won three times for him was Peaceful William and that it was Peaceful William that had been put down after proving untrainable. Stellar City, they claimed, had proved a disappointment but was still in training for pony racing.

The timing of the meatman's visit was interesting. The police investigation did not become public knowledge until mid-March of 1951, but Hill may have become aware of it before then.

It was important to Hill and Morris to satisfy investigators that the surviving horse was, as they claimed, Stellar City. In April, Hill persuaded his head lad and three young apprentices to sign a photograph confirming that the horse in the picture, which had a white star, was Stellar City.

It was true, it was Stellar City, but it was not the horse that Lincoln Close, Alan Harvey, and Dominic and John Forte had previously known as Stellar City. When Peaceful William was winning races, he was the one with the white star.

When they were required to give evidence at Bow Street Court on June 28, 1951, they told the truth. Maxwell Turner, for the prosecution, asked Close, "Thinking about it now, do you think the photograph you signed was the photograph of Stellar City, or not?" "I don't think it was," Close replied.

He was followed by Harvey, an 18-year-old apprentice. "Do you think that the photograph which you signed was a photograph of Stellar City?" "No, sir, I don't." "Had the Stellar City which you knew a star at all?" "No."

The horse sold to the meatman in February was the real Peaceful William. In his summing up at the Old Bailey on October 29, 1951, the Recorder, Sir Gerald Dodson, observed, "Stellar City has survived the turmoil of the prosecution, but Peaceful William perished in February 1951, and that was just when the police were getting active about this matter."

Dodson also referred to Morris's bank statements, which revealed that, over a two-month period, £30,000 had been paid in from successful bets. Morris claimed that he had won only about £4,000 from bets on Peaceful William, that he had had bigger bets on other horses, and had actually lost money betting in 1949.

Neither Dodson nor the jury were convinced. Ringing-in Stellar City for Peaceful William had been highly lucrative. On the seventh day of their trial, Hill and Morris were found guilty, and each was sentenced to 18 months in prison. "This result, on the evidence, was really inevitable," the Recorder remarked.[13]

In December, their application for leave to appeal was rejected and both were warned off by the Jockey Club.

At quarter to two on the morning of March 6, 1950, Bobbie O'Ryan was woken up by a knock at his door. James Rooney and William Lyons had come to see him. All three were due to appear at Dublin District Court the next day, Rooney and Lyons as defendants, O'Ryan as a witness.

O'Ryan had made a statement to the police. Rooney and Lyons wanted him to testify that the statement had been made under the threat of losing his jockey's license. Instead, O'Ryan informed the police, and on March 7 Rooney and Lyons faced a fresh charge, that of conspiring to pervert the course of justice.

When the case moved on to Dublin's Central Criminal Court, Mr. Justice Haugh described O'Ryan as "a terribly important witness," reflected in the fact that Mr. G. Murnaghan, counsel for the defense, attempted to discredit him. "Was he telling you the whole unvarnished truth?" Murnaghan asked the jury. "If he was, why did he not hold his head up, and tell you like a man?" Perhaps O'Ryan was thinking of the early morning visit.[14]

If he was frightened, he wasn't alone. Two other witnesses, Thomas and Doris Cooke, refused to testify because of alleged threats by Rooney and Lyons, who were granted bail only after giving an undertaking not to interfere with witnesses.

They were not men to be treated lightly, but the evidence against them seemed strong. O'Ryan was a well-known Irish jump jockey. On November 27, 1949, he received a phone call from Rooney, who trained at Drogheda, about 30 miles north of Dublin. Rooney wanted O'Ryan to ride for him at Haydock the following Thursday, December 1. O'Ryan agreed, although he wasn't told the name of the horse.

When O'Ryan arrived at Haydock on November 30, he met Lyons, Rooney's head lad, who told him that the horse was Carmeen, running in Division II of the Haydock Novices' Hurdle. Lyons said he thought Carmeen would win.

On the morning of the race, O'Ryan met Rooney. When the

jockey asked if Carmeen was fancied, the trainer replied, "Would Mount Mills win?" Mount Mills was a successful hurdler that O'Ryan had partnered. "It would be a certainty," said O'Ryan. "This one is as good as Mount Mills."[15]

Rooney said that he would not be going to the races himself but introduced O'Ryan to the owner, a Mr. Rowan, who would be representing him. Mr. Rowan was actually a Belfast bookmaker called James Connolly Quinn, and Carmeen was not officially trained by Rooney but by William Parks.

On paper, Carmeen had nothing to recommend him. A lightly raced, maiden nine-year-old, who had never finished better than fourth, Carmeen had made his most recent run eighteen months ago, at Mullingar on May 19, 1948, after which his legs "went bad." Yet he was strongly fancied in a field of 18.

On the eve of the race, John Mescall, a jockey who worked for Rooney and had won on Mount Mills, phoned Dublin bookmaker Joseph Williams and told him that O'Ryan would ride the winner of the 2:30 p.m. race. As a result of the call, Williams travelled to Haydock and put £115 on Carmeen, a bit of it at 20-1. Dublin District Court later heard that, "While at the race meeting, Mr. Williams saw a considerable number of Irish racegoers, many of whom he knew to be associated with Rooney." Williams wasn't the only one who had been tipped the wink.[16]

The Sporting Life reported, "A big plunge took place on Carmeen at all available odds from 5-1 to 13-8."[17] Carmeen won by a comfortable two lengths. It was his last appearance in public. After spending two nights at the racecourse stables, the winning horse was apparently moved to some stables at Altrincham, about 20 miles away, and then disappeared.

Carmeen's success was blatantly suspicious and at Mullingar races two days later, O'Ryan heard rumors that the winner was actually either Fulford or Mount Mills. Shortly afterward, Brigadier Edward Boylan summoned him to appear before the Irish Turf Club.

On December 7, less than a week after walking Carmeen into the winner's enclosure, O'Ryan found himself in front of the stewards, with Detective Andrew O'Connor and Sergeant Kenny in attendance. By the time he left, O'Ryan had signed a statement.

Several times during the following weeks, O'Ryan was approached by Lyons, while the police continued their investigation. Eventually, on January 29, 1950, O'Connor arrested Rooney, Lyons, and Parks. The next day, at Dublin Magistrates Court, they were charged with conspiracy to defraud by pretending that Mount Mills was Carmeen.

Carmeen's history was obscure. Rooney had registered the horse in March 1946, three months after he had been issued with a trainer's license. The owner was allegedly a Mr. M. O'Reilly, who denied all knowledge of the horse.

In January of 1948 Carmeen was reported to have been sold to W. Rowan. He ran four times that year, with the trainer given as Francis Ward, who was one of Rooney's stable staff and Carmeen's trainer in name only.

Ward stated that he had not seen Carmeen since May of 1948, although he was officially the horse's trainer until October 1949 and still appeared as the trainer when *The Sporting Life* detailed the result of the race at Haydock.

By then, Carmeen was trained by Parks, who said that on November 26 some men had arrived to take the horse away, on Rowan's instructions. Parks gave police a description of the horse, which matched that of Mount Mills, not Carmeen.

Mount Mills's history was equally strange. In December 1945 Rooney registered him as being owned by William Carroll, a cousin by marriage who was only 15 at the time and stated that he had never owned the horse nor signed forms that appeared to bear his signature.

In January of 1948, a sale was registered to a Mr. Doherty of Belfast. According to Rooney, on November 27, 1949, eight days after Mount Mills had finished third at Naas, Doherty informed him that he had sold the horse.

When Rooney loaded Mount Mills into a horsebox and sent him to Dublin, where he was met by Lyons, he was acting on the mysterious Mr. Doherty's instructions.

On the night of November 28, the *Kilkenny* carried a horse from Dublin to Birkenhead, where a horsebox driven by Frederick Dias collected it and drove it to Haydock. Lyons was one of two men with the horse, and on their arrival at the racecourse, Lyons told one of Haydock's employees that the horse was Carmeen. After the race Dias was told that his services were not required as the horse was not going back to Ireland.

When Rooney, Lyons, and Parks appeared at Dublin District Court, on March 7, 1950, they were joined by Ward and additionally charged with conspiring to obtain prize money for William Rowan. On March 28 all four men were committed for trial, which opened at Dublin's Central Criminal Court on June 19.

The prosecution case against Rooney and Lyons seemed compelling and their defense correspondingly flimsy. None of the defendants were called to give evidence, and Lyons had refused to make a statement to the police.

Rooney's defense counsel, Mr. Murnaghan, was reduced to pointing out that there was no evidence that the horse that arrived at Dublin docks was the horse that was loaded onto the *Kilkenny*, nor that Rooney or Lyons had backed Carmeen. Murnaghan suggested that if there had been any "funny business," Doherty and Connolly Quinn were responsible.

O'Ryan's testimony that he had met Rooney near Haydock on the morning of the race conflicted with that of Mescall, Rooney's jockey, who testified that the trainer was at home, at Drogheda. After it emerged that Mescall himself had been seen at Haydock, with Lyons, the prosecution applied for him to be treated as a hostile witness.

As Mr. Justice Haugh observed, either O'Ryan or Mescall "was committing contemptible and deplorable perjury."

Mr. T. Odell, representing Parks, protested, "There is not an iota of proof that Mount Mills ran in the Novices' Hurdle at Haydock Park." Not proof but strong circumstantial evidence, including identification evidence.

Since both horses had disappeared, they were not available

for inspection but photographs were. Like the winner, Mount Mills had a large white blaze, whereas Carmeen had a small white spot on its face.

At a later hearing Patrick Lenihan, who had ridden Carmeen twice, was asked, pointedly, "Is it possible for a white spot on a horse's head in 1948 to develop into a great blaze in 1949?"

"No."[18]

On June 26, 1950, the jury found Parks and Ward not guilty but could not agree on a verdict on Rooney or Lyons. A new trial was ordered.

It opened on November 22, with the defense choosing to call no evidence. The jury retired at 5:50 p.m. on November 28 and at 8:35 p.m. announced that they were again unable to agree. Rooney and Lyons walked free.

~

During the course of the first "Carmeen" trial, one of the defense counsel remarked, "You may think it would be very desirable that there should be some proper method of identification."

His view was shared by Tommy Weston, who had been champion jockey in 1926 and in 1920 at Chester, had unwittingly ridden one of Peter Barrie's ringers, Golden Plate.

Weston retired in 1949. In his autobiography, *My Racing Life*, published in 1952, Weston wrote, "It is a surprising thing that no one has yet attempted, in this country, to evolve a system of certain identification of racehorses. Ask any trainer if he could positively identify any horse in a race, and he will find it difficult to provide a definite answer.

"Invariably, when the question of substitution has been raised, the reply will be, 'Oh, there's always someone about who would spot a switch like that.' Is there?

"Other countries, particularly America, have long had methods of combating substitution, chiefly by means of tattoo marks on the upper lip. This method has been found reasonably satisfactory."

Weston advocated a similar system to that adopted in greyhound racing, where an identity book was issued, providing a description of the dog, with details of markings. The book was checked every time the dog ran.

"If the greyhound authorities have gone to such lengths and expense to insure an absolute minimum of substitution, there appears no reason why horse racing authorities could not evolve some such similar system."

Weston added, "There have been many concrete instances of co-operation in other matters between the British Jockey Club and similar Turf organizations in other countries, and in this matter of identifying racehorses there could be similar co-operation. It will never be possible to know just how many horses have been brought from other countries to take part in major or minor races over here which have not been the animals which they were represented to be."[19]

In May of 1951, the Jockey Club set up a committee, chaired by Lord Rosebery, to consider introducing procedures for marking horses. The committee quickly decided that the idea was not practicable.

"There is, in practice," it concluded, complacently, "very little trouble in establishing the identity of a British racehorse running at home. The main trouble is with Irish, French, and other horses. The chances of detection of substitutions are greatly diminished by the use of air transport. A horse nowadays can arrive a few hours before the race, and be back in his own stable before nightfall."

The cases of Liffey Valley, Peaceful William, and Carmeen all involved horses from Ireland, but none were flown in and, a few hours later, flown out. Liffey Valley and Peaceful William were trained in England while Carmeen remained at the racecourse stables for two nights after the race. If the committee was right about the most likely source of ringers, those ringers went undetected.

In 1952 the Thoroughbred Breeders' Association revisited the issue of identification. That May it informed the Jockey Club that the TBA Council accepted, "that the two systems, lip-tattooing and markings-photograph-chestnuts, would, either separately or jointly, be too complicated and expensive for use in this country."

Instead, the TBA concluded, "that a system of visual markings on a form giving a diagram of the head, near and off-sides of a horse, in addition to the descriptive markings in writing, would be of advantage. This, then, is the recommendation."

It received short shrift from the Jockey Club, which replied, "With regard to the identification of thoroughbreds, it was, of course, agreed when the Special Committee reported in 1951, that the marking of horses was not considered practicable."

In November 1952 the TBA returned to the attack. In a letter to the senior steward, Major Reginald Macdonald-Buchanan, the TBA's secretary, F.E. Birch, declared, "This Association considers that the matter is of great importance to the industry, and urges that a register of markings should be officially kept. As this country is the only one of importance that has no satisfactory system of identification, there cannot be any great difficulty in having one."[20]

The Jockey Club disagreed.

The Unrequired Ringer 6

There were five of them, six if you count Leonard Phillips, seven if you count the man who actually cut the cable, but Phillips had never said who that was. Like *War and Peace*, it might be a good idea to make a note of the characters.

You could start with Gomer Charles, a jolly-looking, double-chinned Welsh bookmaker; the same one who had owned Liffey Valley, alias Newtown Rock.

On Sunday, December 11, 1966, at about 9:00 p.m., Patrick Bricknell and Brian Hoggins walked up to the door of number 22, Park Place, Cardiff, and rang the bell. When Charles answered, one of them threw pepper in his face and the other shot him in the chest. And then there were four.

William Rook was already 57 at the time of the trial, in 1954. In 2002 he would have been 105. It was safe to assume that he was dead.

Maurice Williams was ten years younger. Old regulars at the Westport Inn on Malden Road in Kentish Town remembered him indistinctly from the days when the pub was called the Gypsy Queen and Williams lived opposite it, but they told me he was long gone.

That left Victor Dill and Harry Kateley, but Dill was 56 when he was tried, and when I searched for his death, I found it, in 1986. That helped me to find a relative or, rather, a relative's widow, but she told me that Victor had been the dark sheep of the family.

They knew nothing of him, which left Kateley, the ringleader and the youngest of the conspirators. He might be alive.

Kateley was born in 1911. Sometimes, old men like to talk about their past, while they still can. Kateley died in 1999, aged 88, and although I traced two of his sons, neither would talk to me.

There was still Leonard Phillips, a younger man, but Phillips is a common name. What chance did I have of finding him? One day, early in January of 2002, I received a phone call. It was from Tony Morris, Phillips' son-in-law. Leonard was very ill. He had emphysema and had just had a leg amputated, but when he felt well enough, he would talk to me.

Morris rang two weeks later. Leonard had died, aged 79, but May Phillips, his widow, would see me. So I drove to Trebanog, near Porth, in South Wales, not far from where Phillips had lived when he set off in his red lorry for Bath racecourse almost 50 years earlier.

Lieutenant Colonel Victor Robert Colquhoun Dill walked along England's Lane in Hampstead, to the greengrocer's shop. Doubtless smartly dressed, as usual, he climbed the stairs to the office above and waited for his instructions. Later that morning, Maurice Williams rang. He told Dill to put £3,500 on Francasal. It was Thursday, July 16, 1953.

They were a strange pairing, Dill and Williams, brought together by the desperation of one and the greed of the other. Dill had a privileged background but little else; Williams had the money. He kept it at home, roughly £8,000, in banknotes. At that time, a secretary's salary was about £400 a year and a four-bedroom detached house standing in half an acre in London's commuter belt could be bought for less than £4,000.

Dill's father, Thomas Reginald Colquhoun Dill, was a London barrister. Dill had been educated at Eton, where he was a King's Scholar, and at the Royal Military Academy at Woolwich. During the First World War he served in France and was awarded the Military Cross. Afterward, his career took an unlikely course.

He worked as an actor before rejoining the army in 1939. After escaping from France, he was given a job at the War Office, promoted to lieutenant colonel, then invalided out. Dill then returned to the theatre.

For a while, he was manager at St. James's Theatre, which was demolished in 1957. It stood at the corner of King Street and Angel Court, off Pall Mall. In the closing years of the war, it staged a long run of Agatha Christie's *Ten Little Indians*, and in 1945 King George VI visited the theatre to see Emlyn Williams' new play, *The Wind of Heaven*. Perhaps Dill met him.

The following year Dill returned to France, this time as a bloodstock dealer, but he did not prosper. In 1952, age 54, he returned to England and unemployment. Desperate for work, he found it with Harry Kateley, a bookmaker with an office at the junction of Oxford Street and Poland Street.

The legalization of betting shops was still eight years away, and Kateley's office, which he shared with Maurice Williams, was a telephone credit business. It was there that Dill and Williams first met.

Later, at the Old Bailey, his own counsel would describe Williams as "a roughish diamond. One of those characters you have heard of who go around with huge wads of five pound notes on them." He kept the notes in the inside pocket of his waistcoat, and in a second inside pocket, at the top of his trousers.[1]

Williams, 47, a big, shambling man, lived with his sister in Malden Road, Kentish Town, within walking distance of England's Lane. They had a shop that sold decorators' supplies, but that wasn't the source of his banknotes. Williams was a professional gambler.

Four nights a week he went to the dogs, at Harringay and Walthamstow, and also bet on boxing and the horses. Williams didn't study the form but relied on "whispers," passed on to him by informants.

Early in July of 1953, a whisper persuaded Williams to have £100 each way on Nash's Gorse at Newmarket at 8-1. His victory set Williams up for a bigger bet to come, but even in court Williams refused to identify his informant, for he was a man who kept his secrets and liked to stay in the background.

The greengrocer's shop at 38 England's Lane, Hampstead, was owned by Robert James Davidson. For a while, he and his two brothers also ran the turf accountant's office above, but in March 1953 they sold the business to Williams, although it continued to operate under the name of J. Davidson & Co.

Williams installed Dill as manager, but the retired army officer was no bookmaker. He relied on Harry Kateley for advice.

Newspapers sometimes referred to Kateley, 42, as a hairdresser, but it was his wife, Nancy, who was the hairdresser. At the time of their marriage, in 1939, Kateley gave his profession as "greyhound trainer."[2] Perhaps Kateley and Williams got to know each other through their mutual interest in the dogs.

In 1951 Kateley succeeded his father as a bookmaker, inheriting a client called William Rook and a trade account with Gomer Charles. Charles, 46, was a well-known South Wales bookmaker, with offices in Cardiff, Newport, and Pontypridd. Rook, 57, was a very different figure, a prosperous partner in the Bell Engineering Company in Slough.

Rook owned racehorses. At the beginning of 1953, he had four in training with Percy Bailey at Epsom. Rook also bet heavily, placing £100 or even £200 on his own horses, often with Kateley.

That was the cast — Victor Dill, Maurice Williams, Harry Kateley, Gomer Charles, and William Rook. On September 19, 1953, all five, some meeting for the first time, would stand together in the dock at Bow Street Magistrates' Court.

~

On April 1, 1953, Lester Piggott rode Sun Suit to a comfortable victory in a selling race for two-year-olds at Nottingham. On April 13 Sun Suit finished a creditable runner-up to Little Danehurst in another seller, this time at Windsor.

Afterward, Sun Suit was claimed for 300 guineas by a Mr. A.H. Williams. Harry Kateley had a habit of calling himself Williams.

Part of his office in Poland Street bore the name A.Williams, and Kateley had a bank account in that name, but the only real Williams was Maurice Williams, Kateley's associate.

Kateley was a tenant of Alexander Finegold, whose Oxford Street shop bore the name Della's Gowns. Kateley persuaded Finegold to buy Sun Suit, who was then renamed Della's Choice.

Kateley and Williams had a special reason for buying Sun Suit. They wanted to use her as a yardstick to measure the ability of an unraced two-year-old called Santa Amaro, whom they had bought in France for £2,000.

On April 21 Williams entered Santa Amaro for the Merthyr Selling Plate at Chepstow on May 25. Through Rook he then arranged for Santa Amaro to be trained by the exotically named Colonel Frederick Baden Powell Weil at his yard at Twyford in Berkshire, although another "authority to act" form was also made out in favor of Rook's own trainer, Percy Bailey.

Santa Amaro arrived at Folkestone on May 12, but he was not taken to either Weil's or Bailey's yards. Kateley told Rook that there were "too many eyes" at Epsom, and Rook was asked to suggest somewhere quieter.[3]

He suggested Alfred Layton's Cabbage Hill Farm at Binfield, Berkshire, where Rook's own horses were sometimes kept. It was hardly ideal, since Layton was not a trainer, and on May 15 Santa Amaro was moved to Weil's yard.

Two days later Williams visited the yard. Weil, meeting him for the first time, was not impressed. He promptly wrote to Weatherbys informing them that, "having met Maurice Williams, he had decided not to train for him." He asked that any "authority to act" be cancelled.[4]

On May 18 Santa Amaro was driven to Worcester racecourse, which at that time staged flat as well as jump races. At Kateley's request,f Gomer Charles had arranged for a trial to be staged. Three horses lined up, and Santa Amaro, carrying a weight cloth containing up to 21 pounds, finished two lengths in front of Della's Choice. A selling race was clearly well within his compass.

One of the riders, Richard Harrison, who worked for Percy Bailey, asked for the name of the winner, but he wasn't told. Santa Amaro was a secret.

After the trial Santa Amaro was taken to Captain Thomas Hanbury's yard near Swindon. Dill, who knew Hanbury, telephoned and asked if he would train the horse for Maurice Williams. He explained that they desperately wanted to run Santa Amaro at Chepstow the following Monday, May 25. Hanbury pointed out that he only held a jumps license.

Dill's desperation became obvious the next day, when he persuaded Hanbury to go with him to Weatherbys' office in London in an attempt to resolve the problem.

According to Henry Twite, a long-serving employee at Weatherbys, "Colonel Dill was very emphatic that, as Santa Amaro was so fit and well, it must run at Chepstow on the Whitsun* Monday, May 25." Twite held out little hope of a license being issued, and when Hanbury suggested that Dill send the horse to Gerald Balding, Twite cautioned that Santa Amaro would still not be eligible to run, not having been stabled for long enough with a licensed trainer.

Dill was forced to admit defeat. On May 22 Williams informed Weatherbys that Santa Amaro would be returned to France. "In England," he said later, "everybody sees everything; everybody knows everything." On May 29 Santa Amaro was driven to Folkestone and back to France, and secrecy. Della's Choice, her job done, was sold.[5]

The conspirators now changed their plan. Foiled in their attempt to slip in one dark horse, they decided to slip in two. Dill returned to France in search of another two-year-old. He emerged with Francasal, a bay colt trained by Georges Pelat, bought early in June for £820.

Francasal was described in court as "a somewhat indifferent horse," a description fully justified by his record. In six runs, all in claiming races, Francasal had finished in the first six only once.[6]

*A legal holiday in England, Wales, and Ireland

It had proved difficult to arrange suitable stabling for Santa Amaro, and there was another round of musical chairs in anticipation of Francasal's arrival. On July 5 Kateley and Rook visited Norah Wilmot, who trained at Binfield, and told her that they would like to stable some horses with her. She never heard from them again.

A few days later Percy Bailey was informed that Francasal would soon be arriving at his yard and was to run at Bath on July 16. Both Francasal and Santa Amaro had already been entered for the Spa Selling Stakes. Santa Amaro had also been entered for a race at Newmarket the same day.

The conspirators were walking a thin wire because Weatherbys had informed Williams at the time of Santa Amaro's return to France that "It would be advisable that your horse, if he is to run in this country as trained in England, should be in the hands of a licensed trainer at least a month before the race." Instead of a month, it was three days.[7]

On July 11 the two horses arrived at Folkestone, where they were stabled overnight. The next day Sigmund Webster, a horse transporter, drove Santa Amaro to Alfred Layton's Cabbage Hill Farm at Binfield, then took Francasal to his own yard at Carter's Barn, Sonning Common, about 15 miles away.

On July 13 Webster collected Santa Amaro from Cabbage Hill Farm and drove him to Bailey's Grove Stables at Epsom, where the colt was put in the care of stable lad James "Jock" Grant, although Grant was not told the horse's name. Bailey was under the mistaken impression that it was Francasal.

On July 15 Roy Gourley, Bailey's farrier, fitted the horse with racing shoes in preparation for his run at Bath the next day. While *The Sporting Life* indicated that both Francasal and Santa Amaro were trained privately, the race card issued at Bath named Colonel F. Weil as their trainer, much to his annoyance.

That morning, Thursday, July 16, 1953, Leonard Phillips got into his red lorry and set off down the Rhondda Valley. He and his partner caught the ferry across the Severn Estuary and drove toward Bath. At about 1:20 p.m., they turned into

Lansdown Lane, down the hill toward Weston, and parked by the side of the road, about a mile from Bath racecourse.

The two men got out of the cab, raised the extension ladder that rested on the gantry in the back of the open lorry and leaned it against a telephone pole. Phillips held the ladder while his partner climbed to the top, arranged the oxyacetylene torch, and burned through the telephone cable. It was approaching 1:30 p.m.

William Glass, cutting the grass for Bath Corporation, approached them. "What are you doing up there?" he asked. He was told they had a job to do. Suspicious, Glass tried to make a note of the lorry's registration number. He wrote down the number 478.

About 15 minutes earlier, on his way to Newmarket, horsebox driver Sidney Bennett stopped at Stevenage and phoned Gerrard 2290, as he had been told to do. Harry Kateley picked up the phone in his office in Poland Street and told Bennett to turn around and take the horse back to where he had picked him up, in Sonning Common.

Maurice Williams then sent a telegram to Newmarket's clerk of the course, asking him to inform Willie Snaith, who was expecting to ride Santa Amaro in the 2:30 p.m. race, that the horsebox had broken down. Bennett's horsebox actually contained Francasal. Santa Amaro had already arrived safely at Bath for the 2:00 p.m. race.

When the Davidson brothers had run the Turf accountant's office in England's Lane, they had held only three accounts with other bookmakers. It was all a small firm needed, but once Williams had installed Victor Dill as manager, the court was told, "any number of accounts were opened with other bookmakers."[8]

They were opened with references supplied by Gomer Charles, the South Wales bookmaker, and by Kateley, in his guise as Mr. A. Williams, but most of the accounts had not been used. They were used now.

By 2:00 p.m. bets totalling £3,580 had been placed with over 20 bookmakers, all in the name of J. Davidson & Co., and all at Starting Price* (SP). Victor Dill had executed Williams' orders.

Gomer Charles, from his office in Cardiff, had spread another £2,500 around seven bookmakers. According to Charles, he was merely laying off a bet from Kateley's office and did not stand to win any money himself. On the contrary, he stood to lose, having accepted a local client's £25 bet, which he did not lay off.

The sums involved were enormous. According to the Office for National Statistics, £1 in July of 1953 would be worth about £17 today. Between them, Dill and Charles had staked the equivalent of over £100,000 on Francasal.

Bookmakers would normally have used the "blower" service to lay money off into the racecourse ring, an exercise that would have crushed Francasal's SP, but the telephone line was down. Some of those who had taken bets from Dill tried to contact him, but the phones at J. Davidson & Co. were off the hook. At about 1:45 p.m., his work done, Dill went to the pub.

Eventually, a taxi service was started between Bath racecourse and a telephone kiosk about two miles away, but by then the race that mattered, the first, was over.

In *The Sporting Life*, Francasal and Santa Amaro were among the "20-1 others" in the betting forecast for the Spa Selling Plate. Neither had any known form, and Billy Gilchrist, Francasal's rider, was not a fashionable jockey.

The on-course money was for Empire Magic, the 6-4 favorite. Francasal started at 10-1. The conspirators' gamble was for a present-day £1 million.

Percy Bailey passed Kateley's riding instructions to Gilchrist, but Gilchrist, wearing Williams' chocolate-and-white colors, didn't follow them. He was told to wait until the last of the six furlongs before striking for home but took up the running after a furlong and held off the challenge of Pomonaway to win by one and a half lengths. "It was a comfortable but not an easy win," said Gilchrist.[9]

* The price ruling in the racecourse betting ring at the time the race started

While Bailey saddled up William Rook's own horse, Fallow Isle, for the next race, Rook bought Francasal in for 740 guineas.

The following day Bailey's farrier, Roy Gourley, returned to the yard, expecting to replace Francasal's racing plates with exercise shoes, but the horse was not there. Bailey had been told that Francasal was being sent back to France.

That was the intention. Sigmund Webster drove Santa Amaro from Bath to Cabbage Hill Farm and then on to his own stables at Sonning Common to join Francasal. Williams asked Dill to arrange for Francasal to return to France, and on July 17 Dill asked the British Bloodstock Agency to make the necessary arrangements, as a matter of "extreme urgency." Webster was primed to drive Francasal to Folkestone, but it was already too late.[10]

The plot unravelled very quickly. Before the day's racing was over, bookmakers had already asked the post office for an explanation of "the failure of telephonic communication with the racecourse before the first race."[11]

The next day, July 17, the GPO's preliminary report was passed to the Bath police. The National Sporting League, soon to be followed by the National Bookmakers' Protection Association and Tote Investors Ltd., advised their members to withhold payment of winning bets pending the outcome of inquiries.

The Jockey Club and the police acted with commendable speed. On July 18, after racing at Ascot, Bailey was interviewed by the stewards. Bailey insisted that he was not Francasal's trainer but had merely agreed to act for Williams, whom he had never met, if he sent any horses over from France. A horse had arrived at his yard on Monday, July 13, and Bailey had done what he was told — "to give him a trot on Monday, two steady canters on Tuesday, a pipe-opener on Wednesday."

As far as his interrogator, Sir Humphrey de Trafford, was concerned, that made Bailey the horse's trainer.

Earlier the same day, July 18, Detective Inspector Glyn

Evans, head of Bath CID (criminal investigation department), received an anonymous phone call from London. The caller was reported to have said, "Kateley and Charles are the men you want over the racing job."[12]

Perhaps he said a little more because the next day the police descended on Webster's yard at Sonning Common, where they seized Francasal, and on stables at Padworth, about 15 miles away, where Santa Amaro had been transferred. Both horses were driven to veterinary surgeon George Forbes's premises at Epsom.

Bailey described the two bays as "a pretty good pair and pretty much alike," but their former French owners readily distinguished them and so did James Wright, the vet who had inspected the horses at Folkestone on their various arrivals and departures.[13]

While Francasal had one contrary tuft of hair on his forehead, Santa Amaro had two.

Stable lad James Grant recognized white marks on Santa Amaro's withers, and farrier Roy Gourley also identified him, remarking that Santa Amaro was still wearing the racing plates he had fitted.

On July 22 Dennis Bushby, Bath's clerk of the course, sent a telegram to the Jockey Club to lodge an objection to the winner of the Spa Selling Stakes, "on ground that the winner was not Francasal."[14]

The same day, Williams' solicitor contacted Scotland Yard and informed them that his client wished to see them. Detective Superintendent Reginald Spooner, who was leading the investigation, and Chief Inspector Frederick Hodge, obliged. They had been wanting to see him.

Dill had already been interviewed, and *The Sporting Life* was soon able to report that "the information already gathered makes the case reasonably complete."[15]

On August 4 a conference was held at Scotland Yard attended by Major George Baker, the Jockey Club's chief investigation officer, and Bath's Detective Inspector Glyn Evans.

Evans had brought news of progress with his investigation into the sabotage of the telephone cable. Leonard Phillips, a 31-year-old rag and scrap metal dealer from Dinas, in the Rhondda Valley, had been interviewed as early as July 19 but repeatedly denied ever having been to Bath.

Dinas was a rough area and Phillips was a bit of a rogue, with his dining room table liable to have lead in its legs.

The identification evidence was compelling, and on August 5 he was arrested and appeared at Bath Magistrates Court the next day, charged with "unlawfully and maliciously cutting a cable, being part of a certain electric telegraph belonging to Her Majesty's Postmaster General, contrary to Section 37 of the Malicious Damage Act, 1861."

Phillips' case was finally heard on September 18. He had told the police, "A fellow I know as Bill came to see me. He offered me 35 nicker to do the job. An 'easy,' he said." Phillips was generally uncooperative and refused to sign a statement. "I am only a small end in the big wheel," he insisted. "I don't know the big shots."[16]

Phillips was sent to prison for three months, but he refused to name his accomplice and the man who actually cut the cable was never identified.

When I visited his widow, May Phillips, in February of 2002, she explained that Leonard had rarely talked about the case, even within his family. She didn't know who had employed him to cut the cable but assumed that it was Gomer Charles and geographically he was the most likely candidate.

Now that both her husband and his accomplice were dead, she felt able to reveal that the man Phillips had protected was Emrys Bloomfield, a local man. "He was short and stocky, and a strong lad who used to box," she remembered.[17]

Gomer Charles was alleged to have made a wild attempt to escape punishment. On August 17 Lord Eliot, director of a London commission agency, telephoned the police to report a visit by Charles and George Bowden, a former jockey and trainer once employed by Eliot.

Ludicrously, they had suggested that Eliot present himself to the Chief Constable of Bath as a representative of the Jockey Club and discourage further action in the Francasal affair. "Was the Chief Constable's wife interested in a fur coat?" they wondered. "Was Eliot interested in £500?"[18]

Charles denied having seen Eliot. Whether he did or not, on September 19, in the immediate wake of Phillips' hearing, Charles, Kateley, Williams, Dill, and Rook all appeared at Bow Street Magistrates Court, charged with "conspiring to defraud the Bath Racecourse Company Limited of their money by pretending a horse running at Bath on July 16 in the name of Francasal was in fact Francasal, and conspiring by fraud and unlawful devices in wagering on horse racing at Bath on July 16 to win themselves sums of money."

Committal proceedings opened before Sir Laurence Dunne on October 7, and on December 2 the five defendants were formally committed for trial at the Old Bailey.

The trial started on January 12, 1954. Harry Kateley's precarious financial position was immediately revealed when he applied for, and was granted, legal aid. Kateley was the only defendant not to appear in the witness box, choosing instead to make a statement.

"I am wholly innocent of being concerned in any switching of horses," he said. "Any acts which might have appeared to be suspicious were wholly directed to diverting the attention of many persons, particularly those in the racing world, from Francasal to Santa Amaro, and that is why I think Santa Amaro was sent to Newmarket, although I did not know it at the time.

"I did not know on July 16 which of the two horses were running at Bath. So far as I knew, Francasal was the better horse, and if it had been desired to run Santa Amaro at Bath, they could have done so in its own name. The odds would have been longer.

"I had put only £50 on this horse. I was not connected in any way with cutting the blower service, and I know nothing about it. I know nothing of any switching of these two horses."

The judge, Mr. Justice Sellers, told the jury that Kateley was "quite entitled to remain in the dock" but added, "you realize at once, if he had made that statement on oath there are a good many matters which might have been inquired into." By declining to enter the witness box, Kateley avoided cross-examination.[19]

Although 147 witnesses were lined up and the trial extended into February, many of the facts were not in dispute. Maurice Williams accepted that the horse that ran at Bath was not Francasal but Santa Amaro and admitted that when he sent a telegram to Newmarket to inform Willie Snaith that the horsebox had broken down, it was a lie. It was never intended to run the horse at Newmarket.

The defendants' case was that it was "a legitimate betting coup." Santa Amaro had run in Francasal's name but not deliberately. Williams told the court that Francasal was the horse intended for the planned coup, because the colt had experience, which Santa Amaro lacked, and Francasal's connections in France believed that he should already have won a race there.

The two horses had been switched but accidentally. On July 13, as Sigmund Webster prepared to take Santa Amaro to Percy Bailey's yard, at Epsom, both horses had briefly been in adjacent boxes at Webster's stables at Sonning Common, while Webster had breakfast. Cross-examined by Ashe Lincoln QC (Queen's Counsel), for Kateley, Webster admitted that he could have mixed the horses up; a war injury made him forgetful.

The interruption to the "blower" service was crucial, but the police failed to establish a link between Phillips, convicted of cutting the cable, and those set to benefit from his timely vandalism.

In his summing up, Mr. Justice Sellers was very clear. "There is nothing in the evidence," he told the jury, "which associates any one of these accused with that matter. Nothing has been proved to associate any one of these men with that.

You may say it is very suspicious. It looks very fortuitous, but we cannot hold them responsible for it."

On February 2 the jury retired to consider their verdict. The foreman returned to tell the judge that they were unable to agree. Mr. Justice Sellers asked if they could agree in part or not on anything. "Not on anything," the foreman replied. The judge ordered a retrial.[20]

The second trial opened at the Old Bailey on February 16 before Mr. Justice Byrne. In some respects the defendants' position was strengthened, although Dill was now obliged to ask for legal aid.

Sigmund Webster, who had admitted the possibility of mistakenly switching the horses, now testified that this was what happened. "I was in a hurry and I easily get muddled," he said. "I realize now that I took the wrong horse that day." Again cross-examined by Ashe Lincoln QC, Webster added, "I am quite certain I made a mistake."

The next day Lincoln submitted that in the light of Webster's evidence the trial should be stopped. If Francasal and Santa Amaro had been switched unwittingly, the defendants had no case to answer. The judge insisted that the jury decide.

The defense reinforced its position with new evidence from the daughter and wife of Alfred Layton, of Cabbage Hill Farm, Binfield. In the opinion of Margaret and Mary Layton, contrary to the evidence given by Mr. Layton, the horse that arrived at their farm on May 12, Santa Amaro, was not the same horse that arrived on July 12.

The prosecution queried their failure to tell the police or, apparently, discuss the matter with Mr. Layton, but their evidence added to the confusion surrounding the horses' movements.

It wasn't enough. On March 17, 1954, after deliberating for almost four and a half hours, the jury found all the defendants except William Rook, guilty. Maurice Williams, smiling as the verdict was announced, slapped Rook on the back and said, "Good luck."

Mr. Justice Byrne reserved the longest prison sentence, three years, for Harry Kateley. "You are," the judge told him, "quite obviously the head and brain of this conspiracy."

Williams, described as the co-originator of the conspiracy, received two years. "I have no doubt the two of you dragged Dill into it," the judge remarked, sentencing Victor Dill to nine months.[21]

Williams and Charles, also sentenced to two years and the only two of those convicted with any funds, were jointly ordered to pay £4,500 toward the costs.

~

There is no doubt that Santa Amaro was the winning horse. The identification evidence was incontrovertible and defense claims that the horses had been switched by mistake and that Francasal was the intended runner were unbelievable.

Francasal had experience but not ability, a fact reflected in the horses' respective purchase prices. No one would have staked the equivalent of £100,000 on Francasal. Santa Amaro's convincing success in the trial at Worcester on May 18 marked him out as the coup horse, and the conspirators had clearly intended to land a gamble with him, in his own name, at Chepstow on May 25.

Two mysteries remain. One is Santa Amaro's whereabouts in France between May 29 and July 11; perhaps the colt returned to his former trainer, Maurice Wallon. The second is why Santa Amaro did not run in his own name at Bath?

Few people were aware of Francasal's poor form in France, and with the "blower" service cut off, Santa Amaro would probably have started at a similar price.

The key to the coup's success was not running a ringer but cutting the telephone cable. The police were unable to produce evidence to link Leonard Phillips with the conspirators. Without that link they could not have been prosecuted and the bookmakers might have had to pay up. The Francasal case was a case of an unrequired ringer.

Kateley and Williams were greedy. Their greed meant that, in the end, the only conspirator to collect any winnings was William Rook, who claimed that his only bet was £10 each way, on the tote, at the racecourse. It won him less than £200.

In April of 1954, the stewards of the Jockey Club sustained the objection to Francasal and awarded the Spa Selling Stakes to the runner-up, Pomonaway. Francasal and Santa Amaro were disqualified for life, along with Harry Kateley, Maurice Williams, Gomer Charles, and Victor Dill.

On July 26 Francasal and Santa Amaro were sold by auction at Epsom, on the orders of the High Sheriff of Surrey. Francasal was bought by Major E.M. Methven, a retired cavalry officer, for 160 guineas while Gordon Gilbert bought Santa Amaro for 400 guineas, on behalf of a Mr. Bligh, of Gerrards Cross.

It is a long time ago and all the leading players are now dead. In 1966 Gomer Charles was shot dead by burglars on the doorstep of his home in the center of Cardiff. There was £25,000 in cash in the house. The men were sentenced to life imprisonment. Charles's sons, Michael and Peter, owned racehorses until 1963 when, acting on Weatherbys' advice, they sold them.[22]

Harry Kateley, described as a retired council worker, died at his home near Dorking, Surrey, in 1999, age 88.

I wonder if any of the patrons of William Hill's betting shop in Malden Road, Kentish Town, know that Maurice Williams once lived next door.

Victor Dill lived on into old age, retiring to Bognor Regis with his wife, Phoebe. A relative, the late Major Richard Dill, trained as a permit holder from 1964 to 1977. Victor died in hospital in Chichester in 1986, age 89.

The Davidsons' greengrocer's shop in England's Lane, from above which Dill placed so many bets on Francasal, is now an estate agent's office.

Percy Bailey's fitful training career ended in 1953 and Billy Gilchrist retired three years later. Both are now gone, along with Grove Stables, Cabbage Hill Farm, and Carter's Barn. All that remains, a welcome annual reminder, is the Francasal Stakes, run at Bath each year.

In 2002 Tony Morris, Leonard Phillips' son-in-law, named a

two-year-old Santa Amaro with a view to running it in the renamed Len Phillips Memorial Francasal Two-Year-Old Selling Stakes. May Phillips, Leonard's widow, was to present the trophy. Sadly, May died a few weeks before the race, and the long-prepared plan for Santa Amaro had to be abandoned after he ran disappointingly in his preparation races.

A Used Car Salesman 7

"This nefarious design was born in a mind that was primed by greed, nurtured in cunning, and executed with boldness. You decided the stakes were worth the gamble, thinking you could take advantage of the bush people at Casterton."

— Judge Trevor Rapke, Melbourne County Court,
July 7, 1973.

Maybe it was because they lived so far out in the country that city journalists and lawyers couldn't agree on Lawson and his wife Dabee's surname. Whether it was Bettington, Bennington, or Bettingham, one day in July 1971, they had visitors at their farm at Rylestone, in central New South Wales.

They were unexpected visitors, two men from Melbourne. Vittorio David Renzella, in his mid-twenties, slim, dark-haired, with a hooked nose, would have introduced himself as Rick Renzella, a racehorse owner. Confident and talkative, like the used car salesman that he was, Renzella introduced Mr. and Mrs., let us say Bettington, to his trainer, Alan McNamara, a man four years older than Renzella.

They had come to see a horse the Bettingtons had bred themselves, called Royal School. Royal School was an unexceptional six-year-old who had won six of his 41 races, a record that was less impressive than it sounded because the races were all at small, country tracks. Royal School might have won more races if he hadn't been a bit of a rogue, and it was hard to see why anyone would want to buy him, but Renzella did, for $300.

"I was a little surprised," Dabee Bettington remembered.

"He wasn't looking very good and we didn't intend to train him again. He was to be just a horse to round up cattle with."[1]

Mrs. Bettington was even more surprised when, almost two years later, she was shown a photograph of Royal School romping home in a race at Casterton, in Victoria. She could see that the horse in the photograph wasn't Royal School.

Renzella was a con man, with the assets of a ready smile and look-you-in-the-eye reassurance, both of which had helped to fund a nice house in the Melbourne suburb of Brighton and later fooled a prominent QC barrister into believing what Renzella told him.

He had a small string of racehorses, and of convictions, including for the possession of an unregistered firearm and living off prostitutes' earnings.

During October and November of 1971, against McNamara's advice, Renzella insisted on running Royal School four times at country tracks in the Gippsland racing district, east of Melbourne. He finished last twice and second last twice. If anyone was taking notes, they would have noted that Royal School was not a horse to back next time out.

Relations between Renzella and McNamara were strained, and early in 1972 Royal School joined Ross Afflick's yard at Cranbourne, in Melbourne. Afflick was a former jump jockey in his late twenties, who had agreed to work as Renzella's private trainer.

In March of 1972,Renzella asked Ian Baird of the Australian Bloodstock Agency to buy a "well performed" horse, telling him that it was for an unnamed friend who wanted to race in Western Australia. Baird eventually suggested Regal Vista.

A year younger than Royal School, Regal Vista was a well-known sprinter in Melbourne, regarded by his experienced trainer, Brian Courtney, as "a horse just below top class." His owner, Anthony Naughton, was prepared to sell Regal Vista for $10,000, and on April 27 William Burns, a veterinary surgeon, examined the horse on Renzella's behalf. His report was discouraging.

Burns found there to be "considerable, chronic damage to the near foreleg," and although Regal Vista was currently fit to race, he was fundamentally "unsound for racing," being "a horse that could have broken down at any time."[2]

Renzella asked for a second opinion, which merely confirmed the first one, but he was not deterred. A price of $6,000 was agreed, with a further $3,500 payable when and if Regal Vista won. The deal done, Renzella told Baird that he was acting for a Mr. Kourlinis, but on the purchase documentation Kourlinis's name was struck out and replaced by that of Jim Doumtses.

On May 5 Regal Vista was removed from Courtney's stables, but the new owner, whoever he was, made no attempt to register the transfer of ownership. Regal Vista was ready to run — he was pre-post favorite for the following day's Coral Sea Handicap at Sandown — but there was no sign of his new connections wanting to race him.

Regal Vista was taken to McNamara's yard at Mornington, in Melbourne and a few days later moved to Afflick's stables, but the Victoria Racing Club was not notified of a change of trainer and Renzella instructed both McNamara and Afflick not to exercise Regal Vista on the racetrack. It was a strange way to train a racehorse.

On the evening of May 10, Renzella drove a hired float (horsebox) to Afflick's stables, where he had arranged to meet Gary Canavan, a jump jockey attached to McNamara's yard. Canavan had agreed to drive the float to Mildura, about 350 miles northwest of Melbourne.

Renzella then collected Stephen Wood, who had ridden Royal School on his first outing after leaving the Bettingtons. Two horses, one of them called Redline, were loaded on to the float, and Canavan was told that the destination was no longer Mildura but Casterton, about 200 miles west of Melbourne. Canavan and Wood traveled together in the float, which arrived at its destination at about 7:00 a.m. the next morning.

They had difficulty finding suitable stabling and finally left the two horses in trainer Bob Mullen's stables. One of the horses, Mullen noticed, was very heavily rugged.

On Friday May 12, 1972, Royal School made his first racecourse appearance for over five months in the Muntham Handicap at Casterton over six furlongs. It was hundreds of miles from the tracks he had raced on the previous year, and given Royal School's poor form, it was no surprise that not one of the four tipsters in Melbourne's daily paper, *The Age*, thought that he would finish in the first three in the ten-runner field.

Someone disagreed strongly, for Royal School was backed down from as much as 50-1 in places to 7-4 second favorite. He beat Apex Star, the 5-4 favorite, by an easy three lengths.

Jack Barling, Apex Star's trainer, was as stunned as most punters must have been, for Apex Star had won his two most recent starts, and Barling could not believe that Royal School could have swept his horse aside so contemptuously. When Louis Toth, Apex Star's rider, told him what Wood had said when the horses pulled up, Barling's suspicions intensified.

"I'm glad I won," Wood told Toth. "I'm on four thousand." The race was worth $325 to the winner.

Jim Cerchi, the veteran trainer of another runner, said to Barling, "This is a ring-in. I've seen the horse before, boy. It's not the same horse. Fire in a protest."[3]

Barling made a point of watching Royal School on his return from the track and noticed that the brand on his off-shoulder was a one over a five, indicating that the horse had been foaled in 1965 and was a six-year-old. In the race book Royal School was down as a seven-year-old. He informed Douglas McDonald, one of the three stewards, that he had been told the winner was a ringer, but the stewards took no immediate, decisive action.

Their chairman was the Victoria Racing Club's stipendiary steward, William Brewer. He had delegated the pre-race task of examining horses that had not raced in the district before to Francis Beattie. Beattie, like McDonald, was a part-time steward appointed by the South-Western District Racing Association.

Beattie had asked Afflick for Royal School's registration certificate and checked the brands on the certificate, which included a one over a five, with those on the horse. He signed the certificate and handed it back to Afflick.

Beattie had also noticed that in the race book Royal School was down as a seven-year-old, but because the brands matched those on the certificate he did not consider it necessary to query the discrepancy.

Nor did McDonald, who examined the horse again after the race. He later testified, "I had a slight suspicion that it was not Royal School even before the weigh-in. I thought either the horse was doped or it was a different horse." He may have had his doubts, but he didn't stop the "correct weight" signal being given, the all clear for bets to be settled.[4]

At Flemington the next day, racecourse gossip was full of rumors of a ringer, and the name of Regal Vista was already being suggested. On Monday, May 15, the Casterton stewards opened an inquiry, led by Brewer. When Brewer checked the registration records at the VRC's office, he discovered that the correct brand for Royal School, foaled in 1964, was a one over a four. That was also the brand recorded by the steward who had checked Royal School when he last ran, at Moe, the previous November. They needed to take a closer look at the winner's registration certificate.

Brewer and Eric Jeffery, Victoria's deputy registrar of racehorses, went to Afflick's stables and asked to see Royal School and his papers. Afflick told them that Royal School wasn't there nor were his papers, which, at different times, the trainer insisted had either been kept by Beattie or passed on to Renzella. They were never found.

Asked to identify one of the horses, Afflick said it was Royal Manor, although it bore the brands of Royal School. When Brewer and Jeffery returned about an hour later, the trainer admitted that the horse was Royal School; Renzella had told him not to say so. Brewer impounded the horse.

The evidence of the brands alone was enough to satisfy the

stewards that the winning horse was not Royal School, but Renzella was not about to admit defeat. On May 16, smartly dressed as ever, he emerged from an interview with the stewards, completely unruffled.

"I am not worried," Renzella said. "I have a number of witnesses I can produce at the right time to prove that it was Royal School who raced at Casterton. This inquiry has only been started by some stupid rumor. It has caused a lot of fuss over nothing. Royal School was checked by the stewards at Casterton and passed. I was there, and I can tell you I know what my own horse looks like."

Brian Cash, Renzella's solicitor, warned that legal action would be taken if the stewards did not release Royal School within a reasonable period. Shortly afterward, he took out a writ for the horse's return and the stewards returned it, on the condition that the horse remained at Afflick's stable.[5]

Over the next few days the stewards continued their inquiry, interviewing Renzella again, as well as Afflick, Wood, and Canavan. Meanwhile, the search was on for Regal Vista, the suspected ringer.

According to the purchase documentation, Regal Vista was now owned by Jim Doumtses, a local estate and travel agent who, it emerged, was the brother-in-law of John Kourlinis, who ran a cafe. Neither of them appeared to have any knowledge of horse racing, and Doumtses was extremely unhelpful, insisting that the horse had been sent to Western Australia, over 2,000 miles away, but refusing to reveal its location.

"Regal Vista is alive and well in a paddock near Perth. The rest is my business," he told prying reporters. "When he is fit again, he will race. If the VRC does not permit me to race him, then he will be mincemeat."

Kourlinis said nothing. "He can't speak much English," Doumtses, a fellow Greek, said for him. "He doesn't want to talk to you."

Nor did Doumtses. When the stewards asked him to meet them at the VRC's offices on May 24, he refused. "I do not want anything to do with these inquiries," he said. "I have a business to run and have not got time to be going down to the racing center. I am not a gambler. People advised me to buy Regal Vista, so I bought him because I wanted a good horse to race. He is my first horse."

Renzella claimed that he was simply the go-between in Regal Vista's sale, for which he had received a $1,500 commission. He had advised against the purchase, a story at odds with the evidence of the Australian Bloodstock Agency's Ian Baird. Renzella insisted that he had no idea where Regal Vista was and offered a $2,000 reward for anyone who found the horse.[6]

To add a touch of farce, the Western Australian Agriculture Department confirmed that any horse brought into the state required a certificate declaring it free of "noxious weeds." No clearance papers had been received for Regal Vista, whose owners were liable to be fined if the horse was found.

By the end of May, Renzella was predicting that he would be barred for life, "because I won't say 'yes sir, no sir, kiss my ....' to the stewards." If he was barred, he would appeal to the Supreme Court. The stewards, he complained, "are the accusers, judge, jury, witnesses, and the executioners. How can there be any justice in that?" He hoped that the police would investigate the case, "so that the truth will come out."[7]

On June 1, acting on the basis that attack is the best means of defense, Renzella sued the VRC along with Brewer, McDonald, and Beattie, for having suggested that the winner was not Royal School but Regal Vista. He had been presented with the race trophy, worth $20, but not the prize money of $325, so he sued the Casterton Racing Club, too.

Renzella admitted that he had won $33,570 in bets, all from the TAB Double, which coupled the day's main race, the Casterton Cup, won by Gay Demand, at 9-2, with the Muntham Handicap. Off-course bets on the Double had to be placed by 2:00 p.m., 40 minutes before the Casterton Cup and almost two hours before the Muntham Handicap. The pool was closed long before punters became aware that Royal School was the subject of a gamble.

Renzella arranged for three men, including McNamara and Stephen Wood's father, Leslie, to place bets at three TAB agencies, all situated near Renzella's workplace. The bets coupled every runner in the Casterton Cup with Royal School, with bigger bets on the more fancied Cup runners.

The pool contained $120,665, with each of the 1,078 winning 50-cent tickets paying $111.90, odds of over 200-1. Two men with TAB telephone accounts, a Mr. Fox and a Mr. Gardiner, won over $16,000 and $9,000 respectively, but Renzella was the biggest winner. The day after the race he walked into the Balaclava agency and handed over 300 winning tickets.

Less than three weeks later, with lawyers to pay, he claimed that the $33,570 was gone. "I've got a $42 light bill that hasn't been paid," he moaned. "I'm worried they will cut the power off."[8]

At the beginning of June, the Hamilton Racing Club offered Renzella the chance to pay his bill when it issued a $500 challenge for a winner-take-all match between Royal School and Apex Star, who had recently won again at Coleraine and finished fourth at Werribee.

Renzella accepted the challenge, in principle. "I'm not going out there for a miserable $500," he said. "If they put up $5,000, I'll put up $5,000, and I know which horse will win." But the match would have to be postponed because Royal School had a leg injury.

The mystery of Regal Vista's whereabouts and ownership remained unsolved. The deputy registrar of racehorses declared, "I am not speculating who the owner is," and Doumtses continued to be uncooperative.

Having finally submitted an application for the ownership of Regal Vista to be transferred to him, Doumtses told reporters that he "may or may not" attend the meeting, arranged by the VRC stewards to discuss his application. "I'm a busy man, and if I've got clients to attend to; they've got to be looked after."

The stewards waited for him for an hour and then Jim Ahern, their chairman, walked into the waiting area and asked, "Is Mr. Doumtses here?" He wasn't. The stewards issued a statement declaring, “As Mr. Doumstes failed to attend, the application for the transfer will rest in abeyance.”

Doumtses later retorted, “I am going to sell Regal Vista and get out of it. I’m sick of it.” When asked where a potential buyer could view the horse, which Doumtses described as “sick but alive,” he refused to say. They would have to buy him unseen.

Renzella was apparently prepared to, allegedly in an attempt to prove his innocence. “I know everyone says the horse is dead, shot, turned into cray bait, but it’s not true. Why would anyone want to kill a horse they spent a fortune on?”[9]

While Renzella negotiated the purchase of Regal Vista for $7,500, plus the return of the $1,500 commission, the VRC charged Renzella, Afflick, Wood, and Canavan with fraud and conspiracy. Wood and Canavan were also charged with having given false evidence to the stewards.

Canavan claimed that he had traveled alone to Casterton, enabling Wood to claim that he had not arrived at Casterton until the day of the race, May 12. This conflicted with the evidence of two important witnesses, who provided an example of the unforeseen incidents that have a habit of intruding on carefully planned deceits.

On May 11, having unloaded Redline and the other horse from the float and settled them in Mullen’s stable, Canavan and Wood booked into a motel and went to sleep. Their arrival had been noticed by Mullen’s 15-year-old son, David, working at the yard during his school holiday, and Ian Treloar, an 18-year-old strapper employed by Mullen.

Later in the day they went to look at the new arrivals, lifted up one of the horse’s rugs, and noticed a large scar on its rump. When Wood arrived and pulled the rug down, they asked him about the scar. Wood denied that the conversation had taken place.

It was an important conversation because the horse was the one that raced the next day, and Regal Vista also had a large scar on his rump.

The police had now joined the chase, but, true to his word, Renzella welcomed their intervention. Their inquiries, he said, "will only help to prove our case against the stewards' charges."

Those charges, Renzella maintained in an action through the courts, had been pre-judged by McDonald and Beattie and the stewards' inquiry should therefore be stopped.

Supreme Court judge Mr. Justice Adam disagreed. It was true that McDonald had already signed an affidavit that Royal School was not the winner, citing six differences between Royal School and the winning horse, but Adam concluded, "It is not the stewards' fault if they have firm convictions as a result of what they have seen." He did not accept that those convictions would prevent McDonald and Beattie from taking proper account of the defendants' evidence.[10]

While the Supreme Court was preparing to reject Renzella's application, he suddenly produced Regal Vista and invited Brian Maguire of the Australian Bloodstock Agency to examine the horse at a secret location in the Cranbourne district of Melbourne. Maguire stated, "I am convinced beyond a shadow of doubt that the horse is the missing Regal Vista." There was a large scar on the horse's quarters.

Renzella declared himself delighted. "I always knew Regal Vista was alive, and I am thrilled to be able to show him to you. Regal Vista is a key witness in my defense. That's why I have bought him."

Regal Vista was available for the Casterton stewards' inspection, but the stewards, rather surprisingly, declined to inspect him, provoking Renzella into offering Regal Vista for sale, for $3,000. "Regal Vista is no good to me now," he said, "so I may as well sell him cheap. I only bought him so he could be examined by the stewards."[11]

On July 4 Renzella and Afflick were barred for life, along with Royal School. Wood was barred for 20 years, and Canavan for 10 years. All four announced that they would appeal to the South-Western District Racing Association.

To add insult to alleged injury, Renzella's attempts to sell

Regal Vista were hampered by the fact that, officially, the horse was still registered as owned by Anthony Naughton.

The appeal hearing opened on July 25. Two days later all the charges against Wood and Canavan, except those of giving false evidence, were dismissed and their bans reduced to two years.

In his summing up, Brian Cash, Renzella's solicitor, accused the Casterton stewards of being "irresponsible, careless and not competent to hold their positions," a line of attack unlikely to appeal to the SWDRA, which had appointed two of them. Renzella's and Afflick's appeals were rejected.[12]

The police investigation continued, and on June 5, 1973, the four men, plus trainer Alan McNamara, appeared at Melbourne County Court before Judge Trevor Rapke, charged with conspiring to cheat and defraud Casterton Racing Club and others by entering Royal School and then running a horse other than Royal School. All five defendants pleaded not guilty.

Renzella was represented by Philip Opas QC. Demonstrating his credentials as an accomplished liar, Renzella managed to persuade Opas of his innocence. "He had all the attributes of a good salesman or a magsman* or a con man. Undoubtedly, he was all three," Opas reflected later, ruefully.[13]

Perhaps the same skills explain why Renzella's accomplices received such a small share of the winnings. During the course of the trial, which occupied 20 days, it emerged that McNamara, who had agreed to place bets in order to keep Renzella sweet and was frightened of him, received $3,800. Afflick's share was only $920 while Wood received $706 and Canavan $500.

The defense tried to raise doubts in the jury's mind about the identity of the winning horse and claimed that it really was Royal School, but it was hard work.

When Dabee Bettington, who had owned Royal School for almost seven years, was shown photographs of the winner, she observed, "It's a much bigger horse than Royal School.

* A storyteller or swindler.

The whole chest looks much too broad to be Royal School. Royal School is much darker than this horse. Royal School has a more rounded nose, and his star is more in the center. The foot here seems to be a normal sort of foot; Royal School's is much smaller. His action doesn't seem the same. Royal School, when he was walking, was more sweeping."

Royal School and Regal Vista, exhibits Y and Z respectively, were available for the court's inspection, and Opas believed that Renzella might have escaped conviction if he had not resurrected Regal Vista.

"Renzella could be described as cunning but not clever," wrote Opas. "Had he been really clever, he would not have produced Regal Vista. Far from clearing him, that horse convicted him. There was room for suspicion but, in the absence of the horse, I believe proof was lacking. The horse provided the proof."

Treloar and David Mullen told the court about their discovery of the scar on the horse's rump, and Opas admitted, "having cross examined these two young men, I have no doubt that they did see the scar and did ask a question about it. Undoubtedly, the jury believed them."

He was not confident that they would believe Renzella. "He was very confident, even over-confident, of his ability to handle cross-examination," Opas recalled. "I was in no doubt that Crown Prosecutor John Moloney QC would have made mincemeat of him."[14]

Renzella was restricted to making an unsworn statement from the dock, which was unusual largely because it was made in the absence of his senior counsel, Opas having left the trial to meet a long-standing engagement in Europe.

Renzella claimed that Royal School had been "skin and bone" when he bought him and that over the next six months,he had transformed him. It was the real Royal School who had won the Muntham Handicap.

Doumtses gave evidence under an indemnity from prosecution, but he was an unconvincing witness and the relationship between him and Renzella remained unclear.

Opas remarked of the two men, "The tales they told were so incredible that I am unable even to guess at the truth," but "I believe that, from first to last, Doumtses never set eyes on Regal Vista. I feel certain that, from May 5 to June 21, Doumtses had not the faintest idea where Regal Vista was."[15]

Wherever he was, he was almost certainly under Renzella's control. His prospects of winning at Casterton, as a ringer, were spelled out by handicapper Ian Middleton. "Regal Vista is a much better type of horse than we get at Casterton," he said. "If I'd had Regal Vista nominated, he'd have had well in excess of 10 stone (140 pounds)." Royal School was allotted 7 stone 13 pounds (111 pounds).

The jury took over 12 hours to reach their verdicts, which were announced on July 7, 1973. Canavan was acquitted; his four fellow defendants all found guilty.

Judge Rapke was satisfied that Renzella was the driving force behind the fraud and expressed sympathy for both McNamara, who he accepted had been drawn in under extreme pressure, and Wood. "You were used," he told the jockey, "and I feel sorry for you." It was a generous attitude, for Wood must have known that the Royal School he finished last on at Moe in October 1971 was not the same Royal School he won on at Casterton seven months later.

McNamara, Wood, and Afflick were all placed on probation for two years. Renzella was sent to prison for the same period. Opas admitted, "I know now that most of what Renzella did tell me was lies. He almost boasted about misleading me and the court."[16]

Renzella did do one good turn for his barrister. He phoned him from Geelong prison and asked if Opas would give Royal School a home, which the lawyer did, to their mutual pleasure.

Regal Vista was less fortunate. Naughton, Doumtses, and Renzella all claimed that the horse was theirs. A court finally ruled that Renzella was the legal owner, and Renzella then sold Regal Vista, who raced on with decreasing success.

Opas neither saw nor heard from his former client again,

but both Renzella and Wood had more news to make.

On March 22, 1983, almost 11 years after the Casterton ring-in, Wood walked into the Melbourne Police Headquarters and handed Detective Senior Sergeant Russell Bradley a two-page statement. "I take complete responsibility for what happened," he said.[17]

What had happened was that, three days earlier, at the St. Patrick's race meeting at Broken Hill, a horse called Foden won the Orlando Improvers Handicap after being backed from 50-1 to 2-1 joint-favorite. A bookmaker told the stewards that he believed the winner was a ringer and Chief Stipendiary Steward Tom Carroll promptly intercepted Foden and the man leading him in, Gregory Dunn.

Earlier that afternoon another steward, Peter Davidson, had inspected Foden and noted that the chestnut had a white blaze on its forehead, white marks above its hind hooves, an inverted T brand on its near side, and a bent left ear. By the time Foden arrived in the winner's enclosure, it had lost all these identifying marks.

The game was already up. The stewards declined to announce "correct weight" and impounded the winner, while the police impounded Gregory Dunn, a 23-year-old part-time strapper and jockey.

While Dunn made an early appearance in court, the stewards awarded the race to the runner-up, Eastern Crisis, and ruled that all bets on Foden were lost. That was a bitter blow to Wood, who had flown a group of men to Broken Hill and given each of them $500 or $750 to spread around the ring. Early reports suggested a potential pay-out of $200,000 but Wood's own estimate of $55,000 was probably more accurate.

Later, when Wood bumped into one of the men, John Hose, Wood quipped, "Visiting hours are every second Sunday."[18] After handing in his confession, he led the police to the real Foden and admitted that the winner was actually Nordica.

Wood and his stepfather, John Doughton, had bought

Nordica at auction on February 14 for $6,000 and, eight days later, bought Foden privately for $1,000, prices that reflected the horses' relative abilities. They paid cash, which was just as well, because the check for $940 that Wood gave to Kevin Pearce, the pilot of the aircraft that ferried his helpers to Broken Hill, bounced.

Wood told the police that his confession was prompted by a desire to "stop innocent people being dragged in and to save police time. No one was aware that the horses were being swapped." According to Wood, the only guilty party was Wood.[19]

It was a noble gesture, perhaps encouraged by the recognition that he didn't have a leg to stand on, but the police were not prepared to accept that Doughton, Dunn, and his brother Andrew Dunn were ignorant innocents. In September of 1983 all four were committed for trial, finally appearing at the District Court in October of 1984.

They all pleaded not guilty to charges of conspiracy to defraud, including Wood, who argued that he could not be guilty of conspiracy since he had acted alone. After a 14-day trial Wood and Gregory Dunn were found guilty, Andrew Dunn was acquitted, while the jury were unable to agree on Doughton's guilt or innocence.

Describing the episode as a "miserable sort of crime," and Wood as a "plausible manipulator," Judge E.P. Knoblanche sentenced Wood to two and a half years in prison, and Dunn to 300 hours community service.[20]

Having confessed to one ring-in, Wood confessed to others. A month after he appeared at Melbourne Police Headquarters, detectives from Sydney appeared at Orange in New South Wales to investigate a race run at Towac Park over a year earlier.

On January 1, 1982, a horse called Tillant, having his first start for almost five months, finished last of 12 in the Improvers Handicap over 1,200 meters. On January 9 Tillant appeared again, provoking a subsequent headline in the local *Central Western Daily*, "Big Plunge at Towac Park."

Tony King reported, "One of the best organized plunges seen in the west for some time was brought about on Saturday when Tillant won the 1000 meter Improvers Handicap. As much as 33-1 was bet about the horse, who eventually started at 4-1."[21]

The Orange Jockey Club held a cursory inquiry and were satisfied; the police were not. In 1983 they charged Wood; Gregory Dunn, who rode Tillant; and owner-trainer Kelvin Veale with another conspiracy to defraud, this time by substituting the multiple winner Rack's Image for the untalented Tillant.

It wasn't the first time Rack's Image had appeared under a false name. Wood admitted that, on November 3, 1981, Melbourne Cup Day, he had landed a gamble at Wentworth, in Victoria, by running Rack's Image in the guise of Blue Mirage.

While Wood was misbehaving with horses, Renzella was misbehaving with his first love, used cars. By the 1980s he had graduated from changing the identity of racehorses to changing the identity and ownership of stolen cars.

In 1998, after pleading guilty to conspiracy to defraud, Renzella, already serving one jail sentence, told the court that he had been dogged by his association with the Royal School scandal. The judge gave him another six months, with a release date of January 1, 2001.[22]

The Return of the Ringers

8

"It was a scenario that might have been authored jointly by an Alfred Hitchcock and a Damon Runyon."

— Judge Jacob Fuchsberg, Court of Appeals, New York, June 10, 1980.

In 1972 Spencer Drayton, president of the Thoroughbred Racing Protective Bureau, delivered a statement to the House Select Committee on Crime. Drayton recalled the situation in the early days of the TRPB, just after the Second World War. "The TRPB's initial study of thoroughbred racing had found the methods of horse identification in use throughout this country to be grossly inadequate," he told the Select Committee.

"In some instances the identifier was presumed to know all the horses that came to the paddock. In other cases a 'clocker,' that is a person who records the time of a horse's workout or race, was employed as identifier, on the theory that he could recognize every horse on the grounds by sight.

"Unscrupulous horsemen took advantage of this situation to run ringers. In 1946, the year prior to the development of the lip tattoo system of identification now in use at all Thoroughbred Racing Association tracks and most tracks throughout the country, there had been no less than 26 cases under investigation by the TRPB, several of which proved to be blatant frauds."

As a result, a lip-tattooing program had been introduced for horses and a fingerprint scheme for racetrack workers, to weed out people using false names and having criminal records.

"For 25 years," Drayton reported, "this solved the ringer problem and, during this time, there was never a horse which had been tattoo branded involved in a ringer case." Drayton was now obliged to report that the long period of grace was over.[1]

Several months earlier, Paul Berube, one of the TRPB's special investigators, now its president, had been questioned by the same Select Committee about a fresh outbreak of ringers.

Early in 1972 it had been discovered that the winner of a race at the Fair Grounds, New Orleans, staged on December 10, 1971, was not Idle John but Lins Dr Joe. This was not a huge surprise since Idle John had raced five times at tracks in Arkansas and New Mexico that year and been beaten an average of over 20 lengths, whereas Lins Dr Joe had won five races in California. Both horses had subsequently disappeared.

On March 16, 1972, a group of men from New York went to Narragansett Park in Rhode Island and cashed substantial winning bets on Oriennel, a longshot trained by Robert Servideo. The foal certificate Servideo had presented bore Oriennel's name but the registration number and markings of a different and better horse, Transponder. Servideo and owner Paul Bast were suspended, although Servideo was later exonerated.

The authorities were dealing with counterfeit foal certificates, and good ones. The counterfeiters used the same type of paper used by The Jockey Club, complete with counterfeits of The Jockey Club and TRPB seals.

Jockey Club chairman Ogden Phipps, having studied Oriennel's certificate, remarked, "The phony certificate was unbelievably real. It had all the expected validation marks and even had the perforated stamp indicating application of the lip tattoo on September 9, 1968."[2]

By the time Berube presented his testimony on May 25, 1972, the TRPB's "very active and very pending investigation" had uncovered six horses used as ringers, racing in nine states, under 12 different names, in 41 races, 14 of which they had won. The races embraced the period from November 1970 to March 1972.[3]

The Select Committee was looking particularly at the involvement of organized crime in sport, and Berube was not reassuring. "It would be my opinion that organized crime is definitely involved in the perhaps financing of this whole operation," he said. "The whole thread is organized crime."

The sums involved were "substantial." Using false names, the conspirators were prepared to pay large sums to buy good horses and to buy off trainers. The horses the ringers were substituted for were sometimes cynically killed.

Serious criminals were involved and potential witnesses were fearful. Congressman Larry Winn Jr. asked Berube, "You are saying, then, that they fear for their lives, if they give you the information that you are seeking?" "There is no question about that," replied Berube.

The most prolific ringer was Rule Away, who ran and won under at least three different names. On May 17, 1971, at Suffolk Downs near Boston, the three-year-old gelding was bought by D. Gordon for $11,000. Gordon vanished, but nine days later Rule Away resurfaced at Garden State Park in New Jersey under the name of El Toro Tortuga, owned by William Foley and trained by Al Forman.

When the track vet went to the barn to inspect the horse, it was in the care of Pat Catrone, a trainer not licensed in New Jersey. El Toro Tortuga was not allowed to run.

Early in June at Suffolk Downs, a horse called Native Mud was well beaten in a lowly $2,500 event. On July 13, Native Mud appeared at Liberty Bell Park in Philadelphia and won in $5,000 company, then repeated the performance on August 4. By then, the real Native Mud had probably been destroyed. The winning horse was Rule Away.

Native Mud's owner was listed as John O'Connell and his trainer as Charles Coco. Coco told the stewards that he had never met O'Connell, had been hired over the phone, and was paid through the post.

Later in August, racing at Atlantic City, New Jersey, Native Mud was claimed for $3,500. Five days later, when Native Mud ran for his new trainer, Robert Durso, Coco, acting on the telephoned instructions of the mysterious O'Connell, reclaimed the horse for $5,000. Coco forged O'Connell's signature on the claim form.

On September 10, still running in the name of Native Mud, Rule Away won a $6,500 race at Atlantic City before moving on to Laurel, Maryland, where he reverted to the disguise of El Toro Tortuga. In December of 1971 and January of 1972, in the new name of Intask, Rule Away won another two races at Narragansett Park.

The fraud was again based on counterfeit foal certificates. The forged certificate for Native Mud bore the tattoo number X8525. So did the horse presented as Native Mud, because that tattoo number was actually Rule Away's.

On May 25, 1972, the same day that Berube was giving evidence at Capitol Hill, William Foley and John O'Connell were barred from New Jersey's tracks, although both names were believed to be aliases.

Coco, who was real, was initially suspended for 60 days for breaching the rules governing claims. The penalty was subsequently reduced to 20 days suspension and a $600 fine.

On May 26 the stewards at Hazel Park, Michigan, revoked trainer Gary Hemmerling's license. Several months earlier, on November 17, 1971, Hemmerling's Radio Bay had caused an upset when winning at the Detroit track. Radio Bay had arrived from Shenandoah Downs with an unimpressive record. The reason for the upset was that the winner was actually Polo Field. Again, a counterfeit foal certificate had been used.

Hemmerling had owned and trained horses in Michigan for many years and had run Radio Bay in his own name at the request of the shipper. The TRPB accepted that some of the trainers involved were innocent and had been used.

Before long, owner-trainers George Shearin, Frank Sampson, and James Collins joined Foley, O'Connell, Coco, Hemmerling, and Catrone on the suspended list.

On October 5, 1972, in Rhode Island, a federal grand jury indicted Paul Bast, Martin Rolnick, and Arnold Rosenbaum, also known as Allan Rosen, on charges of obtaining money under false pretenses, interstate transportation of forged securities, and conspiracy. Bast and Rolnick owned horses together, while Rosenbaum worked for a New Jersey printing firm.

That summer The Jockey Club announced three changes to the system for identifying horses. First, a master list of horses and their foal certificate numbers was prepared for distribution to every racing authority, for use by identifiers at racetracks. Second, new bonded paper, with special watermarks and dyes was introduced for foal certificates. Third, future supplements to the *American Stud Book* were to carry registration numbers.[4]

It wasn't enough.

At one time during the afternoon, over 12,000 had been at Belmont, but it was the last race, it was 5:30 p.m., and it was wet. When the race fans who had left early looked at the result in the next day's *Daily Racing Form*, they were glad they hadn't stayed. They'd never have picked Lebon, not even for the show.

That Friday, September 23, 1977, Lebon went into the $10,000, one and a quarter-mile turf race with a record to flick through and quickly discard. The five-year-old had been a poor sprinter in Uruguay, the winner of one race and $711 in the last two years. His recent export to the United States hadn't improved him. On September 9, having his first run since April, Lebon finished 11th of 12 over one mile and a sixteenth, in a $9,500 claiming race at Belmont on the dirt. The close up in the *Daily Racing Form* reported, "Lebon showed nothing."

Not in the race. Inexplicably, he had shown up much better in the pre-race betting, kicking off at a meager looking 7.4 to 1. That was because of the blonde woman. She had bet $7,000 on Lebon. Maybe she liked Uruguay.

It was a straw no serious punter could cling to. On September 23, there was nothing to recommend Lebon, which was why Jack Morgan's horse started at 57-1, the rankest of rank outsiders.

Larry Adams, a 41-year-old journeyman jockey, had taken over from Tommy Wallis. "Lebon took over with a rush from the outside midway along the backstretch," the *Daily Racing Form* reported, "saved ground after drawing clear and won with something left." The winning margin was four lengths,

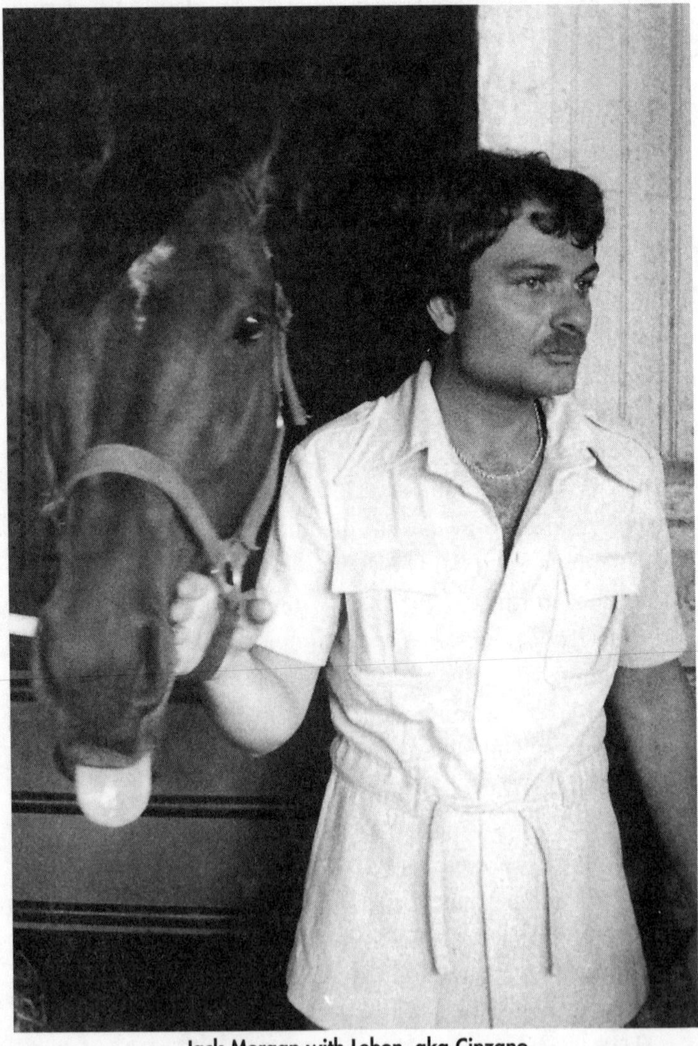

PHOTO COMMUNICATIONS

Jack Morgan with Lebon, aka Cinzano

the queue at the $50 pari-mutuel window, one deep. It consisted of Dr. Mark Gerard, veterinary surgeon and clairvoyant.

Gerard presented his tickets; $1,300 win and $600 show, $80,440 to come; cash, please. They didn't have $80,000 sitting in the till, so they collected it from the safe. Phil Maxwell brought it. Maxwell had once been a jockey, and he recognized Gerard. "Doc, how did you bet this horse?" he asked. "I had a dream," replied Gerard. Not really a dream, more a spot of forward planning.[5]

Gerard was a 43-year-old New York racetrack vet whose equine clientele had once included Riva Ridge, Hoist the Flag, and the mighty Secretariat. More recently, he had been active in importing Thoroughbreds from South America.

That spring Joseph Taub, a wealthy computer executive and future owner of the New Jersey Nets basketball team, told Gerard that he was in the market for a good horse. Two weeks later Gerard told him that he had found one. It was a champion in Uruguay, four years old, might cost $200,000, and was called Cinzano.

Taub told Gerard that he was prepared to pay $150,000; $100,000 on delivery and $50,000 at the end of the year. Gerard promptly bought Cinzano for $81,000 and billed Taub for the initial $100,000, plus $12,000 expenses. He liked money.

On June 3, 1977, Cinzano was loaded onto a plane at Carasco airport, near Montevideo, along with another of Gerard's purchases, the five-year-old Lebon. At $1,600, about $1,000 more than he had recently been sold for, Lebon was the bottom branch of the tree. Although he had won his first three starts, that was a long time ago. On his latest outing, Lebon had broken down; he was a racehorse without a racing future. All that the two bay horses had in common when they landed at Kennedy Airport on June 4 was their appearance.

Gerard was waiting to meet them, together with Dr. Robert Gale of the Department of Agriculture. Taub's vet would have been there, too, but Gerard had told him, incorrectly, that he wouldn't be allowed to enter the receiving area.

The documentation that accompanied the horses indicated that Lebon had a large, diamond-shaped white star on his forehead, while Cinzano had a small star, slightly lower down, and elongated by a stripe. He also had a scar on his left shoulder.

Gerard took the necessary blood samples and filled out the description forms required by The Jockey Club. If the horses had been bred in the United States, they would have had tattoos, but they weren't, and they hadn't.

Cinzano and Lebon were taken to a quarantine station to await the results of the blood tests. On June 11, after having been cleared, they were driven to Gerard's farm at Muttontown, Long Island. Lebon's halter had his name on it, while Cinzano's did not.

Gerard no longer lived with his wife, Alice, but Alice still kept a horse at the Muttontown property, an old jumper called Lake Delaware, whom she exercised regularly.

Alice was at the farm on the evening of Sunday June 12 but did not join her husband, Mona Smith, and trainer Frank Wright for dinner at a local restaurant. During the meal Gerard received a phone call. There had been an accident at the farm. He left, asking Wright to follow later if he didn't return.

When Wright arrived at the farm, Gerard told him that Cinzano had fractured his skull and broken an ankle in a freak accident. He had been forced to put the horse down. Wright saw the body of a bay horse.

Through the General Adjustment Bureau, Cinzano had been insured for his purchase price of $150,000. When filing a claim, two vets had to be consulted, one representing the owner, the other the insurance company. Gerard phoned Dr. Harry Hemphill, who also worked at New York racetracks, and asked him to look at Cinzano's fractured leg, to certify that it was a fracture requiring euthanasia. Hemphill asked if Gerard wanted him to come over that night? Gerard said no, he would bring the leg to his Belmont office the next day. Macabre, but not, perhaps, to a vet.

On June 13, Hemphill inspected the leg at Belmont but certified that he had been in attendance at Gerard's farm the previous night, and that the horse involved was a four-year-old called Cinzano.

The horse's carcass was collected by Anthony Minieri and taken to a public dump at Huntington, where it was soon submerged under a mountain of garbage. The insurance company, declining to be difficult, paid Taub $150,000, less the initial premium of $15,000.

On June 15 the surviving horse, said to be Lebon, was moved to trainer Sidney Watters at Belmont, but Watters did not train the horse. Gerard did that himself, with Alice as an exercise rider.

Several weeks later Lebon was shipped to Joe McMahon's barn at Saratoga, with a halter bearing the name Lake Delaware. Every morning Gerard was at the barn, issuing instructions. He was vague about the horse's identity and told an exercise boy that if the clockers asked for the horse's name, he was to tell them it was Denim and was trained by Jack Morgan. Later, Gerard told McMahon that the horse's name was Lebon.

On August 28, at the end of the Saratoga meeting, the horse was moved back to Watters under the name of Denim.

As a vet employed at the New York Racing Association's tracks, Gerard was not allowed either to train or own racehorses, so he sold Lebon to Jack Morgan for $8,500. It was a purely paper transaction. The money was never paid, and Gerard continued to pay the horse's training fees and dictate its program.

Morgan, 32, had worked as Gerard's assistant for about eight years. In 1977 he obtained a trainer's license, and Gerard told him that he might give him a South American horse for them to train together, then sell. Morgan didn't see Lebon until early September, and when he did, Gerard was in command.

A nearby trainer who regularly arrived for work at 4:30 a.m. reported finding Mr. and Mrs. Gerard already washing their horses down. "They were working them in the pitch black," he said.[6]

Gerard told Morgan to enter Lebon in a particular race on September 9 and to book jockey Tommy Wallis.

The race was more successful than it appeared. Fred Burlew was working as the track's horse identifier, and he was a diligent one. Burlew compared the horse with the description on the certificate The Jockey Club had issued for Lebon. The horse had a star with an extending stripe, but the written description suggested a star without a stripe.

Burlew contacted The Jockey Club. Barbara Calvo confirmed that the documentation from Uruguay and the forms completed on the horse's arrival in the United States indicated a star but no stripe. She consulted photographs of Lebon. At least, Lebon's name was on the back of the photographs. When Gerard submitted them, together with the forms, he submitted photographs of Cinzano.

Dr. Manuel Gilman, NYRA's chief examining vet, became involved. Gilman matched the horse against the photographs. He assumed that the written description was an error and allowed Lebon to run. After all, such errors were commonplace. Every year, 6,000 registration certificates were corrected by The Jockey Club to bring them into line with descriptions supplied by track identifiers.

A new certificate was issued for Lebon to include not only the stripe but also the scar on the horse's left shoulder. No one examined the horse's teeth to confirm that it was a five-year-old.

The amended certificate ensured that no difficult questions would be asked when Lebon reappeared on September 23, nor when he finished a creditable fourth in a $25,000 allowance race at the Meadowlands on October 12. All seemed well, but not for long.

The Hipodromo de Maronas in Montevideo, where Cinzano had won seven times, is a long way from Belmont. Unfortunately for Gerard, two Uruguayan racefans who knew Cinzano well were at Belmont on September 23. They were curious about Lebon; so curious that, when they returned home, they discussed it with Julian Perez of *El Pais*.

Through the Associated Press, *El Pais* obtained a picture of Lebon in the winner's circle. On October 14 Bud Hyland, a

New York steward, received a phone call from Uruguay. He was told that the winner could not have been Lebon but was probably Cinzano.

Lebon was immediately imprisoned at Belmont in barn 59. An examination of his teeth indicated that they belonged to a four-year-old rather than a five-year-old. With the help of Cinzano's Uruguayan connections, it was soon established that the horse posing in the winner's circle on September 23 was Cinzano.

On October 24 Dr. Mark Gerard and Jack Morgan were both suspended indefinitely. As inquiries continued, the bona fides of other horses imported from South America by Gerard were questioned. Chirico, Sundoro, and As De Pique II were placed under guard. It was suspected that As De Pique II, a winner at long odds at Monmouth Park, New Jersey, might really be Enchumao, who had been destroyed after breaking a leg at Gulfstream Park.

While Gerard challenged his suspension in the courts, Morgan told reporters, "So far as I know, the horse I was training was Lebon. I never heard of Cinzano until this thing happened. If it is Cinzano, the substitution was done without my knowledge. If I was set up by Gerard, the like I had for him would really turn into hate." Morgan, who had a penchant for loud, checked jackets, said that he was prepared to take a lie detector test.[7]

Instead, he was required to give evidence at Gerard's trial, which finally opened at Nassau County Court, before Judge Raymond Harrington on September 8, 1978.

Gerard faced a string of charges, all stemming from the allegation that he masterminded the substitution of Cinzano for Lebon, an exercise that involved killing Lebon, stealing Taub's horse, executing an insurance fraud, causing another vet to swear falsely that the dead horse was Cinzano, and tampering with witnesses as well as with a sports contest. During the investigation Gerard had twice called Dr. Hemphill to ask him to stick by the story that he had actually seen the dead horse.

Hemphill taped the calls and testified that he had not seen the horse and had falsely signed an insurance form signifying that the horse was Cinzano.

The defense, conducted by F. Lee Bailey, accepted that the winner was Cinzano but maintained that Gerard was unaware that the horses had been switched. Gerard's situation, already unpromising, became perilous when the prosecution, led by Thomas Davenport, played a tape of Gerard's interview with the New York State Racing and Wagering Board.

Asked whether he could tell the difference between Lebon and Cinzano, Gerard replied, "I never had any question in my mind. Lebon looked like a cheap horse and Cinzano looked like a good horse. Cinzano looked bigger and better."[8]

It seemed a small step from establishing that when Gerard backed Lebon, he had known that he was backing Cinzano, to finding him guilty of having organized the substitution.

When the jury retired on September 20, they asked for the testimony of trainer Joe McMahon to be read to them. His evidence had highlighted Gerard's evasiveness about the identity of the horse and his intense interest in its training. It didn't look good.

Yet none of the prosecution witnesses really mattered. F. Lee Bailey, with the dapper Dr. Gerard carrying his boxes into court for him, had called only one witness, but it was the one that counted.

Alice Gerard, in her early 30s, looked thin and drawn, in her beige dress. It wasn't difficult to believe Bailey when he told the court that Dr. Gerard's wife had suffered "emotional problems" and "mental instability." She was receiving psychiatric treatment in California.

Mrs. Gerard had been given limited immunity from prosecution. She testified that it was she, not her husband, who had been responsible for Lebon's purchase. She had told Robert Forne, Cinzano's former owner, that she wanted Lebon to ride, not to race. Forne considered it an odd and expensive way of acquiring a saddle horse.

Alice wasn't looking for any horse; she was looking for a horse "that looked like Cinzano." "Why?" she was asked. "So that I could switch them, substitute one for the other." According to Alice, it was Alice who had hatched the plot. Her motive, she said, was not money. "I didn't do it for the money. I had all the material things I wanted." She did it because she didn't like horse racing and wanted to discomfort the racing authorities.

"I didn't think my husband would be blamed," she said. "I wanted to show them, and everyone else, that they (NYRA and The Jockey Club) could be wrong at least one time." It was a curious motive, but then, Mrs. Gerard had been presented as a person with problems.

On June 12 she had switched the horses' halters and turned the two horses out in a paddock. In the evening, while Dr. Gerard was out for dinner, she brought the horses in, but as she was leading Lebon into his stall, "there was about a dozen cats chasing this little rabbit. They ran under Lebon's feet."

The alarmed horse reared up, cracked his skull on an iron crossbar above the stable door and fell down, breaking his leg. Alice phoned her husband at the restaurant, and when he got home, she went into the house. The horse Dr. Gerard euthanized was wearing the halter he associated with Cinzano; the surviving horse's halter had Lebon's name on it.

Mrs. Gerard tearfully insisted that she would not have agreed to a horse's murder. "I'm a vegetarian," she said. "I don't eat meat. I wouldn't have any part of killing a horse." It had been a terrible accident.

The blonde woman who had put $7,000 on Lebon when he ran for the first time at Belmont, on September 9, was at one time thought to have been Crista Mancuso, the Florida-based owner of several of Gerard's South American imports, including Sundoro and Enchumao.

It was rumored that after Lebon won, an irritated Mrs. Mancuso, who had not backed the horse the second time, tipped off a Uruguayan newspaper, but Mrs. Gerard told the court that she was the blonde punter. She had backed Lebon in order to get money, "to start a humane society for race-horses."[9]

Since Alice was insistent that she was responsible for the ringer, Davenport asked her if she was also responsible for two other alleged substitutions, involving other horses imported by her husband; Chirico for Sundoro, and As De Pique II for Enchumao? Flustered, Mrs. Gerard was allowed to consult with her attorney outside the courtroom. When she returned, she took the Fifth Amendment and declined to answer.

The jury's verdict rested on their view of Alice Gerard's testimony. In his closing address, Davenport told the jurors, "I could not bring myself in any way to attack this poor woman. I think she is pathetic, but not believable. I think it is sad, but not credible. It is based on fiction. I think it is an insult that you would be asked to believe it." Mrs. Gerard jumped up, glared at the prosecutor, and strode out of the courtroom.

Bailey, having attacked the racing authorities' inadequate identification procedures, pleaded, "Only ask yourself whether her story could be true." In a performance regarded as one of Bailey's best, he pounded away at the notion of "reasonable doubt."

One juror later explained, "I didn't necessarily believe she did it, but there was always that possibility."

That possibility persuaded the jury. It delivered its verdict on September 21, to find Dr. Mark Gerard not guilty of the more serious charges leveled against him but guilty of two misdemeanors involving "fraudulent entries and practices in contests of speed."

According to Davenport, "The decision was a compromise. They said Gerard found out about the switch somewhere along the line but were not convinced that he planned it back in June."[10]

In November, sentencing Gerard to one year in prison and a

$1,000 fine, Judge Harrington told him, "The message must go out that people in your position that involve themselves in this kind of activity are facing substantial penalties; these penalties must be a deterrent from engaging in such conduct."

Gerard was released on bail pending an appeal, which, in June 1980, he finally lost. Judge Jacob Fuchsberg concluded that the jury had "a solid basis for inferring that Gerard knew Lebon was Cinzano and, in consequence, that he masterminded the plan to race the ringer."

The wayward vet had a final throw of the dice. Due to move into prison on June 20, he appealed for a stay of sentence until a hearing could be arranged to consider whether imprisonment would seriously impair his health, because Dr. Gerard was suffering from a circulatory disease.

Judge Raymond Harrington ruled that Gerard had failed to prove that there had been "some catastrophic change" in his health since he was sentenced in November of 1978. He was forced to keep his appointment with prison.[11]

In a curious postscript, at the Meadowlands on October 15, 1981, the stewards ordered that As De Pique II, by then a ten-year-old, be scratched from the second race because he was believed to be Enchumao.

By then, another plague of ringers had appeared.

Barely two weeks after Dr. Gerard was sentenced, the grandstand at Hawthorne burned down. There had been another shock at the Chicago track the previous day, November 18, 1978, when Charollius had punters tearing up their past-performance pages.

Charollius approached Hawthorne fresh from a convincing defeat in $2,500 claiming company at Thistledown, Ohio, and with a record for the season of one win from 21 starts. Expected to leave the gates at about 30-1, Charollius started at 4.4 to 1, and won.

The race was added to a list embracing nine tracks in six states, where investigators concluded that poor horses were being replaced by better ones. Clifford Wickham, president of the TRPB, reported, "TRPB agents in several East Coast and Midwest States have been engaged in virtual round-the-clock duty in order to complete all logical leads as swiftly as possible. It has been established that all of the horse substitutions have been accomplished by means of counterfeit foal certificates."[12]

About 25 blank certificates had been stolen from The Jockey Club's offices in New York. These certificates, which lacked the watermarks found on bona fide documents, were being used to run ringers, including Charollius, an alias for the superior Roman Decade.

On December 13 Mike Reavis, William Combee, and Charlie Wonder were ordered to appear before the Illinois Racing Board to show cause why their owner and trainer licenses "should not be suspended or revoked."

When Charollius won at Hawthorne, Reavis, 32, was listed as its owner and trainer. Combee, 40, was the owner and trainer of Roman Decade while Wonder, 50, himself a trainer, had delivered the winning horse to Reavis, along with its counterfeit foal certificate.

When the board met again, on December 28, Reavis was the only one of the three accused men to appear, although Combee and Wonder were represented by attorney Arthur Engelland.

Reavis told the board that, early in November, he had agreed to take Charollius as a favor to Wonder, who had supplied him with horses in the past. Instead of charging Wonder training fees, Reavis asked him to put $200 on Charollius, Wonder having told him that the horse ought to win. The horse did win, but Reavis never received any money.

Wonder asked Reavis to present himself as Charollius's owner and trainer, "because Charlie believed he would get better odds if his name was not used. I knew that I was doing something wrong by having my name listed as owner, when I knew that Wonder was the owner," said Reavis, "but it wasn't until the Tuesday after the race that I got any suspicions that there was the question of a ringer."

That morning, November 21, Reavis was asleep in his truck at the stables. He was woken up by Wonder tapping on the window. "Wonder told me that Charollius had been moved, and that he may have been a ringer," said Reavis. "I was shocked and upset because it was my name on the foal certificate as owner and trainer.

"Wonder told me to go to the racing secretary's office and get the papers. I did, and the racing secretary, Pat Farrell, said, 'No, that horse is not to leave the grounds.' Wonder had told me to tell Farrell, in that case, that the horse had already left. Farrell said, 'Oh, no.'

"Later that day at the barn, two law enforcement agents questioned me. Wonder had told me to say that I had purchased Charollius from a man called George Bowers. I was so upset that I forgot the name, and I could see the agents didn't believe my story. So Wonder, who was stabled nearby, was called down to my part of the barn. He told them that Bowers had asked him to train the horse but that he hadn't been interested and that he had recommended me."[13]

The next day Reavis decided to tell the truth and approached the Hawthorne stewards.

The board believed Reavis and restricted his punishment to a six months' suspension, whereas Wonder and Combee were both suspended for 25 years and barred from the clubhouse and grandstand areas of all the state's tracks.

Wonder had already been ruled off indefinitely by the Kentucky Racing Commission. That summer at Ellis Park he had persuaded another trainer friend, William Price, to take two horses, Prince Sappir and Eagle Heights, with Price's wife listed as the owner of the former and Wonder's wife as the owner of the latter.

On August 7 Prince Sappir won by eight lengths at a heavily backed 4.2 to 1. On September 4 Eagle Heights won at a similarly heavily backed 5.8 to 1. The enthusiastic support was due to the fact that Prince Sappir was actually Jimmy Reb, while Eagle Heights was Beau Bronze. The counterfeit certificates displayed the names of Prince Sappir and Eagle Heights, but the description and tattoo numbers were those of the ringers.

Price told the commission that he had known Wonder for a long time and was "just trying to do the man a favor. I did not know, and I'll take a lie detector test or anything you want me to, that I was running a ringer."

The commission was "inclined to believe his protestations that he was a dupe, rather than a villain," and, taking Price's good record into account, suspended him for 60 days.[14]

On September 24 the gang ran a ringer at Great Barrington Fair, in Massachusetts on October 29 they were ringing the changes at Thistledown; on November 11, the venue was Waterford Park, West Virginia. That day Bay Batim ran in the name of Born a Great Count. Although the ringer finished second, the stewards were suspicious, and the FBI joined the investigation.

They arrived too late to prevent the next deception, which was the very next day, at Beulah Park, Ohio, where Stoned Crow cruised to a seven-length success in a $2,000 claimer, at 5.6-1. Both the odds and the result were a surprise since, in his previous start, in a $3,000 claimer at Hawthorne, Stoned Crow had finished last of 12 at 94-1, when listed as owned and trained by Charlie Wonder.

After Stoned Crow had won at Beulah Park again, it was discovered that Stoned Crow was really Piperazine Pete, the winner of a $7,000 claimer at Hawthorne the previous month.

Stoned Crow was listed as owned and trained by Myles Neff. Neff fared less well than either Reavis or Price, whose claims to have been innocent dupes had been accepted. In January 1979 the Ohio Racing Commission suspended Wonder, Combee, and Neff for 25 years.

The FBI's investigation rumbled on. In 1980 George Bowers of Florida and Eugene Martin of Massachusetts pleaded guilty to charges relating to the substitution of Bay Batim for Born a Great Count at Waterford Park and were given suspended prison sentences.

Later that year Wonder, from Indiana; Combee, from Florida; and Burley Clouston II and III, both of New York, were charged in connection with the fixing of 14 races, using forged foal certificates.

That December, at a U.S. District Court in Kentucky, Combee was sent to prison for one year and a day, in company with Burley Clouston II. Wonder was not present, preferring to visit Manitoba in Canada, where he was safe from extradition.

No sooner had one cache of ringers been exposed than another was unearthed. In July 1980 some tattoo equipment was stolen from River Downs in Ohio. The following May a steward at Agua Caliente informed the TRPB that a group of Americans, including Glendo Sullivan, were trying to buy Mexican horses, horses without tattoos or conspicuous markings. The TRPB launched an investigation and were soon joined by the FBI.

Sullivan was a recently licensed trainer in Kentucky. Investigators discovered that he was an associate of Omar Fannin Jr., also a trainer. One of Fannin's horses was Mamma's Clue, who had won a maiden race at Jefferson Downs in Louisiana on September 20, 1980, at 6-1. It was a startling result because Mamma's Clue had lost his previous two races by a total of 50 lengths.

Two months earlier Glenn Kopp had delivered the stolen tattoo equipment to Sullivan. When Mamma's Clue was entered for a race at Churchill Downs on June 17, 1981, his tattoo was compared with a photograph of Mamma's Clue's tattoo, taken when the horse's details were first registered. The number was the same, but the nature of the tattoo was different.

The stewards ordered the horse to be scratched from the race and impounded. Blood tests confirmed that it was not

Mamma's Clue. The horse turned out to be Dantetta, a winner in Mexico.

Early in 1983, at a U.S. District Court in Louisville, Kentucky, seven men, including Sullivan, regarded as the ringleader, and Fannin were charged with criminal conspiracy.

Sewing and Reaping 9

"Be not deceived. God is not mocked. For whatsoever a man soweth, that shall he also reap."

— Galatians, chapter 6, verse 7.

The reaping began at Mothecombe House, on the beautiful Flete Estate in South Devon, with an evening phone call. Marshalla Ali Salaman made the call on August 28, 1978. Anthony Mildmay-White received it. The two men were from different decks of racing society. Mildmay-White, delicate featured, fresh-faced, was a privileged young man with a marked lack of arrogance and strong sense of duty.

They were qualities reminiscent of his uncle, Anthony Mildmay, the 2nd Baron Mildmay of Flete, a legendary, heroic figure in national hunt racing who had drowned off the estate's coastline, age 41, in 1950.

Mildmay had been champion amateur rider five times and, in the early 1970s his nephew was also a successful amateur jockey. In 1976, at the unusually young age of 28, Mildmay-White was elected to the Jockey Club. He was born to represent the establishment; Salaman, to kick against it.

Three years older than Mildmay-White, "Taffy" Salaman had been brought up in the poverty of Cardiff's ethnically diverse docklands, Tiger Bay. Swarthy, compact, a likeable rascal, hot-tempered and pugnacious, a former stable lads' boxing champion, Salaman had been a jockey and trainer, sometimes both, scratching along.

In 1977 he trained Churchtown Boy to finish second to Red Rum in the Grand National and was now combining training and riding from a yard at Lambourn.

When Mildmay-White picked up the phone, Salaman told him that the Jockey Club had better send someone to John Bowles's yard at Crickhowell straightaway. The horse that had won the selling hurdle at Newton Abbot that afternoon was not In the Money.

"I did it to get my revenge," Salaman told me 23 years later. "It's a terrible thing to say, a shameful thing to say, but I admit that was the only reason. I'm from Tiger Bay. We don't shop each other. I wouldn't have shopped him if he hadn't done the thing with the passport."[1]

It was "the thing with the passport" that ruined trainer John Bowles's plans, for In the Money was the story of a relationship gone bad.

~

Salaman and Bowles met at Colin Davies's yard at St. Arvans, near Chepstow, where Davies had trained Persian War to a hat trick of champion hurdle victories. In the early 1970s Salaman was the stable jockey and Bowles one of Davies's owners, a South Wales builder adept at winning contracts from local councils.

Bowles was ambitious, and his ambitions included race riding. In 1975 he entered into a partnership with Salaman to run a racing yard at Court Farm, Llangattock, near Crickhowell. Salaman would train the horses and ride some of them, while Bowles would manage the business and be the stable's amateur rider.

The enterprise got off to a good start, with over 30 horses. That autumn Falcon's Boy supplied an early three-timer, with Salaman in the saddle for Falcon's Boy's first win, at Newton Abbot, and Bowles following up at Wincanton and Ludlow.

A few months later, on April 14, 1976, Bowles won on Falcon's Boy again, but this time the winning trainer was Dr. Arthur Jones. The previous day Salaman's trainer's license had been withdrawn for a year. The cause was Westwyn.

Westwyn, a moderate and aging chaser, had been transferred from Colin Davies's yard to Bowles's new training establishment at Court Farm.

"He wasn't going to win a race," said Salaman, "so I told John to send him point-to-pointing. Westwyn was given to Captain David Walsh and his girlfriend and they trained him, although I gave them advice and made the mistake of not scratching Westwyn off the list of horses I had in training."

On March 13, 1976, with Walsh on board, Westwyn finished second in an Adjacent Hunts' race at the Brecon point-to-point meeting at Llanfrynach. Five days later Walsh partnered the 11-year-old in the prestigious Kim Muir Memorial Challenge Cup Chase at the Cheltenham Festival. Starting at an ungenerous 66-1, Westwyn fell when tailed off.

Two days later, on March 20, Westwyn seemed in such good form that Bowles decided to run him that afternoon at the Gellygaer Farmers' point-to-point at Lower Machen.

Westwyn won the Open race and on April 3 finished fifth in another Open at the Radnor and West Herefordshire point-to-point at Bredwardine, but the clerk of the course for the Gellygaer meeting lodged an objection to Westwyn's victory, on the ground that the winner had been in the yard of a licensed trainer after November 1, 1975, contrary to Regulation 34 (iv).

The Jockey Club fined Bowles £200 and, punitively, withdrew Salaman's trainer's license for 12 months. James Lambie, writing in *The Sporting Life*, remarked, "By any criterion, the stewards' judgement seems extraordinarily severe."

Salaman, not for the last time, felt a deep sense of injustice. When the Jockey Club turned down his application for a fresh hearing, he recruited the help of Newport's MP (Member of Parliament), Roy Hughes, now Lord Islwyn. "This appears to be a technical infringement of the rule," Hughes suggested to the stewards, "with no fraudulent deception intended. Salaman was not legally represented at the inquiry and to refuse him a rehearing, in view of the particularly heavy penalty imposed, seems a very arbitrary way of doing things."

Peter Twite, head of the Jockey Club's rules department,

was unapologetic. He informed Salaman's solicitor, bluntly, "Your client manifested a recklessness and lack of regard of the rules which made the decision perfectly fair and just." Salaman was certainly capable of fiery displays. Perhaps he had produced one, injudiciously, in front of the stewards.[2]

Nevertheless, on July 15, the Jockey Club held a fresh inquiry. After a three-hour hearing, Salaman emerged with his ban reduced to four months. On August 13, 1976, his license was returned, but the seeds of another unwelcome appearance before the stewards had already been sown. This time, the cause was Womble.

Womble came from Ireland. In May 1975 the five-year-old had won a maiden hurdle race at Gowran Park. The following season he had just two unplaced runs for Salaman, but Paul Kelleway, who rode Womble on both occasions, told the trainer that he had a decent horse.

Questioned in court, Salaman stated, "Womble was showing a great deal of promise."[3] It wasn't obvious from the form book, which recorded that in October of 1976 Womble was given four runs in quick succession, partnered each time by Salaman and well beaten each time. Maybe Salaman had the horse's handicap mark in mind.

There was something else about Womble. He closely resembled one of his stablemates, In the Money. "He was the spitting image," said Salaman. "I'd have had to get up close to tell the difference."

On two occasions toward the end of 1976, Bowles allegedly suggested running Womble in the name of In the Money. Salaman was to testify, "He suggested if we swapped them he would be able to ride Womble, who would be running as In the Money, and have a good bet and have a coup. That was the reason I finally decided to leave Crickhowell."

Bowles claimed that the suggestion came from Salaman. "I dismissed it as a lunatic suggestion from a lunatic," he said.[4]

In January of 1977, Salaman left Court Farm for Lambourn, taking most of the staff and horses with him, including

Womble, while Bowles applied for his own trainer's license.

Womble was sold to Wilfred Sherman, a 66-year-old bookmaker. Sherman was a small man but a large gambler. The plan was to land a coup with Womble in a selling hurdle and then run him in the Knight, Frank & Rutley Opportunity Handicap Hurdle at Hereford on March 5, but throughout February wet weather produced a spate of abandonments. Eventually, although Womble had not raced since the previous October, it was decided to go straight to Hereford.

Sherman was in Australia. According to Salaman, the owner left instructions for him to phone a Mr. Green at Ladbrokes. Green would know the size of his stake. All Salaman had to tell him was whether the bet was win or each-way.

When Salaman rang, he was told that Green was away. His secretary said that Sherman's standard bet was £40 each way. To be on the safe side, Salaman asked for £100 each way, equivalent to about £400 each way today. Salaman himself had £400 on Womble.

Ridden by Mark Floyd and backed from 25-1 to 14-1, Womble landed the gamble, but Sherman was unhappy, claiming that he would have had £1,000 on the winner.

Sherman, now 90 and living in retirement in Spain, flatly denied Salaman's account. "I was in Australia," he told me, "but didn't even know the horse was running. When I got home, my secretary said that Salaman had rung to say that the horse had won and he had put £50 on it for me."

According to Salaman, a few days later, he and Sherman fell out comprehensively when the owner insisted on running Womble in the County Hurdle at Cheltenham, despite the trainer's advice that the ground was too soft. Womble was backed from 33-1 to 16-1 but broke down. Salaman told Sherman to take his horses away.

Sherman's recollection was different. "Good God, no. I was against the horse running. It didn't belong in that class of race and it was muddy going. I said, 'Why are you racing him in this? You must be mad.' "

Three years later, in March of 1980, Salaman claimed that Bowles had "conspired with somebody else and tried to destroy me and tried to get my license taken away." The "somebody else" was allegedly Sherman, and the conspiracy involved In the Money's passport.[5]

~

John Bowles bought In the Money in Ireland for 750 guineas. "I expected it to do well," he testified later, without obvious reason.

On August 27, 1975, he was due to partner the six-year-old on his British debut at Haydock, in an amateur riders' flat race, but there was a problem; neither Salaman nor Bowles had brought In the Money's passport.

Bowles told the Haydock stewards that a racecourse vet had checked the passport at Hereford on May 26 and the stewards allowed In the Money to run. A rank outsider, he was well beaten.

Over two and a half years later, in 1978, Bowles and Salaman, their partnership long ended, were summoned to a disciplinary inquiry into an alleged "deliberate falsification of a vet's signature on a horse's passport."

Later Salaman claimed that Bowles had confessed that it was Wilfred Sherman who had encouraged the Jockey Club to investigate the episode. Sherman denied any involvement. "I swear to God I don't know anything about it," he told me.

In June, the stewards decided that the signature of Mr. I.R. Barker, the Hereford vet, had been forged by Colin Webley, a commercial artist. Webley, who had no racing connections, was "severely cautioned." Salaman and Bowles were deemed to have deliberately misled the Haydock stewards. Salaman was fined £500 and Bowles £200.

Salaman was incensed. According to Bowles, "After the inquiry, he was raving like a lunatic in front of his barrister that he'd get me one day. He had to be restrained in front of his barrister by witnesses."

Salaman didn't deny it. "I blew my top," he told me. "I was fuming. I said, 'John, you're a villain. You'll never change.

Sooner or later you'll step out of line and when you do, I'll be there; I'll do you. You know the truth of what happened over the passport.' "[6]

After the Jockey Club inquiry Salaman claimed that there had been "a gross miscarriage of justice." The stewards had allegedly ignored the evidence of Brian Fitzgerald, a director of a Crickhowell printing firm of which Bowles was also a director. Fitzgerald had admitted approaching Webley on Bowles's behalf and stated that the forgery had nothing to do with Salaman.

In court in March of 1980, Salaman admitted that he was determined that the moment Bowles "stepped out of line," he would do something about it. "I told John Bowles words to that effect," he said. "I'm not trying to hide it."[7]

Less than three months after Salaman's outburst at the Jockey Club, Bowles did step out of line.

By then, In the Money was a nine-year-old who had not raced for almost three years. In three runs over hurdles in the autumn of 1975, when trained by Salaman and ridden by Bowles, he had been pulled up twice and slipped up once.

Yet on Bank Holiday Monday, August 28, 1978, In the Money led from the start, drew clear, and won the Hatherleigh Selling Handicap Hurdle at Newton Abbot by an easy 20 lengths, at a well backed 8-1.

John Bowles, in a flamboyant jacket and large-collared open shirt, just had time to celebrate his long-awaited first success as a trainer and buy the winner back for 1,100 guineas, before being summoned to a stewards' inquiry.

In the Money had no form. The stewards asked Bowles to explain how he had acquired some. Bowles told them that, in the past, In the Money had broken down and broken blood vessels but that he had finally got him right. The stewards "recorded" Bowles's explanation, indicating that they remained to be convinced.

Anthony Mildmay-White was one of the stewards. When Salaman telephoned him at Mothecombe House that evening, adamant that the winner could not have been In the Money, Mildmay-White replied that if he made such a serious allegation, he had to be prepared to repeat it in court.

"Salaman said that he'd have to think about it," Mildmay-White recalled. "He rang back and said, 'Yes, I will.' "

Mildmay-White had a guest staying with him, Lieutenant Colonel Sir Martin Gilliat, private secretary to the Queen Mother and a Jockey Club grandee. The young steward asked Gilliat's advice. What should he do?

Gilliat advised him to contact Major General Sir James d'Avigdor-Goldsmid, the Jockey Club steward responsible for security.

"By then, it was about 1:00 a.m.," Mildmay-White told me. "I rang d'Avigdor-Goldsmid and said, 'You need to get your boys to Bowles's yard now, or in the morning.' " But no one went. It was a fatal delay.[8]

Incredibly, it was not until four days later, on Friday September 1, that Bob Anderson, Racecourse Security Services' chief investigator, finally arrived at Bowles's yard near Crickhowell and asked to see In the Money. "Oh, didn't you know?" replied Bowles. "I let the Jockey Club know on Wednesday. He has been put down."

Bowles subsequently testified that immediately after the race, John Williams, who rode In the Money, had told him, "Don't get too excited. I felt him go at the second last."

Bowles conceded that there was no sign of lameness when the horse returned to the winner's enclosure, and so did the man who led the horse in, William Glyn Morgan Jones.

"After a seller, for the auction, you have to take any bandages off," said Mildmay-White. "It was obvious the horse wasn't lame. He was certainly sound when he walked around the winner's enclosure." Yet, less than 24 hours later, In the Money had been put down, without reference to a vet, because of crippling lameness.

Bowles told Anderson that the morning after the race, In the Money's near-fore tendon had "gone completely. He couldn't put it to the ground. He was in great pain. It would have been cruel to keep him."

On September 8 Bowles was visited by another Jockey Club official, in company with Colonel Dean, a veterinary officer. "Our surprise visit did not appear to disturb Mr. Bowles in any way," the official reported. "As a matter of fact, he was very cooperative and gave us every assistance.

"He was aware that Taffy Salaman was going around the racecourses telling people that In the Money was a ringer, and put it down to the fact that he had given evidence for the Jockey Club in connection with the recent case of a forged passport, in which Salaman was involved, and in connection with the same horse, In the Money."[9]

Bowles told his visitors that he had just given his version of events to *The Sporting Life*'s John McCririck, for publication the next day.

McCririck reported Bowles as saying, "In the Money seemed all right when we got home, but the next morning he could hardly hobble. It was pathetic. I couldn't watch the old boy suffer any more, so I took him down to Lawrence Potter, a Bristol butcher, to have him put down."

Bowles blustered against the "small-minded individuals who have it in for me and are jealous of the way I got the horse right. I certainly wasn't in the money after the race, though of course I fancied the old horse. I made no secret of that. He was much better than a plater, and I told lots of people he'd win from here to the church if his legs stood up."[10]

But they hadn't, so off In the Money had gone to Potter's abattoir at Bishops Sutton. Potter himself was away at the Ascot Sales, and the horse had been shot by one of his employees, Simon Chidzey. But which horse?

The official photographer at Newton Abbot that day was Colin Wallace. He took photographs of In the Money jumping the last hurdle and being led into the winner's enclosure. The winner's style of running reminded him of a horse he had once owned, called Cobbler's March.

Cobbler's March had passed through several trainers' yards — Earl Jones, Richard Tinney, Tommy Craig, and, latterly, Walter Charles — but, regardless of the trainer, the form book invariably recorded, "led."

Cobbler's March was an inveterate front runner, with five wins to his name. In the first of them, at Hereford in 1971, he was in front after the second flight of hurdles; for the other four, most recently at Worcester in April 1976, he "made all." That was his style.

In May 1977 Charles asked Leslie Harries to carry out a split tendon operation on Cobbler's March, from which the 10-year-old recovered well. The operation did not leave scars, but Cobbler's March had two distinguishing features: a white mark on his forehead and a dimple, a "prophet's thumb," on his right flank.

Harries had noticed the dimple when carrying out the split tendon operation and stated that it was unusual for it to be in that area. In the Money did not have such a mark, yet Wallace noticed it on his own photographs of the winner.

Officially, In the Money did not have a white mark on his forehead, either, yet the winner did. On September 8, when Bowles was asked for an explanation, he said, "The old horse knocked his forehead in the stable and grazed the skin. It was caused by a piece of wood near the stable door."

When Detective Chief Inspector Geoffrey Booth visited the yard, Bowles offered the same explanation. "If you look at Aparicio," he said, "you'll see he also has one from throwing his head back." Booth did look at Aparicio but could not see a mark.

By a strange coincidence, the same vet had also operated on In the Money. In December of 1975, Harries had acid fired the six-year-old's forelegs. The operation left distinctive scars. No one noticed any such scars on the winner at Newton Abbot.

At the time of the operation, Harries found that In the Money's tendons were badly damaged. "My prognosis was very guarded," he said. "It was a very bad case of broken down tendons."[11]

Carl Coughlin, an apprentice who had ridden In the Money at Court Farm during Salaman's spell there, was adamant that the horse in the photographs taken at Newton Abbot was not the horse he had ridden.

Salaman himself was unequivocal. The horse in the photograph was "definitely not" In the Money.

Salaman testified that after In the Money had been acid fired, "He never came sound again. A year later, we did get him back into training to see if he would improve with exercise, but it didn't work, so John gave the horse to his uncle as a hack. He rode him a couple of times up the road and he was still lame. He returned home and we turned him back out. I suggested he should be put down. He had no future, but John wouldn't put him down."

Asked what the chances were of In the Money racing again, Salaman replied, "A million to one. He was crippled."

Jeffrey Kear, who worked for Salaman, told a similar tale. When he last saw In the Money, late in 1976, the horse was in poor condition and sharing a corrugated iron shed with a cow. "Personally, I could never see him racing again," Kear said.[12]

Salaman told me that even if In the Money had been sound, which he could not believe, he could not have won the Newton Abbot race in the style of the winner. "He was an out-and-out plodder," he said. "He didn't have the speed to make the running. Anyway, In the Money could not have cantered 20 yards, let alone won by 20 lengths."

In September of 1977, Charles sent Cobbler's March to the Ascot Sales, where he fetched 620 guineas. Rebecca Beaumont signed as the purchaser, but her friend John Bowles paid. He said he had bought the horse for Beaumont to ride in point-to-points. Such a powerful front runner seemed a strange choice for an inexperienced amateur rider, and the plan came to nothing.

Bowles testified that Cobbler's March had suffered from increasing lameness, although he had never been seen by Anthony Pavord, Bowles's vet. "It died in the second or third week of May 1978," he testified. "I found it one morning. It had died of a twisted gut. There were marks on the ground where it had been thrashing its head about in agony."[13]

A local farmer, Ralph Games, loud and aggressive in the witness box, said that he had seen a dead horse lying near a muck heap when visiting Court Farm and had cut the horse up with an axe. He took some pieces of meat for his dogs, and Bowles fed the rest to his pigs.

On October 12, 1978, Bowles was arrested and bailed to appear at Crickhowell police station on December 7. "They asked me about Cobbler's March," he said. "A horse I last had in my yard in May. I expect to receive a letter from the police confirming the matter is closed, well before December 7."

Instead, on July 20, 1979, Bowles and John Williams, the jockey, were jointly charged with three offenses, and Bowles with a fourth. It was alleged that they had conspired to defraud Newton Abbot racecourse, Weatherbys, other racehorse owners, bookmakers, and the tote, by falsely representing that the horse they ran was In the Money. Both men pleaded not guilty to all the charges.

Their trial began at Exeter Crown Court on March 3, 1980, with Bowles detained in custody on the ground that he might attempt to contact prosecution witnesses. He had already telephoned Wallace, the racecourse photographer and former owner of Cobbler's March. During the course of their conversation, Bowles told Wallace, "the offer still stands."

A week into the trial Williams was acquitted, leaving Bowles to face two remaining charges. He stuck firmly to his story, supported by a dubious assortment of witnesses.

Lord Jeremy Hutchinson QC, for the Crown, dismissed Bowles as a liar and a cheat. "There have been a number of witnesses in this case who have not been telling the truth," he said, making it clear that he counted trainer Mick Killoran and Bowles's assistant, William Glyn Morgan Jones, among them.[14]

The prosecution produced no evidence of a substantial betting coup, although there was enough interest at the course to persuade some bookmakers to wipe their prices off their boards completely, or to cut In the Money's odds to his eventual starting price of 8-1.

Proof of a coup was not required. When Judge Hazel Counsell summed up, she told the jury, "The only issue is whether the horse that ran in that race at Newton Abbot in the name of In the Money was, in fact, that horse."

Lord Emlyn Hooson QC, a former Liberal MP, acting for Bowles, told the jury that the case was "absolutely racked with doubt," but after deliberating for almost five hours the jury found Bowles guilty on both charges, by a majority of 10-2.

The judge was in no doubt. She told Bowles, "You have been found guilty and I say at once on what I consider to be overwhelming evidence."

Bowles was sentenced to 18 months in prison, suspended for two years, fined £1,500, and ordered to make a legal aid contribution of £1,500. "I am too sick to say anything, but I shall definitely be appealing against the conviction," he said.[15]

The evidence on which Bowles was convicted was compelling. The winning horse was clearly Cobbler's March, but mystery still surrounds the execution of the plot, and of the horses.

The day after the race Bowles and his casual helper, William Glyn Morgan Jones, took a horse to Lawrence Potter's abattoir, where Simon Chidzey shot it. But which horse was shot?

Bowles and Jones claimed that it was the horse that had won at Newton Abbot, In the Money. Since the winner was actually Cobbler's March, the obvious assumption is that it was Cobbler's March who was taken to the slaughterhouse and that In the Money had been fed to the pigs three months earlier, an episode based on the unreliable testimony of Bowles and Ralph Games.

Bowles had invested a lot of time and effort in preparing Cobbler's March and had bought him back after the race for 1,100 guineas. He may have intended to race the horse again under its real name, knowing that Cobbler's March's most recent run was not in December of 1976 but August of 1978.

To be on the safe side, Bowles may have decided to stable Cobbler's March somewhere other than Court Farm for a few days after the race, while taking In the Money to the slaughterhouse.

There were suspicions that Cobbler's March had been driven from Newton Abbot to Mick Killoran's yard near Cheltenham and that, once the investigation started, Bowles had arranged for the horse to be killed. Perhaps Cobbler's March was, after all, fed to Bowles's pigs and Games's dogs.

Bowles did not attend the Jockey Club hearing on July 15, 1980, at which he was declared a disqualified person for 20 years, which meant that he was barred from any premises licensed by the Jockey Club, including trainers' yards and racecourses.

The disqualification was a source of lasting frustration to Bowles, who made it a source of lasting irritation for the Jockey Club.

In 1986 the disgraced trainer was thrown out of Newton Abbot racecourse. In 1987 he applied, unsuccessfully, to have the term of his disqualification reduced, and in 1988 the Disciplinary Committee fined him £500 for having attended a meeting at Cheltenham on May 4 and three point-to-points.

The following February Bowles issued a writ against the Jockey Club and applied for an injunction to prevent him being restrained from attending a point-to-point meeting. The injunction was refused.

In May of 1989, Bowles was given leave to appeal against his original conviction. Two months later the Court of Appeal rejected his appeal. In August Bowles was fined £1,000 after admitting having attended another point-to-point meeting. The fine was not paid, and in November Bowles's name was added to the forfeit list.

In January of 1990, the Jockey Club agreed to register three horses in his son Lee Bowles's name, subject to Lee signing a declaration that the horses were his own property, were not stabled at his father's farm, and that no disqualified person would be involved in their care or training.

That July Bowles paid the £1,000 fine and in December applied to the Irish Turf Club for a permit to train in Ireland. His application was refused.

A month later, in January of 1991, Bowles asked the Disciplinary Committee to reconsider his disqualification. The committee considered Bowles's request but were unwilling to reduce the period of disqualification.

Bowles's situation reached a low point in 1992. In March, his court action against the Jockey Club was finally struck out as frivolous. In June he appeared at Merthyr Crown Court, charged with rape.

Bowles, 48, was alleged to have invited a 16-year-old girl and her 14-year-old friend to Court Farm, plied the older girl with whisky, shown her a pornographic film, then raped her. Bowles claimed that the girl had consented. He was found guilty and sentenced to seven years in prison but in November 1993 lodged a successful appeal and was released.

In 1994 Bowles appealed to the Jockey Club to lift the ban on his attendance at race meetings, to enable him to watch Lee's hunter-chasers in action. The request was refused, but in 1996 the Jockey Club agreed to end the disqualification in return for an undertaking that Bowles would not apply to own, train, or ride horses under Jockey Club rules for at least four years.

Having returned to Ireland, Bowles again applied to the Irish Turf Club for a trainer's license. In January of 1998, his request was granted. It was unusual for a Jockey Club ruling not to be applied equally in Ireland.

Cahir O'Sullivan, Keeper of the Match Book, confined himself to saying, "Mr. Bowles was interviewed in the presence of his lawyer and our lawyer. Lee Bowles surrendered his permit last October due to ill health. It was as a consequence of this that Mr. Bowles applied for a license."[16]

Bowles established his yard at Killucan, Co. Westmeath and in April of 1998, Back to Bavaria gave him his first winner, at Ballinrobe. The following month Back to Bavaria won again, at Killarney, but, along with Altregan Boy, who had won at Limerick, tested positive for a prohibited substance. In January of 1999, Bowles was fined IR£1,000, although it was accepted that there was no evidence that Bowles had administered the drug.

On March 2, 1999, Bowles had his first runners in Britain since his disqualification almost 19 years earlier, when Back to Bavaria and Willyyelkra ran at Catterick.

In August of 2000, Bowles achieved the biggest win of his career when Drewstown Lady won a division of the IR£30,000 High Speed Data Handicap Hurdle at Galway, but the following May he was fined IR£300 for "unacceptable behavior" during an argument with a member of the racecourse security staff.

Salaman, Bowles's nemesis, had a checkered subsequent career. He relinquished his trainer's license in 1981, resumed it in 1983, relinquished it again in 1985 and, after several years in Saudi Arabia, resumed training at Baydon, near Lambourn, where he has since trained a small string.

A Detective Story 10

"Well, members of the jury, I am sure that you must have found in this case, as I have, that it is both curious and fascinating, and you may have thought more than once, 'Well, this would make a very good book, a very good detective story.' "

— Judge Harry Bennett, York Crown Court, May 30, 1984.

The reason that Paul Dumbleton, Ken Richardson's solicitor, approached me in September of 1992 was because of Jo n Jack. On September 8 Jo n Jack had won a selling race at Lingfield at 33-1. The Betting Office Licensees' Association was suspicious and advised its members to withhold payment pending an inquiry. Richardson's name appeared in the press.

The publicity was particularly unwelcome because the home office was considering a petition from Richardson calling for the Flockton Grey case to be referred back to the Court of Appeal. Dumbleton wanted to distance his client from Jo n Jack and focus attention on the petition.

On September 21 BOLA finally advised its members to pay out, and the flurry of excitement died down. No evidence was produced to link Richardson with Jo n Jack's racing career, but there was a link. Jo n Jack was bred by the East Riding Sack and Paper Company, a subsidiary of the East Riding Holdings Company, of which Richardson was a shadow director and major shareholder.

Some of the betting shops used in the Flockton Grey coup 10 years earlier had been targeted again, and some of the winning punters were the same. One man, suspected of involvement in the Flockton Grey case, had £200 each-way on Jo n Jack.

When the men behind the coup revealed themselves, claiming to have won £33,000, one of them was Peter Haran. His father, Ken, was a friend of Richardson's who had given evidence at the Flockton Grey trial.

Nine months later Richardson was back in the news. On June 29, 1993, Old Hook landed an off-course gamble when winning a selling race at Folkestone at 20-1. BOLA again advised its members to withhold payment, before giving the all-clear 48 hours later.

Old Hook was trained in Belgium by Allan Smith, who had once trained for Fallig Farms, a controversial operation in which Richardson had been involved.

These coups were intriguing, but it was the case of Flockton Grey that engaged my interest. After studying the petition, I set to work gathering and considering the evidence. Perhaps the trial at York Crown Court had resulted in a miscarriage of justice, a cherished prize for a journalist.

Later, Richardson felt that I had betrayed him, but my commitment was not to promote a cause but to seek the truth. By training, I am a historian. Historians gather evidence and assess its significance. They must go where the evidence takes them.

One day in the spring of 1996, I turned into a rutted, leaf-covered track, which twisted through woods that finally cleared to reveal a farmhouse, Horn Hill Farm, near Temple Guiting, in Gloucestershire.

Peter Smiles, lean and healthy, was sitting in a sun lounge. Smiles had recently returned from Macau, where he had gone after falling out with the Jockey Club. When the case of Flockton Grey was under investigation, Smiles was head of Racecourse Security Services. Maybe he remembered something, had kept something; he didn't, he hadn't. I would have to ask George Edmondson, the investigating officer.

I already had. A touch gruff in his retirement in Harrogate,

Edmondson had nailed down the lid on Flockton Grey, and my patient attempts to ease it open ended abruptly.

"Dear Mr. Ashford," the final letter began. "I refer to your letter of the 14th inst. I do not wish to discuss the matter, either verbally or in writing."

The letter did answer one question. Before the case was handed to the police, was it investigated by George Edmondson or George Edmundson? "Yours sincerely, Geo. V. Edmondson." On the other hand, he had been wrong about Ashford.

Not every excursion was fruitless, and eventually, enough people answered enough questions for me to gather sufficient evidence to draw conclusions. The conclusions were not the ones I had set out hoping to reach, but they were where the evidence took me.

Kevin Darley was Britain's champion jockey in 2000. In 1978 he had been champion apprentice, but in the early 1980s he was scratching along on 14 winners a year. What spared Darley from suspicion was the ease of Flockton Grey's success. If he had known that he was riding a ringer, Darley would surely not have won by 20 lengths.

It was March 29, 1982, a cold, wet, miserable Monday at Leicester, a few days into the new flat season. A raceday made to be forgotten, but when Flockton Grey galloped away with the Knighton Auction Stakes, it marked the start of a case that would rumble curiously on for almost 15 years and leave one question still unanswered.

Questions were certain to be asked because 20 lengths was an exceptional winning margin, particularly for a two-year-old trained by a man who had held a license for over two years yet was scoring his first success on the flat.

Stephen Wiles was a 34-year-old former jump jockey who had taken over from his father, Fred, in 1979. Wiles trained a poor band of racehorses at Langley Holmes Stables in Flockton, between Wakefield and Huddersfield; so poor that it was January of 1982 before he finally arrived in the winner's circle, when Fallig Schnell won a selling hurdle at Catterick.

Wiles was an unfashionable trainer and Flockton Grey an unlikely star. As a foal, the Dragonara Palace—Misippus colt had been sold for 900 guineas, then resold as a yearling to Ken Richardson for 1,700 guineas. Yet there was plenty of money for him on his debut at Leicester.

Trainer Pat Haslam acknowledged having put either £200 each-way or £300 each-way on Flockton Grey, on Richardson's behalf, while another trainer, Mick Easterby, backed the winner with a credit bookmaker in York.

Flockton Grey was believed to have been backed to win about £200,000, at a starting price of 10-1, and the Jockey Club quickly launched an investigation. On March 31 George Edmondson, an investigating officer with Racecourse Security Services, arrived at Langley Holmes Stables.

There was a gray two-year-old gelding in the yard, and Wiles had allowed his staff to believe that it was the Leicester winner, but he didn't try to persuade Edmondson. Wiles knew, and Darley soon confirmed, that the grey in his yard was not the winning horse.

A blood test taken on April 6 established with 97 percent certainty that the gray was by Dragonara Palace out of Misippus, the breeding of Flockton Grey, but it was not the winner. Flockton Grey's passport described a horse with a conspicuous scar on its off-fore leg, below the knee. The gray in Wiles's yard had no such scar.

Wiles told Edmondson that Flockton Grey was at Jubilee Farm, 70 miles away at Hutton Cranswick, between Driffield and Beverley, a property owned by Richardson.

Edmondson drove to Jubilee Farm and spoke to Terry Wilson, the manager, but there was no sign of a gray gelding. Flockton Grey had vanished.

If the winner was not a two-year-old by Dragonara Palace out of Misippus, named Flockton Grey, which horse was it? If it was an older horse, its teeth might have given it away, but no one had examined the winner's teeth.

Brian Abraham was the veterinary officer on duty at Leicester, with Pat Morrissey and Ken Carpenter assisting him. Every horse running for the first time had to have its passport examined. Since all nine runners in Flockton Grey's race were unraced, there were a lot of passports to be checked, and Flockton Grey was a late arrival.

Abraham checked the vaccination record in Flockton Grey's passport but not the horse. Morrissey checked that some of the horse's markings matched those in its passport, but he did not look at its teeth nor check its off-fore leg for a scar. Flockton Grey was wearing bandages.

Edmondson had a stroke of luck. Ken Bright, the racecourse's official photographer and sole source of photographs of the winning horse, supplied him with seven pictures. In one, the winner had his mouth open.

In young horses, teeth provide a remarkably accurate guide to a horse's age. John Hickman, a distinguished veterinary surgeon, and Douglas Witherington, the Jockey Club's chief veterinary officer, examined blown-up photographs showing the development of the horse's incisor teeth. They were agreed that, in racing terms, the winner was undoubtedly a three-year-old.

At Weatherbys' offices in Wellingborough, David Mitchell and Peter Perry, a colleague of Edmondson, waded through thousands of naming forms and certificates looking for three-year-old grays with a scar on their off-fore leg. There were only three candidates. Dick 'E' Bear and Wednesday Morning were quickly eliminated. That left Good Hand.

In 1979 Colin Tinkler Jr. had bought Good Hand as a foal for 600 guineas. The gray colt was cheap but not without promise; a half sister, Setmark, had been sold for 500 guineas and won three small races for Geoff Toft.

A few months after arriving at Tinkler's yard, at Boltby, near Thirsk, Good Hand broke out of the yard he shared with other young horses and injured his leg on a gate. The injury took a long time to heal and left a prominent scar on the front of his off-fore leg, below the knee.

Tinkler sold Good Hand to his brother Nigel, whose training career got off to a spectacularly bad start. In December of 1980, he was banned for six months after Nickadventure was deemed to have been a non-trier in a hurdle race at Newcastle.

For awhile, Good Hand was kept at Jack Calvert's nearby yard, and it was there, on May 21, 1981, that Peter Calver, a vet as well as a trainer, examined the horse and noted its markings on the naming form needed to obtain a passport. Calver duly noted the scar on the anterior aspect of the off-fore cannon bone. On June 5, 1981, Weatherbys issued a passport for Good Hand.

With Nigel Tinkler's license restored, on July 22 Good Hand made his debut in a selling race over five furlongs at Catterick. Backed from 5-1 to 2-1 favorite, the gray did well to finish third after missing the break. Third again at Thirsk later that month and fourth at Ripon in August, there was a race to be won with Good Hand, but not from Tinkler's stable.

The race at Ripon was a selling race, and acting on Richardson's behalf, Colin Mathison claimed Good Hand for £3,100. When Tinkler asked Mathison where the horse was going to be trained, Mathison replied that he might be going to Belgium but for the time being he was stabled at Richardson's Jubilee Farm.

Ken Richardson was a self-made Yorkshireman. In 1963 he was declared bankrupt but soon afterward established a successful business processing jute and paper sacks. He became a regular visitor to the Malton area, collecting sacks, and got to know the racing community.

By the early 1970s Yorkshire Paper Converters and the East Riding Sack and Paper Company were turning Richardson into a multimillionaire. At the time of his trial, in 1984, his wife's shareholding was said to be worth at least £4 million.

Richardson's interest in horse racing was a gambling interest, and a highly successful one. He claimed to have won over £48,000 in 1968 and £70,000 four years later, thanks to Sovereign Bill's victory in the Lincoln. During the late 1970s and early 1980s he reported winning between £70,000 and £90,000 a year.

Richardson used up to 20 people, including trainers, to place his bets and controlled a string of racehorses and a training operation in Belgium, but it was difficult to keep track of his racing interests because the horses were run in other people's names.

As an undischarged bankrupt, Richardson was unable to register as an owner, but in 1975 he paid the debt and the adjudication against him was annulled. From 1976 it was through choice that he did not race his horses in his own name.

Richardson believed that women were luckier than men, and horses were racing in his wife Josephine's colors from 1967, when her first racehorse, Rockfire, was trained at Wetherby by Eddie Duffy.

In 1970 Mrs. Richardson had horses with Eric Collingwood at Malton and Geoff Toft at Beverley. Later, Richardson was associated with Pat Rohan, Mick Easterby, Jimmy Etherington, Ken Whitehead, Jock Skilling, and Derek Garraton, all in the Malton area; and at Newmarket with Peter Robinson, Clive Brittain, Pat Haslam, Brian Lunness, Paul Kelleway, and Mick Ryan.

Richardson made it clear that the purpose of racing horses was to land gambles. In 1973 Lunness had a two-year-old filly called Jubilee Girl, who raced in the colors of Mrs. P. Cross but had been bought by Richardson for 1,100 guineas.

Lunness told Richardson that Jubilee Girl might be good enough to win the Brocklesby Stakes at Doncaster, the most valuable early season two-year-old race. Richardson preferred to run her in the seller. He had £10,000 on Jubilee Girl, causing her price to tumble from 4-1 to 13-8. She won by seven lengths and later beat Alexben, the winner of the Brocklesby.

At the beginning of December of 1981, the two-year-old Good Hand and the unnamed yearling by Dragonara Palace out of Misippus, both grays, were at Jubilee Farm.

According to Richardson, he arranged for Stephen Wiles to take Good Hand away with a view to selling him, and on about December 18 Elaine Wiles, Stephen's wife, allegedly collected the two-year-old. A busy man, Richardson did not subsequently inquire about the horse and heard no more of Good Hand until after the Leicester race.

In the same month, again according to Richardson, Wiles bought the Dragonara Palace—Misippus yearling and asked Richardson to make the bill out to his father, Fred Wiles. Richardson told Terry Wilson, the manager at Jubilee Farm, to arrange for the yearling's transport, and Peter Boddy, who had worked for Richardson for seven years and often drove the horsebox, delivered the yearling to Wiles early in January 1982.

What could not be disputed and was vital in pointing to the truth was a visit paid to Wiles's yard on January 5, 1982, by Philip Dixon, a local veterinary surgeon. Dixon had been asked to complete a naming form for a horse brought to the yard by Boddy in Richardson's horsebox.

Later, at York Crown Court, Richardson was asked which horse he had sent to Wiles on January 5. He replied, "To my best knowledge and belief it was a Dragonara Palace—Misippus, but I couldn't say that it actually went because I did not see it loaded up and I didn't see it arrive there."[1]

When Dixon arrived, the horse was already there. He was handed a foal certificate in a plastic folder brought by Boddy for a Dragonara Palace—Misippus gelding born on June 6, 1980.

The vet did not take the certificate out of the folder nor examine the horse's teeth. He accepted the date of birth on the part of the certificate visible through the plastic and completed the naming form. He entered details of whorls on the horse's head and of a scar on the front of the cannon bone on the off-fore leg.

The gray was then loaded back into the horsebox and driven away. Dixon was to testify, "I thought it was rather odd that the horse had been brought specifically for me to mark up. I had assumed the horse would be broken and trained by Mr. Wiles and that once it had arrived for being marked up, it would carry on. I found it fairly odd that it was going straight off again."[2]

Richardson claimed to know nothing of the horse's subsequent movements. When he asked Boddy where he had taken the horse, Boddy replied that he had left it at Wiles's yard, but both Stephen and Elaine Wiles, and Stephen Pleasant, a stable lad, testified that no horse by the name of Good Hand, or like him, ever appeared at the stable after January 5.

If the horse was Good Hand, then he was not, as Richardson claimed, removed from Jubilee Farm by Elaine Wiles on about December 18.

Stephen Wiles sent Flockton Grey's naming form and foal certificate to Weatherbys, with Fred Wiles named as the owner. At the end of January 1982, Weatherbys issued a passport bearing the markings of Good Hand but with the name Flockton Grey and a date of birth indicating that the horse was a two-year-old.

According to Wiles, several weeks later Colin Mathison, Richardson's right-hand man, told the trainer to make race entries for Flockton Grey. He said that the "little gray" would be sent to him. A few weeks before the Leicester race, a little gray did arrive at Wiles's yard.

Wiles later testified, "I did believe it was the horse which I had seen for an hour in the January. I thought it was the horse then named Flockton Grey, and then we started to canter it and found it was absolutely useless, green, nowhere near ready to race, didn't know how to gallop straight, nowhere near fit for entering into a race."[3]

The trainer looked at Flockton Grey's passport and was reminded of the scar on its fore leg. The horse he had been sent did not have a scar. When Wiles phoned Mathison, he was told that the gray he had been sent was by Morston but that Flockton Grey would be with him in time for it to race.

Flockton Grey never arrived. Mathison nevertheless told Wiles to declare the horse for the Leicester race and to book Kevin Darley or, according to Elaine Wiles, to confirm the booking that had already been made by someone else.

Early on the morning of Sunday March 28, the day before the race, Boddy arrived and told Wiles he had come for the little gray. Later that morning a horsebox arrived at Geoff Toft's yard at Malton. According to Toft, Richardson had asked him to gallop a two-year-old for him. He had been told that it was a gray.

Andrew Harrison, who rode the horse, confirmed Toft's verdict that it was weak and backward and nowhere near ready for racing.

The horse stayed at Toft's until the day after the race, Tuesday March 30, when the same driver arrived to take it away. The same day, the little gray that had been taken from Wiles on Sunday was returned by Boddy.

Wiles allowed stable lad Stephen Pleasant to believe that it was the Leicester winner, although Pleasant was very surprised. "When I heard it had won," he testified, "I said, 'You must be joking.' I just couldn't believe it. It just didn't look like a winner."

During the trial it was put to Richardson that the gray delivered to Toft was the Dragonara Palace—Misippus two-year-old. Richardson denied it. "That gray was nothing to do with the Wiles," he said. "It was a colt belonging to an owner." When asked who the owner was, Richardson replied, "Mr. Mel Brittain. I don't expect him to confirm this because he has asked me to keep his name out of it because he is trying to get a license to train."

Brittain had horses in training with Peter and Mick Easterby but had ambitions to obtain a license himself, which he did in 1985. According to Richardson, Brittain had asked him to arrange for a two-year-old to be tried, and Richardson had arranged for it to be tried at Toft's. He was unable to explain why Brittain could not have made the arrangement himself nor why Brittain had not used his own horsebox.

Brittain was not questioned by the police nor called to give evidence. He told me that Richardson was only a casual acquaintance and that he had not asked him to arrange a trial. It was not Brittain's two-year-old that had been sent to Toft.[4]

On the day of the race, Monday, March 29, 1982, Peter Boddy drove a horse to Leicester racecourse in Richardson's horsebox. According to Boddy, he had picked the horse up from the Wiles's yard the previous day as a favor, their horsebox having broken down.

That Sunday he drove the horse to Newmarket, along with another two-year-old gray from Jubilee Farm, which he had to deliver to Pat Haslam's yard. At that time Haslam trained in Newmarket.

Boddy arrived at Haslam's Pegasus Stables between 6:30 p.m. and 7:30 p.m. John Hammond, now a leading trainer in France but then Haslam's assistant, was there when the horsebox was opened.

Boddy maintained that there were two horses in the box, one intended for Haslam, the other for Leicester. Peter Martin, Haslam's head lad, did not see inside the horsebox but was of the opinion that there were two horses inside, but Hammond testified that there was only one, which he led out himself.

"I don't think I am wrong about this," he said. "My clear recollection is there was only one horse in this box when it arrived and that horse was delivered to us and then the box went away."

Boddy claimed that he had then driven to the nearby Moat House Hotel and parked the horsebox there overnight. If Boddy was telling the truth, the winner of the Leicester race had either spent about 22 hours standing in the horsebox or somehow been switched by Wiles at Leicester.

At the subsequent trial Geoffrey Rivlin QC, for the prosecution, accused Boddy of "lying through his teeth." His evidence was "quite ridiculous and untrue."[5]

Richardson was also at the Moat House Hotel that evening, although he claimed that he had hardly spoken to Boddy and did not know that his driver had collected a horse from Wiles. He was there to see Haslam and Allan Smith, his trainer in Belgium.

At the event he did not see Haslam but had dinner with Smith and made a number of phone calls, including to Kevin Darley. Richardson advised Flockton Grey's rider that the best piece of ground at Leicester was next to the inside rail.

On Monday morning at 8:30 a.m., Boddy left for Leicester, where Wiles had been told to meet the horsebox, with Flockton Grey's passport. Richardson left Newmarket at 9:30 a.m. and drove to Chelmsford for a business appointment. He heard the result of the race on his car radio while driving back to Jubilee Farm.

Richardson was questioned closely about bets on Flockton Grey but only accepted responsibility for win bets totalling £1,200 and place bets totalling £850, very modest sums by his standards.

He agreed that Ken Haran, a close friend, often placed bets for him but denied that he had done so on this occasion. In a statement to the police, Haran himself said that he had put substantial bets on for Richardson but in the witness box retracted his statement.

After the race the winner was loaded into Boddy's horsebox. Stephen and Elaine Wiles passed it on the M1 on their way home and Boddy waved to them. They expected Flockton Grey to be delivered to their yard, and that is what Boddy claimed to have done, but a gray horse did not arrive at Langley Holmes Stables until the next day, and then it was the hopelessly backward Dragonara Palace—Misippus two-year-old.

On Thursday, April 1, the day after George Edmondson's first visit, Stephen and Fred Wiles went to see Richardson and Mathison. They demanded to know where the winner was but were given the briefest of audiences. Mathison would not allow them beyond his front door.

Mathison admitted having staked £600 each-way on Flockton Grey for himself while his son, Neil, had gone to Ayr with Richardson's son, Andrew, where they placed further bets.

At the trial Geoffrey Rivlin QC, referring to Mathison's bet, said, "You had 7,000 good reasons for talking to the Wiles. You had just won £7,000 and you should have been pleased with them, but you turned them away from your door." Mathison replied, "I told them I knew nothing and had just had a bet on the horse."[6]

Neither the Jockey Club nor the police could find Good Hand, who they were already convinced had run as Flockton Grey. It was feared that he was dead.

Months passed until, on December 4, 1982, the front page headline in the *Daily Star* proclaimed, "We Trace The Ringer — *Star* solves riddle of Flockton Grey." It was the end of one riddle but the start of another.

The newspaper had received an anonymous telephone call. They would find the horse they were looking for in a field just beyond Beggar's Bridge, near Glaisdale, on the North Yorkshire moors.

Reporters David Hudson and Frank Curran made their way along a narrow path by the River Esk to a railway arch. Beyond was a solid wooden gate secured by a heavy chain and padlock, topped with barbed wire, leading to a small, secluded field. In the field were two horses. One was a gray with a distinctive scar on his off-fore leg.

Later that day, Hudson and Curran returned with the police, who took the horse away. On December 6 Brian Abraham, the Jockey Club's veterinary officer, took a blood test that confirmed, with 97 percent certainty, that the horse was Good Hand. But how had he got there?

The field in which Good Hand was finally found was leased by Sylvia Jones, who lived with her husband Peter and daughter Romney at a house called Lavericks, between Egton and Glaisdale. Their son, Greg, worked for trainer Stan Mellor, and Sylvia liked to give the impression that she was in with the hunting and racing fraternity.

Sylvia, Peter, and Romney all belonged to the Goathland Hunt, and Peter occasionally rode in point-to-points. When the police interviewed Sylvia, they found her unhelpful and felt that Romney, then 19, was being shielded from questioning.

Sylvia stated that on March 25, the Thursday before the race, she had gone to the sales at Malton, where she told several people that she was looking for a horse as a companion for a foal. Subsequently, she was away from home for a few days, and when she returned on the evening of Wednesday March 31, Romney told her that a man had phoned that afternoon to say that he would be bringing a horse.

A man wearing a tam-o-shanter arrived in a horsebox, dropped off the horse subsequently identified as Good Hand, and left. A police officer noticed that Peter Boddy wore a tam-o-shanter during committal proceedings, but the description Romney provided was insufficient to identify the driver.

Sylvia stated, unconvincingly, that she assumed someone had heard that she was looking for a horse and had responded to her appeal. They were doing her a favor, and in return, she was providing the horse's keep. She did not think it strange that she had not heard from the horse's owner since.

According to Sylvia, the horse had a winter coat and was undernourished; it could not have raced two days earlier. But Susan Simpson, a friend of Romney, and Brian McKibbin, a local farmer with a racing background who looked after Jones's horses and saw the gray regularly, stated that the horse was not undernourished.

Shortly afterward, Romney was riding out with Julia Foster and Ivy Cook. When Ivy dropped back a bit, Romney turned to Julia and said, "Guess what?" She confided that they had a horse that was a ringer.

Sylvia subsequently contacted Derek Gardiner, the huntsman who looked after the hounds for the Goathland Hunt. Gardiner, short and wiry with rough black hair, lived in a stone cottage next to the kennels.

That day, when Gardiner picked up the phone, Jones

offered him £200 to shoot a horse. "If she had just asked me to come and shoot a horse, I'd have done it for nothing," he told me. "I'd have skinned it, fed it to the hounds, and no one would have known. It was offering me £200. That's why I smelled a rat. I made the excuse that I had run out of bullets."[7]

Sylvia denied having contacted Gardiner but when both gave evidence during an appeal hearing in 1986, Lord Justice Lane made it clear that he believed Gardiner but not Jones, whose evidence the judge described as "incredible and untrue."

Both Sylvia and Romney proved elusive witnesses. When Richardson's trial approached in 1984, Sylvia disappeared, apparently to a cottage in Ireland. Soon afterward, Lavericks was put up for sale.

The police were looking for a connection between Jones and Richardson. They couldn't find one. Jones told them that she didn't know Richardson, although she might have bumped into him, unwittingly, at the races.

But there was a link. On one occasion when the police visited Lavericks, Peter Concannon was there. Concannon, once Pat Rohan's traveling head lad and Geoff Toft's jockey, was assistant to Malton trainer Derek Garraton, formerly Toft's head lad.

Garraton was a close friend of Jones and trained for Richardson. After Flockton Grey's victory, Garraton received a phone call. He was asked to suggest where a horse might be kept. He suggested Sylvia Jones.

In May of 1984, Ken Richardson, Colin Mathison, and Peter Boddy appeared at York Crown Court before Judge Harry Bennett QC, charged with having conspired to substitute Good Hand for Flockton Grey with the intention of defrauding bookmakers.

Richardson was represented by George Carman QC, already a highly prized barrister who later established an unrivaled reputation as an advocate in libel cases. On this occasion the case for the prosecution, presented by Geoffrey

Rivlin QC, depended heavily on the evidence of Stephen and Elaine Wiles. Carman sought to persuade the jury that, as "self-confessed liars," their evidence could not be trusted.

They had lied. Stephen testified that much of the first written statement he made to George Edmondson on March 31, 1982, was untrue, notably his assertion that Fred Wiles had bought Flockton Grey from Richardson at the end of 1981 and that Stephen had subsequently trained the horse.

Wiles and his wife admitted that they had done nothing to disabuse staff and neighbors of the belief that the gray two-year-old in their yard was the winner of the Leicester race.

When asked why they had lied, they replied that it was partly through fear and panic and partly because of the knowledge that they had broken Jockey Club rules, which stipulated that a horse had to be in a trainer's yard for 14 days before it raced. They knew that the winner had not been trained at their yard, although they had submitted forms to Weatherbys reporting that Flockton Grey was in training with them.

During his summing up, the judge told the jury, "It is one of the strongest points made by the defense against the prosecution case that you are being asked to return verdicts of guilty on the basis of the evidence of witnesses, namely the Wileses, who are self-confessed liars in the sense that they told untruths, or were responsible for written untruths, before the race and since the race."[8]

Corroboration of the Wiles's evidence was in short supply, which lent additional significance to Philip Dixon's testimony concerning his visit to their yard on January 5, 1982.

Carman had a fine time tying Dixon and others in knots over whorl positions and documentary discrepancies, but even he could not finesse away the evidence of the scar on the off-fore leg of the horse presented to Dixon that day.

The defense accepted that the winner was a ringer but insisted that Richardson had had nothing to do with the deception. It had not been proved that the winner was Good Hand, and Good Hand had, in any event, been removed from Jubilee Farm by Elaine Wiles in December 1981. The Wiles were the guilty parties.

The jury disagreed. By a 10-2 majority, they found all three defendants guilty. Richardson was given a nine-month suspended sentence and fined £20,000, with costs estimated at £25,000. Mathison was fined £3,000 while Boddy escaped with a conditional discharge.

Richardson protested his innocence. In 1986 the Court of Appeal rejected his appeal, and later that year the Jockey Club warned him off for 25 years, but he did not give up.

Richardson and his associates had been convicted on the basis that the winner was Good Hand. If evidence could be produced throwing doubt on the winner's identity, their conviction might be rendered unsafe.

In 1991 Richardson submitted a petition to the Home Secretary, Kenneth Baker, calling for the case to be referred back to the Court of Appeal. The petition claimed that Richardson was "now in a position to prove that the winning horse could not have been Good Hand."[9]

In 1993 the home office informed Richardson that the petition had not been successful, but Richardson submitted additional evidence and in 1995 obtained permission to apply for a judicial review of the Home Secretary's continued refusal to refer the case back to the Court of Appeal.

Finally, the Home Secretary, by then Michael Howard, relented. In June of 1995 he agreed to return the case to the Court of Appeal.

The appeal was heard in December of 1996, when the crucial evidence was presented by Dennis Bellamy, emeritus professor of zoology at the University of Wales, and Dr. Alfred Linney, head of the medical graphics division at University College, London.

Bellamy had subjected photographs of Good Hand and of the winner to computer analysis. He concluded that they were different horses, largely because a whorl on the winner's forehead appeared to be situated on the opposite side of a midline to the whorl on Good Hand's forehead.

Linney had reached the same conclusion because, using image analysis, he was unable to match up the head shapes of the horses in the photographs.

Their evidence was challenged by the Crown's expert witness, Michael Harrow, an imagery analyst. He claimed to have established that the whorls were on the same side of a central line and questioned the reliability of Bellamy's and Linney's conclusions, which were based on the study of unsatisfactory photographs.

Lord Justice Rose, sitting with Mr. Justice Keene and Mr. Justice Poole, largely accepted Harrow's critique and observed, "Scientific evidence has to be looked at in the context of all other evidence. Having regard to the 1984 trial, there was a very strong case indeed against the appellants, not only that they had participated in a conspiracy to defraud but also that the winner was Good Hand.

"Any other conclusion means that, somewhere, untraced, is another three-year-old gray gelding with a scar on its right fore leg. Such a conclusion beggars belief. We do not think these convictions unsafe and the appeals are therefore dismissed."

Richardson was ordered to pay £50,000 costs. A few days later he declared, "I will continue the fight to clear my name while ever there is a breath in my body, no matter how long it takes or how much it costs. We are going to the Lords, and no doubt that will be kicked out and then we will go to the European Court of Justice."[10]

Richardson's dogged determination to overturn his conviction had more to do with his unusual personality and the depth of his pocket than with the strength of his case.

Lord Justice Rose's observations when delivering judgment in the Appeal Court were well founded because, cumulatively, the grounds for believing that the winner was Good Hand were compelling.

• Beyond reasonable doubt the horse presented to Philip Dixon on January 5, 1982, was Good Hand. On the defense's own admission, Boddy had driven the horse from Jubilee

Farm to Wiles's stable. Richardson acknowledged that the Dragonara Palace—Misippus two-year-old, whose foal certificate was brought by Boddy and handed to Dixon, did not have a scar on its leg and that Good Hand was the only gray Richardson had possessed which did have a scar.

• Exhaustive searches of Weatherbys' records found only three three-year-old grays with a potentially matching scar. Two were readily eliminated; the third was Good Hand.

• If the ringer was not Good Hand, which horse was it? No other credible candidate has ever been suggested. Grey Desire, a talented sprinter owned by Mel Brittain and trained by Mick Easterby, has been mentioned, but Grey Desire was not yet two years old when Flockton Grey ran at Leicester.

• The passport generated by the naming exercise carried out on January 5, 1982, showed a two-year-old gelding bearing the markings of the three-year-old Good Hand. It would have been bizarre for the conspirators to have presented this passport to racecourse officials, yet run a different three-year-old, with different markings.

• Two days after the race Good Hand was delivered to a field leased by Sylvia Jones. Less than eight months earlier, Good Hand was considered to have been worth £3,100. If the gelding was not the ringer, why would someone make an anonymous gift of him to a lady no one acknowledged knowing?

• Nigel and Colin Tinkler Jr., who trained Good Hand for over 20 months, were adamant that the horse photographed in the winner's enclosure and found in Sylvia Jones's field was Good Hand. In 1996 Nigel Tinkler told me, "If the horse had been pink, I would still have said it was Good Hand, by the horse's expression. I can barely read a book but when you have been brought up with horses, you know them. I never had any doubt that the winner in the photograph was Good Hand."[11]

Richardson maintained that Stephen and Elaine Wiles were the guilty parties, but, although they had been untruthful, the suggestion is not credible.

• Stephen Wiles lacked the intellectual and financial resources to have organized the coup, and there is no evidence that they were involved with other conspirators.

• If Elaine Wiles collected Good Hand from Jubilee Farm in mid-December, as Richardson alleged, where did the Wiles keep him? No one saw a gray fitting Good Hand's description at their yard.

• If Good Hand was already in their possession, how is any sense to be made of Boddy's involvement in the naming exercise on January 5, 1982?

• If the Wileses were responsible for obtaining a fraudulent passport bearing Good Hand's markings, why did they allegedly then use a different horse as the ringer?

• There was no evidence to link the Wiles to a single bet on Flockton Grey, beyond the testimony of Richardson himself. He stated that he had never known Stephen Wiles to have more than £5 on a horse but claimed that Wiles had asked him to put £100 on Flockton Grey for him.

• Why did Stephen and Fred Wiles drive 70 miles to confront Richardson and Mathison, demanding to know where the winner was, if they already knew?

One question remains tantalizingly unanswered. Where was Good Hand between January 5, when Boddy drove him away from Wiles's yard, and March 29, when he reappeared at Leicester? Who trained the ringer?

Rumors circulated and suspicion fell on several trainers, among them Mick Easterby. Easterby had backed Flockton Grey with a credit bookmaker who paid him shortly before BOLA asked its members to report any bets they had taken on Flockton Grey.

The bookmaker did not believe that Easterby would have backed an unraced two-year-old trained by Wiles unless he knew something about it. If Easterby had suggested that the bookmaker back Flockton Grey himself, he would have felt less aggrieved, but Easterby hadn't suggested that.

He told Easterby about BOLA's request and gave him until

6:00 p.m. that evening to return the money. Easterby's new secretary, Elaine Sellwood, promptly delivered an envelope to the bookmaker's home, containing his winnings. The bookmaker did not report the bet.

Darley rode work at Easterby's yard but was adamant that he had not sat on Flockton Grey until the race. Easterby himself insisted that he had never seen the horse and had no idea who had trained it. "I wouldn't know anything about it," he told me. "I never saw the gray horse in my life. I have 110 percent no idea who trained it."[12]

Easterby's bet was merely evidence that, in company with several others, he preferred to draw a veil over the fact that he had backed Flockton Grey.

So had Pat Haslam, who was at Leicester that day, betting on Richardson's behalf. Boddy had been at Haslam's yard the evening before the race, but Haslam was equally insistent that he had not trained the winner. Other trainers employed by Richardson also came under suspicion, but there was never more than circumstantial evidence to link any of them to the ringer.

Perhaps Good Hand had been prepared in Belgium. Mathison applied for a duplicate passport so that Good Hand could be exported to Belgium and Boddy made regular trips to Fallig Farms stable in Ostend. He had returned from Belgium on Friday, March 26, and Allan Smith, Richardson's trainer in Belgium, was with Richardson in Newmarket the evening before the race.

Smith also denied any involvement, and there is no evidence that Good Hand ever crossed the Channel.

Terry Wilson, who managed Jubilee Farm, had been known as a good work rider at Clive Brittain's, but there were no training facilities at Jubilee Farm. Wilson, like everyone else, denied having prepared the ringer.

Maybe, when the trainer is an old man, he will tell his tale.

Banned from racing, Richardson turned his attention to football, buying control of Bridlington Town and then Doncaster Rovers.

Colin Mathison and Peter Boddy were ultimately installed as the sole directors of Bridlington Town, while Ken Haran was made chairman at Doncaster Rovers.

Richardson's reign at Doncaster, which started in 1993, was highly controversial. In June of 1995, the main stand at the Belle Vue ground was badly damaged by a fire that had been started deliberately.

Richardson was arrested the following year and later charged with conspiracy to commit arson. The case was heard at Sheffield Crown Court in 1999, when it was alleged that Richardson, by then age 61, had offered a former SAS man £10,000 to set fire to the stands.

After Richardson had been found guilty, his counsel, Gilbert Gray QC, in mitigation, told the court that his client was suffering from a psychotic disorder. While in the hospital wing of Doncaster prison, awaiting sentencing, he had become paranoid and suffered hallucinations. Judge Peter Baker ruled that a substantial prison sentence was still called for and jailed Richardson for four years.

Many years before, at the Old Bailey in 1920, "Ringer" Barrie had held his hands up and pleaded guilty. As former trainer Colin Tinkler Sr. suggested in his autobiography, *A Furlong to Go*, Richardson would have been well advised to have held his hands up.[13]

It would have saved himself and others, particularly Stephen and Elaine Wiles, a lot of strife and money. In 1986 Stephen Wiles finally appeared before the Jockey Club's disciplinary committee. He was banned from holding a trainer's license for five years for having entered and run Flockton Grey, knowing that the horse had not been in his care for 14 days preceding the race.

A few months after Stephen lost his license, he and Elaine split up and both struggled to remake a life in racing, which was the only life they knew.

Stephen eventually trained point-to-pointers from the same yard in Flockton, while Elaine worked for trainer Steve

Norton and, after his retirement, held a number of jobs within the racing industry.

The police kept Flockton Grey and Good Hand in custody until 1986. Since no one claimed ownership of Flockton Grey, he was sent to the December 1986 Wetherby Sales, where he was bought by trainer Robin Bastiman for 680 guineas.

Flockton Grey never raced and in 1989 was sold to Sharon Dick, who worked part-time at Bastiman's yard. Flockton Grey, now 22, is still in Dick's care. Good Hand was claimed by Richardson and was subsequently stabled at the Aike Grange Stud, a few miles from Jubilee Farm.

11 Fine Cotton

A petite, energetic woman got out of the jeep and dashed through the pouring rain to the quarantine center to check that all was well with Juggler, Australia's runner in the 1997 Dubai World Cup.

While Gai Waterhouse checked Juggler, I sat in the jeep with her husband, Robbie Waterhouse; handsome, immaculate, steely bright. Robbie couldn't go to the track because in 1984, the year of Fine Cotton, he had been warned off.

I knew that because two months earlier my friend John Mort Green, a bit player in the story, had given me an extraordinary book. It was called *The Gambling Man*, by Kevin Perkins, complete and unabridged. It is worth reading.[1]

Much later, for Fine Cotton was a case that affected many people, I received a phone call from Alan Brown. Brown was living at a stud farm in Ireland, but he had been brought up on a cattle farm in Queensland with his brother George, who later became a trainer.

In April of 1984, four months before Fine Cotton's fateful race, George Brown was brutally murdered. He had paid a terrible price for failing to run a ringer. Eighteen years later his brother was still seeking justice, the killers still unnamed.

I got another phone call, from a man called Peter Hume, who also lived at a stud, in Shropshire. He called to tell me about his dealings with John Gillespie, who had been jailed over the Fine Cotton ring-in, and how he had lost $50,000.

By then Robbie Waterhouse was in trouble again, for Fine Cotton would not lie down.

As one Australian, George Moore, rode victoriously past Epsom's winning post on Royal Palace, another stood at Wilfred Sherman's pitch on the rails. He was a tall, hawk-nosed man with dark eyebrows and slab teeth. His name was Bill Waterhouse.

After Royal Palace had won the 1967 Derby, Waterhouse moved on to Royal Ascot. He returned to Epsom for the next two Derbys, but Waterhouse wasn't impressed, not by the betting. In England it was just a little boys' game, and Waterhouse was used to playing grown ups.

When he returned to Sydney, Waterhouse played with the biggest gambler in the world, the billionaire Felipe "Babe" Ysmael. The Filipino Fireball had helped Ferdinand Marcos to power in 1965 and was reaping the benefits.

A slight, dapper figure, Ysmael had scores of horses in training and a betting bank the size of China. When the Babe said he wanted 10 cents on a horse, he meant $10,000, but even that was just a warm-up. When Ysmael and Waterhouse played the game on Caulfield Guineas Day, in October of 1967, Ysmael played with $100,000 chips.

No one knew for sure how big the stakes became, but the biggest bet Waterhouse laid Ysmael was said to have been more than $1 million. Waterhouse was the biggest bookmaker in Australia, the man who shaped the Sydney ring when the ring was at its strongest; a brave player, tough, mean, more respected than liked.

Robbie Waterhouse, Bill's son, was dapper, too. In 1980 he married Gai Smith, the vivacious daughter of legendary trainer T.J. Smith. Tommy Smith won the Sydney trainers' premiership 33 consecutive times between 1952 and 1985, winning six Golden Slippers, seven Cox Plates, and two Melbourne Cups along the way.

The marriage brought two formidable racing dynasties

together. Gai had ambitions to train, and, by 1984, age 29, Waterhouse was a significant racecourse presence in his own right, ready to step into his 62-year-old father's king-sized shoes. Not that Bill was planning to retire; he wasn't that sort of man.

And then their lives, and Australian horse racing, suddenly changed.

~

John Patrick Gillespie spent a lot of time in jail, the home of unsuccessful con men. Inevitably a former used car salesman, Gillespie threatened to break all records with 358 convictions for obtaining money through false pretenses. Late in 1983 he was in a Brisbane jail for armed robbery.

Brisbane in the early 1980s was rife with corruption and race fixing. Gillespie had already tried his criminal hand at running one horse in the name of another. In 1982 at Doomben, he arranged for Apparent Heir to race in the name of Mannasong. The intended winner failed to win, and trainer Bill Steer was disqualified for life.

Later the same year Gillespie bought Captain Cadet with a similar exercise in mind but was interrupted by a jail sentence. By the time he was released, Captain Cadet had been injured.

In jail Gillespie met Pat Haitana, Bert Kidd, and Graham Tabe. Kidd and Tabe were associates of Michael Sayers, a notably violent Sydney criminal, illegal starting price bookmaker, and reputed race-fixer. Haitana was the brother of Hayden Haitana, a heavy-drinking rascal who trained a few horses at a yard near Coffs Harbour in northern New South Wales.

On his release from prison, early in 1984, Pat Haitana introduced Gillespie to his brother, Hayden. Gillespie told Hayden that he would like him to look after a horse for him. Later, at the Nelson Hotel in Bondi Junction, Gillespie met Sayers.

Both men needed money. Sayers had debts, including a rumored $120,000 to Albert Tabone, another SP bookmaker, and to George Freeman, an influential criminal reputed to be the biggest illegal bookmaker in Sydney.

In May Gillespie acquired a sprinter called Dashing Soltaire for $10,000 and sent the horse to Wendy Smith, a girlfriend who also trained at Coffs Harbour. Soon afterward, he paid $2,000 for a nine-year-old lookalike called Fine Cotton, who had been racing at bush tracks. Gillespie told the owner that he wanted Fine Cotton as a lady's hack.

He sold one half share to Tomaso Di Luzio and the other to Mal McGregor-Lowndes, who boasted a conviction for selling yellow-painted sparrows as canaries. Fine Cotton was sent to Haitana, who was told that the newcomer was to be used in a ring-in and that Haitana would be paid $20,000 if it went to plan.

It didn't. Act One was designed to familiarize Queensland punters, bookmakers, and officials with a new, untalented performer. On August 1, 1984, Fine Cotton appeared at Bundamba racecourse near Brisbane. After leading for an uncomfortably long time, he faded out of contention.

That Saturday, August 4, with payday approaching, Dashing Soltaire joined Fine Cotton at Haitana's yard. The race that mattered was at Eagle Farm, Brisbane, the following Saturday.

On Monday, August 6, Fine Cotton was galloped hard in the morning to take the sparkle out of his second run, again at Bundamba that afternoon. Two days later Fine Cotton ran again, this time at Doomben, but disaster had already struck.

On August 7 Dashing Soltaire injured his leg badly on a barbed-wire fence, putting him out of action for several months. The following evening Gillespie reported the injury to an associate of Sayers. The man made a phone call and returned to tell Gillespie that he was in serious trouble.

Gillespie could not afford to abort the ring-in. He owed Sayers $8,000, and Sayers was not a good man to owe money to. There was something else troubling Gillespie and Haitana; the gruesome fate of trainer George Brown. In case they had forgotten, they were reminded.

On March 31, at Doomben, Brown's filly, Risley, had been heavily backed but finished unplaced. On April 2 Brown's body — arms, legs, and skull broken — was found in his burned out car. Brown was believed to have been murdered for having run Risley, when he had been told to run a ringer.

For Gillespie a desperate situation demanded a desperate remedy. Rather than abandon the ring-in, he delayed it for a week, to August 18, while he searched for a replacement for Dashing Soltaire.

A few months earlier he had almost bought a decent sprinter called Bold Personality from owner-trainer Bill Naoum, but his backer refused to put up the necessary $20,000. Now Gillespie went back to Naoum and supplied him with a check, planning to run Bold Personality and then cancel the check and return the horse.

It still left a big problem. Bold Personality was a bay, while Fine Cotton was dark brown, almost black, with white socks. Gillespie couldn't afford to be fussy; he pressed on.

The evening before the race he set to work with some dye, but Gillespie was no Peter Barrie. Bold Personality emerged a curious ginger color, like a Hereford bull.

When Gillespie sprayed white paint on Bold Personality's pasterns, the result was such a mess that, in the end, he covered it up with bandages. They would have to rely, not on persuasive disguise, but on the Brisbane stewards' notorious laxity.

Fine Cotton was entitled to be a 33-1 shot for the 12-runner Second Division Commerce Novice Handicap, and he was, but only briefly. Gillespie had tipped Fine Cotton widely, in return for a percentage of punters' winnings; Haitana's tongue, regularly loosened by beer, had wagged. Even at Warwick Farm racetrack, in Sydney, where Robbie Waterhouse was standing, the gossip centered on Eagle Farm.

With 25 minutes to post-time, 2:25 p.m., Fine Cotton had already tightened like a drumskin, to 7-2. Everyone wanted to follow the money. John Mort "The Butterfly" Green, a colorful Brisbane punter who had been tipped off about the ring-in, had agents backing the horse in both Queensland and New South Wales.

Tomaso Di Luzio, Fine Cotton's part-owner, flew to Rockhampton, north of Brisbane, where he backed his horse, while Glenis Clarke, the wife of punter Garry Clarke, flew to Brisbane with a big plastic bag full of money, destined for Fine Cotton. Father Edward O'Dwyer, a punting priest, having spoken to Waterhouse, went to the greyhound track at Appin and bet $1,000 on Fine Cotton.

Commission agent Jack Honey placed $4,600 on behalf of a Queensland Turf Club Committeeman and even senior police officers backed Fine Cotton, prior to investigating him.

The biggest action was at Warwick Farm, where Ian Murray, one of the game's big players, staked over $50,000. When Garry Clarke walked up to bookmaker Mark Read, wanting to bet $6,000, Read remarked, "If this isn't a ring-in, I'm not here."[2]

The gamble spread across Australia to Fiji and to Papua, New Guinea. It threatened to relieve bookmakers of $2 million.

At Eagle Farm, Gillespie and an associate of Sayers distracted Bold Personality's former trainer, Bill Naoum, while his rechristened sprinter negotiated the pre-race preliminaries. Even some of the jockeys suspected that apprentice Gus Philpott's mount was really Bold Personality.

The race itself almost completed the fiasco, with Fine Cotton barely hanging on to win by a half-head from Harbour Gold.

No ringer has ever been exposed as quickly. As Fine Cotton passed the post, a group of men shouted, "Ring-in, ring-in, wrong horse, wrong horse, official inquiry." In the winner's enclosure, assistant judge Lester Grimmett cried out, "This horse is not Fine Cotton."[3]

The stewards told Haitana to fetch Fine Cotton's papers. Haitana, recognizing defeat, strolled out of the gate and disappeared. Dr. Robert Mason, a Queensland Turf Club vet, compared the winning horse with the details on Fine Cotton's identification card. They didn't match, but when Bold Personality's name was mentioned and his card retrieved, the horse and the card did match.

Fifteen minutes after Fine Cotton's victory, the stewards announced his disqualification, with all bets to stand. Punters who had backed Fine Cotton lost their money; bookmakers brave enough to have laid him, kept it, but the Fine Cotton affair had only just begun.

When Hayden Haitana resurfaced, a few days later, it was on Channel Nine's *60 Minutes* program. Fine Cotton's trainer implied what was already rumored, that the Waterhouses were involved.

On August 30 Independent MP Lindsay Hartwig named Robbie Waterhouse in the Queensland Parliament. "Is he the Mr. Big in the scandal?" he asked. Waterhouse appeared on television to deny the allegation, but the rumors persisted.[4]

In Brisbane, the Queensland Turf Club launched an inquiry, soon followed by a police investigation. Across the state border, in New South Wales, where Sydney's Warwick Farm racecourse had been the scene of much of the betting, the Australian Jockey Club opened its own inquiry under chief steward John "The Sheriff" Schreck.

About 60 witnesses were questioned. All were asked if they knew that Fine Cotton was a ring-in, and all said "no." Ian Murray, tracked down in Tasmania, testified that his $50,000 bet was made after seeing the market move for Fine Cotton. Brisbane tracks were notorious for form upsets. He had simply climbed on the back of another "Brisbane plunge." Fifty thousand dollars was a hell of a piggy-back.

Murray claimed that he had asked Bill Waterhouse for a bet of $40,000 to $2,800 and been given $14,000 to $1,000, a bet that sat uneasily with allegations that the Waterhouses were behind the ring-in. The AJC decided the bet was fictitious, then focused on punters with links to Robbie Waterhouse.

Robbie testified that he had not been involved in the betting on Fine Cotton, testimony that would return to haunt him.

Convinced that the Waterhouses were deeply involved but lacking credible evidence, the AJC adopted an unconventional approach. It served the two men and seven others, including Murray, Clarke, and Father O'Dwyer, with notices calling on them to show why they should not be warned off for "prior knowledge" of the ring-in.

On October 30, 1984, Bill and Robbie Waterhouse were warned off indefinitely. The biggest bookmakers in Australia were branded as cheats; their business, closed.

Robbie immediately appealed to the Racing Appeals Tribunal. Ian Murray, also warned off, did not appeal but agreed to give evidence in exchange for an early return to the racecourse.

Murray had told the AJC inquiry that the $50,000 bet he struck at Warwick Farm was for himself, but he told the Racing Appeals Tribunal a different story. Murray testified that Waterhouse had asked him to place the bet on behalf of a friend and that three days after the race Waterhouse had refunded the $50,000, in cash. Waterhouse stuck to his original story, knowing that it wasn't true.

The truth appears to have been that about six months before Fine Cotton's race, Garry Clarke approached Waterhouse and asked for advice in placing a large commission on a horse due to be racing in Brisbane. Waterhouse eventually suggested approaching Murray, but Clarke and Murray distrusted each other, so it was agreed that Waterhouse would act as an intermediary.

On about August 8, Clarke handed Waterhouse $40,000. Waterhouse added $10,000 of his own and passed it to Murray, but the $40,000 hadn't come from Clarke's own pocket. Another man had given it to Clarke. Although neither Clarke nor Waterhouse knew it, the money came from Sydney criminal Michael Sayers.

The tribunal rejected Waterhouse's appeal. Judge Goran remarked, "I find it difficult to reconcile the clean-cut, grammar school-educated, ethical young millionaire with the sort of people with whom he is pleased to associate."[5]

In February of 1985, Sayers was murdered, the victim of underworld debts or a drug dispute. John Gillespie, Hayden Haitana, Tomaso Di Luzio, and fellow plotters Robert North and John Dixon were charged with conspiring to defraud the public. The charge against Dixon was dropped, Di Luzio was found not guilty, while North and Haitana were each jailed for one year.

Gillespie, who absconded while on bail, was subsequently jailed for four years. He told the court that Sayers was behind the ring-in and that Waterhouse was ignorant of it.

The AJC had no substantive evidence against the bookmaker, and the determination with which they pursued him took on the appearance of a witch-hunt. Waterhouse told me, "Racing is a wonderful sport. Its fault is that 99 percent of participants make no money, or very little. Anyone perceived to have done well is looked at with great suspicion. How could other bookmakers find it so difficult, yet the Waterhouses flourish?"

Neither father nor son was a fool, and the incompetent organization and execution of the Fine Cotton ring-in made it unlikely that either orchestrated the plot. "The scheme was so stupid, only stupid people would be involved," Waterhouse told me. "It was so amateurish. There was no Mr. Big." Just Sayers and Gillespie and their motley crew.[6]

But the AJC and the police marched on. In 1986 Waterhouse appeared at Sydney's St. James Court to face 97 charges. He was cleared on most counts but committed for trial, in company with Garry Clarke and Father O'Dwyer, on charges of attempting to obtain a financial advantage by deception and conspiracy to defraud. In 1988 the charges were quashed.

It didn't end the Waterhouses' problems. The AJC did not give up and lurking in the background was the lie Robbie Waterhouse had told.

Despite his acquittal, the AJC refused to lift Robbie's disqualification, a punishment with serious consequences for the bookmaker's wife. As the spouse of a disqualified person, Gai Waterhouse was barred from owning racehorses and had to sell the 13 she part-owned.

In 1989 Gai applied for a trainer's license, for which she was clearly well qualified. In response, she received a curt reply. "Dear Mrs. Waterhouse, Reference is made to your recent application to this Club for a trainer's license. I am directed to advise you that this matter was considered by the Committee at its meeting today, Thursday September 7, and the Committee decided to refuse your application."[7]

No explanation was given, although a possible reason quickly emerged. Immediately before considering Gai's application, the AJC Committee was informed that Robbie was about to be charged with perjury. The charge related to the evidence he had given to the Racing Appeals Tribunal five years earlier.

In 1990 Gai Waterhouse took her case to the Equal Opportunities Tribunal, claiming that the AJC had discriminated against her because she was Robbie Waterhouse's wife.

When AJC chairman Jim Bell was asked why her application had been rejected, he replied, "Because Robbie Waterhouse is a warned off person and we believe he would be an influence on his wife. As far as we were concerned, he was a crook."

It was the view of fellow AJC Committee member Peter Capelin QC that "Robbie Waterhouse was the axle on which the huge wheel of betting operated in the Fine Cotton affair. I considered he was a deceitful man with a commanding personality, with the capacity to influence others."[8]

Gai lost the case but in 1991 won her appeal to the New South Wales Court of Appeal. In January 1992 the AJC finally granted her a trainer's license.

That summer, at the NSW District Court, her husband pleaded not guilty to perjury but guilty to false swearing. Waterhouse admitted having passed the money he had been given by Clarke, plus some of his own, to Murray, and to having placed additional bets on Fine Cotton through other people.

Waterhouse claimed that at the time of the AJC's original inquiry, it was Murray who had persuaded him to support the story that the $50,000 was Murray's, in order to distance Murray from the ring-in. When Murray changed his story and revealed the truth, Waterhouse, not wanting to expose Clarke, felt obliged to stick to his original tale.

He told me, "My error was that I should have said straight away that I had arranged to put a bet on for someone else. If I had done that, I wouldn't have been warned off. I was untruthful about it, which was wrong and I regret it. I wouldn't do it ever again."

Waterhouse was adamant that he did not know that Fine Cotton was a ring-in. "I most certainly was not aware that a ring-in was involved," he said, forcefully. "I couldn't believe that a ring-in was possible on a metropolitan track; it was unthinkable."[9]

Judge Ducker concluded that when giving evidence to the Racing Appeals Tribunal in 1984, Waterhouse had told "deliberate lies" in the hope of ending his warning off. He sentenced him to eight months periodic detention, which obliged Waterhouse to spend weekends at a detention center.

The AJC's dubious handling of the Fine Cotton affair reinforced calls for a more democratic and accountable authority. In 1996 the Thoroughbred Racing Board Act created a new body to control racing in New South Wales.

By then, Gai Waterhouse had established herself as one of Australia's top trainers, with a succession of group I successes with Te Akau Nick, runner-up in the 1993 Melbourne Cup; Pharaoh; All Our Mob; Stony Bay; Nothin' Leica Dane; Electronic; and Sprint By.

In 1995 she was presented with the Archer Award for outstanding achievement and contribution to the racing industry, but her husband was unable to share Gai's racecourse triumphs. It was not until 1998 that the racecourse bans on Robbie and Bill Waterhouse were finally lifted. That October, Robbie was at Randwick with Gai to see In Joyment win the group I Metropolitan, but he was still barred from operating as a bookmaker.

Before he could receive his license, there was a final hurdle to be crossed, erected by other bookmakers. In June of 2001, the Thoroughbred Racing Board granted Waterhouse a license, subject to him joining the Bookmakers' Co-operative and securing the associated financial guarantee, but the co-op rejected Waterhouse's membership application.

Bookmakers were divided. One anonymous Sydney bookmaker explained, "Even though it was 17 years ago, there is still a lot of animosity for him. Remember, he was one of us, yet he was prepared to fleece us. It's a bit like Ronnie Biggs going to British Rail and asking if he could get a job as a train guard."[10]

In August the TRB accepted an alternative financial guarantee and issued Waterhouse with a bookmaker's license. It was a time for double celebration because, a few days earlier, when the season ended, Gai had trained 153 winners, just three short of her father's record of 156, set in 1975-76.

On Saturday August 11, 2001, almost exactly 17 years after Fine Cotton's infamous victory, Robbie Waterhouse, 46, returned to the ring at Sydney's Rosehill Gardens.

"I am really enjoying it," he said. "Surprisingly, it's easier than when I started out. The bookmaker to punter ratio has gone up in the bookmakers' favor and the competition is less severe, because they are a more cautious bunch. I am exhibiting a bit of flair and issuing twice as many tickets as any other bookmaker."[11]

On February 23, 2002, Bill Waterhouse, age 80, followed his son back to the betting ring at Warwick Farm, but by the time the second Waterhouse returned, the first was already heading for the exit. For a man as sharp as Waterhouse, and as closely watched, he did a very silly thing.

After the last race at Canterbury Park on February 6, betting steward Terry Griffin carried out a routine inspection of Robbie Waterhouse's betting sheets. He spotted a string of unusual bets, very unusual.

When Griffin informed Ray Murrihy, the TRB's chief steward, Murrihy immediately opened an inquiry. There were 13 bets, each with a $20 stake, entered on behalf of Peter McCoy. They were all on horses running at tracks in other states. Six were winners and seven losers, which wasn't surprising, because the 13 horses were all short-priced favorites. What was unusual was that Waterhouse had given McCoy odds of 500-1, on every horse, an act of astonishing generosity. As a result, Waterhouse had lost — and McCoy had won — almost $60,000.

Murrihy summoned Waterhouse to the stewards' room and interrogated him at length. It emerged that Waterhouse, not McCoy, had chosen the horses. Asked how he had selected them, Waterhouse explained that he had used rating sheets. Where were they? They were in a bag, which was with his assistants, who had gone home. His assistants included his children, Tom and Kate, who Waterhouse knew were waiting for him in his car.

Griffin was sent to the car park, but the ratings sheets could not be found. Waterhouse said that they must have been thrown away.

McCoy was a former bookmaker who, like Waterhouse, had been warned off in the wake of the Fine Cotton affair and, in 1997, had gone bankrupt. Why had Waterhouse offered him such wildly excessive odds? "To do him a favor. I'd like to see him get out of trouble."

The trouble McCoy was in featured in Waterhouse's betting ledger. It was a debt of $900,000, recently capped at $500,000, but it was not a gambling debt but a debt that related to past business and property deals. Nor, since his bankruptcy, was it a legally enforceable debt. "What's it doing in the betting ledger?" Murrihy asked.[12]

The bets, Waterhouse explained, were a dignified way of reducing McCoy's debt of honor. The stewards could not understand why, if Waterhouse wanted to reduce the debt, he couldn't simply have written it off. They suspected that the bets were a ploy to evade tax.

When Murrihy asked Waterhouse for McCoy's address or phone number, he was unable to supply them but said that he thought McCoy lived somewhere in Braidwood. He would provide details the next day. In fact, McCoy was the manager of

Waterhouse's betting business in Fiji, yet it was 48 hours before Waterhouse supplied the stewards with contact details.

Waterhouse's already fragile reputation was seriously, irrecoverably, damaged. As Ray Chesterton remarked in Sydney's *Daily Telegraph*, "People risked their own credibility to ensure Robbie got a second chance in racing. They must be wondering why they bothered."

Chesterton quoted an uncharitable barroom critic. "The blokes who hand out bookmaking licenses might know a lot about horses and punting," he said, "but they know bugger all about leopards."[13]

At a series of hearings in February and April, Waterhouse insisted that the bets were legitimate, were not entered for tax evasion purposes, that he had not misled the stewards, had not acted dishonestly, had damaged no one, and had broken no rules.

On April 15 the New South Wales Thoroughbred Racing Board Stewards Panel, chaired by Murrihy, delivered its verdict. Waterhouse was found guilty of having entered bets that were not legitimate wagers, guilty of having given misleading evidence, and guilty of having engaged in conduct "prejudicial to the image of racing."

The legacy of Fine Cotton echoed on, for the stewards ruled "that the adverse effect on the image of racing was exacerbated by the fact that Mr. McCoy and Mr. Waterhouse had both been previously warned off due to the notorious Fine Cotton affair, and the knowledge of the members of the industry and the general public of that fact."

Speaking before the stewards announced their decision on penalties four days later, Waterhouse insisted that he had "already been punished very severely" over the Fine Cotton case and urged the panel not to take it into account.[14]

He was fined $6,000 for each of the 13 illegitimate bets, a total of $78,000, disqualified for a year for providing misleading evidence about the whereabouts of his staff, disqualified for two years for providing misleading evidence about

McCoy's address, and disqualified for a year for conduct prejudicial to the image of racing, the disqualifications to be concurrent.

Waterhouse immediately lodged an appeal, which triggered a stay of the penalties and enabled him to carry on working. On July 25 the TRB's Appeals Panel, chaired by Tom Hughes QC, upheld the bookmaker's appeal against the two charges of giving misleading evidence but dismissed his appeal against the remaining charges.

The following month the Appeals Panel reduced the 12-month disqualification for conduct prejudicial to the image of racing to a nine-month suspension, and cut the total fine from $78,000 to $19,500.

Neither the TRB nor Waterhouse was satisfied. Both appealed to the Racing Appeals Tribunal. For Waterhouse, it was an appeal too far.

On September 6 Judge Barrie Thorley confirmed the fines and, describing the offending betting transactions as "sullied by a considerable degree of deviousness," converted the nine-month suspension into a nine-month disqualification, with a starting date of August 16.

The alteration was crucial. Under a suspension, Waterhouse could not work as a racecourse bookmaker but could visit the racetrack and resume business after nine months. Disqualification meant that he was barred from racetracks and stables, and would have to reapply to the TRB for his bookmaker's license. Odds of 500-1 were quoted against Waterhouse being granted another license. Waterhouse indicated that he would appeal to the Supreme Court.

In November, Justice Peter young ruled that the Racing Appeals Tribunal was not entitled to substitute its own penalty of a nine-month disqualification for the appeal panel's penalty of a nine-month suspension. To Waterhouse's delight, the suspension was reinstated. He would be able to return to the betting ring in May 2003.[15]

While the disgraced bookmaker remained headline news,

other leading players in the Fine Cotton scandal drifted into obscurity, periodically unearthed by curious journalists.

In 2002 Hayden Haitana, 56, was working as an odd-job man on the coast of South Australia. Wendy Smith, subsequently Wendy Fahey, who had prepared Dashing Soltaire and been warned off for life for giving misleading evidence, moved to the Northern Territory.

John Patrick Gillespie pursued his suspect ways. In 1996 he arranged to buy some horses from Peter Hume's stud in Shropshire to export to Thailand and was also active in Ireland, but more active with promises than payments. Hume claimed that the experience cost him £50,000.

In 1998 three men were arrested in the Philippines. Claiming to be officials from the Dominion of Melchizedek, Dennis Oakley, Chew Chin Yee, and Stuart Mason-Parker were accused of having duped hundreds of local Filipinos, Chinese, and Bangladeshis into paying up to $3,500 for Melchizedek passports, sometimes with additional payments for arranging jobs on a Pacific island within the Dominion.

The gang had collected an estimated $1 million, but their ringleader escaped. According to the Philippine police, he was John Gillespie, the brother-in-law of Chew Chin Yee, and the self-proclaimed President of the Dominion of Melchizedek. The Dominion existed only on the Internet.

Ian Murray, known as The Sunshine Kid, had major heart surgery in 1998 and is now a rare visitor to the racecourse. Father Edward O'Dwyer and Garry Clarke still live in Sydney, but John Mort Green has moved to England. John Schreck, the AJC chief steward, occupied a similar role with the Hong Kong Jockey Club until retiring at the end of 2002.

Fine Cotton and Bold Personality are both still alive and living near Brisbane, Bold Personality in the care of his former trainer Bill Naoum.

12 Au Revoir

Given a dozen attempts, you still wouldn't have picked the winner. That day at Thirsk, July 29, 1995, there were 18 runners for the six-furlong Rocom Selling Handicap for lady amateur riders. One of the first names punters crossed out was Pretty Average. There was nothing to recommend her.

The maiden five-year-old's form figures read 000/0. Pretty Average had never started at less than 25-1 and never finished better than eighth. She had recently returned from a three-year break, to finish 11th of 13 in a lowly sprint handicap at Southwell's all-weather track. Even in a weak field, Pretty Average was a no-hoper.

She didn't race like one. Ridden by Margaret Morris, Pretty Average led from start to finish, winning at a seemingly ungenerous 20-1, although the tote paid 89-1.

Patricia Hamilton, wearing a pretty floral dress, a big smile, and a head full of curly hair, stood proudly in the winner's enclosure, holding her horse's head, while Jim McDonald, her partner, boasted of having landed a touch. At one time Pretty Average had been 50-1.

At the post-race auction no one wanted to buy the winner, and the triumphant couple dashed off to the evening meeting at Hamilton to watch another of their horses, Elite Number, run badly.

It soon emerged that there was more to Pretty Average than

met the eye. McDonald, who ran a small engineering business at Stonehouse near Glasgow, had bought Pretty Average as a foal for 1,250 guineas and sent her to trainer Tommy Craig. "She was a small filly who needed more time," Craig remembered. "After we had tried her in three races without her showing much, McDonald said he'd take her back."

Three years later, in June of 1995, another small trainer, Basil Richmond, received a phone call from Fergus Jestin. Jestin was a north-country permit holder who knew McDonald and Hamilton through the point-to-point field.

"Pat is a friend," Jestin told me. "She had a horse she wanted to run on the all-weather. I suggested she send it to Basil Richmond, who trains not far from Southwell."

Richmond knew Jestin but not Hamilton or McDonald. Pretty Average arrived at his yard at the beginning of July, Richmond checked its passport and submitted the necessary forms to Weatherbys.

Pretty Average had a conspicuous scar on one of her forelegs. "Her leg had been badly cut," Richmond concluded. "It was obvious. You could see the gash where she had probably been caught on barbed wire."

The same scar had caught the eye of John Hughes, a former jump jockey who had met McDonald and Hamilton earlier in the year and been shown two of their horses, Hotspur and Short and Sweet. When Hughes rode work on Short and Sweet, he noticed "she had a very bad scar on her foreleg. It stood out."

So did her speed, which surprised Hughes. "Why are you flapping with her," he asked McDonald, "she's good enough to win under rules." "Aye, I know," replied McDonald.

A few days later Short and Sweet disappeared from her box at Maudslie Castle Stables, at Ashgill near Stonehouse. "Where's the filly?" Hughes asked. "Oh, she's away," McDonald replied.[1]

In the border country north of Carlisle, there is a special kind of horse racing. It is not licensed by the Jockey Club, and drugs that are prohibited under the Rules of Racing, such as bute, are permitted. It is called "flapping."

There are fewer flapping tracks in Britain today than there were when Peter Barrie resorted to them, in the 1930s but in 1995, between April and September, about seventeen flapping meetings were held in the Borders, at Hawick and Langholm, Irvine, and Selkirk.

After Tommy Craig had returned Pretty Average to McDonald, the filly joined the flapping circuit under the name of Short and Sweet. In 1994 she raced in the ownership of A. and D. Bell. Darren Bell lived with Angela McDonald, Jim's daughter.

Short and Sweet made little impression that year but did better in 1995. She won four races and on July 1 won the Stella Artois Handicap at Hawick, on the same day that Hotspur won the Murphy's Mile for McDonald.

After joining Richmond, who was unaware of Pretty Average's flapping past, the mare was entered at Southwell on July 22, where she was ridden by apprentice Claire Balding. "Mr. Richmond told me that she had shown speed at home," Balding recalled, "and to jump out and be up with the pace. She did break well, but the first two furlongs hadn't been watered and she got a bit lost in the dry ground. When she met watered ground, she went much better but had lost too much ground to make it up. Although she finished 11th, she ran quite well."

Richmond tried to book champion lady amateur rider Diana Jones for the race at Thirsk, but Jones had already been booked. Margaret Morris had ridden a winner for Richmond before, so he booked her. "I had a few pounds on Pretty Average on the tote," Richmond admitted, ruefully. "I wish I'd had more."

The following Monday, July 31, Pretty Average finished third, under Claire Balding, in another selling race at Ripon, where she started at a less appealing 4-1.

On August 6 Hamilton removed Pretty Average from Richmond's yard, telling him that they had received an offer they couldn't refuse. Hamilton, the horse, and McDonald disappeared, although they were in hiding from the press rather than from the authorities, who soon established contact.

David Pipe, the Jockey Club's spokesman, declared, "The Security Department is making inquiries into allegations concerning the history of Pretty Average. It is a serious offense for anyone to run a horse under Rules, knowing that it has previously been flapping."[2]

The inquiries revealed that Short and Sweet was not the only flapping horse to have raced under Rules. In 1992, one of Pretty Average's stablemates at Craig's yard was a three-year-old called Bluefaulds, also owned by McDonald, and equally unpromising.

He had more success racing on flapping tracks under the name of Hotspur, taking time out during the winter of 1994-95 to run, unsuccessfully, over hurdles from Jack Birkett's and then Fergus Jestin's yards.

Jestin insisted, "I was duped, the same as Basil Richmond. I bought the horse from Darren Bell, who I met at a point-to-point in the company of Patricia Hamilton. I wouldn't have

JEAN RAFTERY

Almost Impossible, aka Forty Two

touched it if I'd known it had been flapping. How do you tell? The flapping people should stamp a horse's passport."[3]

The Jockey Club's Rule 181 (i) was clear. "A horse is not qualified to be entered to start for any race if it has run at any unrecognized meeting." Flapping meetings were unrecognized. In April 1996 Hamilton and McDonald were warned off for ten years.

Strictly speaking, Pretty Average wasn't a ringer at all. The horse that ran in the name of Pretty Average was Pretty Average, although she had raced under a different name outside the Jockey Club's jurisdiction.

Even though Hamilton and McDonald knew that Pretty Average had been racing successfully at flapping tracks, they could not have been more than hopeful of success at Thirsk. McDonald landed a gamble, but not a big one.

Kelly Winter landed a bigger one, and needed to. On July 17, 1998, Winter was in Las Vegas with some friends. The friends were alleged to have promised to wipe out Winter's gambling debts, about $30,000, in return for the New Mexico horseman running Forty Two in the name of Almost Impossible.

The race was for maidens. Almost Impossible was a $600 unraced three-year-old with nothing but two slow work times to his name. Forty Two cost $17,000 and had two wins at Sunland Park, New Mexico, to his name.

Winter had two brothers, Emmett and Floyd. "I met Emmett Winter through his stepbrother, Floyd, a blacksmith in Tampa," trainer Joaquin Schafers testified. "I got the horse about six weeks before the race. When I worked him about two weeks before the race, he popped out of the gate like a rocket, like he'd been doing it all his life. Their explanation was that the horse had run and won races at the bush tracks of New Mexico."

Schafers made sure he had money in his pocket for the trip to Calder racetrack. "I figured, with no published works and being by nobody out of nobody, he'd be 20-1. When I walked out of the paddock, I looked at the board and he was 2-1. I was so shocked at the price, I didn't even bother to bet him."[4]

If he had, the unknowing Schafers would have been paid at odds of 4-1 for when horse identifier Ken Masters checked the tattoo number under Almost Impossible's upper lip with the number on his foal certificate, the numbers matched. That was because Kelly Winter had changed the number on the certificate.

Emmett was listed as the winner's owner, but Floyd said that he and Kelly had hidden the truth from Emmett until the last minute, for fear that their brother would ruin the odds. Someone did, but the payout nationwide on Almost Impossible was still almost $300,000, much of it thought to have filtered back to the Winters. In Las Vegas, the bookmaker owed money by Kelly won a reputed $35,000. He had got his money back.

The Winter brothers might have melted away, unnoticed, but when gamblers win once, it makes them think, why not again? They told Schafers that they were taking the horse north. Later, he got a call to say that Almost Impossible wouldn't be running, but to back Swing a Tune at Philadelphia Park.

Kelly had bought Swing a Tune for $2,000 and inscribed Forty Two's tattoo number on his foal certificate. He took Forty Two to Charles Town races in West Virginia and prepared him for a race at Penn National, Pennsylvania. When the race was cancelled, Winter switched his attention to Philadelphia Park.

On September 21 the track's horse identifier checked Swing a Tune's lip tattoo against his foal certificate and was suspicious enough to arrange for a check of all the tattoo numbers allotted to the offspring of Swing a Tune's dam. None matched the number on the horse's lip. Swing a Tune was scratched from the race.

Emmett phoned Floyd to tell him that their ruse had been rumbled. "I'm out of here," he said. It took investigators a long time to catch up.

Almost four years later, in May of 2002, the FBI arrested Kelly and Emmett Winter. Floyd had already struck a deal, pleading guilty to lesser charges in exchange for his testimony. Emmett eventually struck his own bargain, leaving Kelly to face trial alone.

It was a losing battle. Kelly Winter was convicted on a string of charges relating to running Forty Two as a ringer and sentenced to 28 months in prison. The history book could not be closed on ringers yet.[5]

There was an element of romance about Pretty Average's victory, something I had been hoping to find in my research into ringers. I didn't find it. The ring-masters were not romantic figures but generally seedy, sometimes deeply unpleasant characters, crooks without concern for others, or regard for their horses.

The motivation was often the obvious one, of greed, or need; greed in the case of Dr. Mark Gerard, Jack Morris, Maurice Williams, and Ken Richardson, none of whom needed the money; need in that of Peter Barrie and Hayden Haitana, who did.

Yet greed was rarely the only motive. Men like John Bowles enjoyed the trickery, which was a sort of defiance of authority. Some, like Barrie and Rick Renzella, wallowed in the attention, which boosted their misplaced faith in their own cleverness.

Arrogance, accompanied by incompetence, was a regular stumbling block, for the conspiracies featured here were all exposed, although some of the guilty parties were extraordinarily reluctant to acknowledge their guilt.

Not everyone was punished. James Rooney and William Lyons escaped conviction, while the mysterious Mr. Graham and Mr. Stedworthy simply escaped. The most successful ringers were the ones who have not been mentioned because they escaped detection altogether, and kept quiet about it.

Peter Christian Barrie was a fraudster and a cheat, and his reputation as "King of the Ringers" was not based on success, yet he dominates the modern history of ringing. With the forgiving passage of time, it is easier to accept him as an engaging rascal, as well as a dedicated crook. For over 30 years Barrie plied his race-fixing trade, a pioneering internationalist, indifferent to rules wherever he found them.

Barrie was a unique figure in horse racing and a sadly neglected one. He may not deserve to be celebrated, but he deserves to be acknowledged. If I have succeeded in resurrecting the "King of the Ringers," I am content.

There may yet be another Kelly Winter, but there will be no more Barries. Tattoos and brands, passports and blood testing, microchips and DNA, as well as much improved security and stewarding, have tipped the scales powerfully against ringers. Yet skulduggery's strange appeal persists. I confess, although not as often as Barrie, that part of me hopes that today, at a racecourse somewhere…

Notes

Abbreviations:
JCR — Jockey Club Records.
Pinkerton — Pinkerton's National Detective Agency Records.
NSWTRB — New South Wales Thoroughbred Racing Board.

The Dark Pool

1. Wray Vamplew, "Odds Against: The Punter's Lot Is Not a Happy One," *Sporting Traditions*, Vol. 5 No. 1, November 1988, p. 54; *Racing Post*, June 15-16, 2002.
2. For brief accounts of the Trodmore case, see James Lambie, "The strangest race meeting as never was," *The Sporting Life*, February 20, 1978; John Stubbs, "The Race Meeting that Never Was," in Richard Onslow (ed.), *Great Racing Gambles & Frauds*, Vol. 2 (1992), pp. 45-50; John Randall, "Racing's most brilliant betting coup," *Racing Post*, August 2, 1998.
3. There is some material on Benjamin Chilson in Pinkerton, containers 150-152.
4. For the Running Rein affair, see Michael Seth-Smith, *Lord Paramount of the Turf* (1971), pp. 81-128.
5. Memorable, but the original source for the quotation is not known. It is reproduced, among other places, in John Welcome, *Infamous Occasions* (1980), p. 177.
6. *Racing Post*, November 19-20, August 22, December 12, 1998.

Part One

Chapter 1 — Heating Up

1. Richard Onslow (ed.), *Great Racing Gambles & Frauds*, Vol. 3 (1993), p. 129.
2. *Census of Scotland*, 1891, 1901; *The People*, February 4, 1951; JCR. Australian Jockey Club to Weatherby & Sons, May 17, 1920.
3. For Barrie's wartime record, see National Archives of Australia, World War I Service Records, Series B2455, No. 384.
4. C.R. Acton, *Silk and Spur* (1935), p. 86.
5. *John Bull*, June 9, 1923.
6. Ibid., February 17, 1923; JCR. Statement by Gilbert Marsh, December 29, 1920.
7. *John Bull*, February 24, 17, 1923.
8. Ibid., February 24, 1923.
9. *The Times*, June 9, 1920; *John Bull*, March 3, 1923.
10. *The Times*, June 28, September 14, 15, 1920.

11. *John Bull*, March 3, 1923; *The Sporting Life*, October 27, 1919.
12. JCR. Weatherby & Sons to A.W. Pearson, November 7, 11, 21, 1919; A.W. Pearson to Weatherby & Sons, November 11, 24, 1919; *The Sporting Life*, June 8, 16, 1920.
13. *John Bull*, March 24, 1923.
14. *The Times*, September 23-25, 1920; *John Bull*, March 10, April 14, 1923.
15. JCR. Statement by Gilbert Marsh, December 29, 1920.
16. Ibid., Cyril S. Lawley to Weatherby & Sons, December 16, 1919.
17. *The Times*, September 23, 1920; *The Sporting Life*, December 30, 1919.
18. *The Sporting Life*, July 7, 1920; *John Bull*, March 10, 1923; *The Times*, July 16, September 24, 1920.
19. *John Bull*, March 17, 1923; *The People*, June 16, 1935.
20. *John Bull*, March 31, 1923; *The Sporting Life*, April 20, 27, 1920.
21. *John Bull*, May 19, 1923.
22. Ibid., February 17, 1923; JCR. Statement by Gilbert Marsh, December 29, 1920; Charles Russell & Co. to Weatherby & Sons, November 22, 1920.
23. John Welcome, *Neck or Nothing: The Extraordinary Life & Times of Bob Sievier* (1970), p. 59. Sievier was the controversial owner and trainer of Sceptre; Gill, his implacable opponent.
24. *The Times*, September 14, 15, 1920.
25. *John Bull*, April 14, 1923; JCR. Norman Weisz to Weatherby & Sons, September 5, 1919; Rena Stephens to Weatherby & Sons, December 31, 1919; *The Sporting Life*, September 28, 29, 1920; *The Times*, September 29, 1920.
26. Margaret Lane, *Edgar Wallace: The Biography of a Phenomenon* (n.d. 1938), p. 282. Barrie's name appears among those listed as having helped the author; Jack Leach, *Sods I Have Cut On The Turf* (1961), pp. 118, 116; Meyrick Good, *The Lure of the Turf* (1957), p. 83.
27. Frank Atherton Brown, *Sport From Within* (1952), pp. 136-7. For Bottomley, see especially, Julian Symons, *Horatio Bottomley* (1955; 2nd ed. 2001). Also, Jack Waterman, "England's Superman Alights on the Turf," in Richard Onslow (ed.), *Great Racing Gambles & Frauds*, Vol. 4 (1994), pp. 89-99.
28. *John Bull*, February 17, 1923.
29. Christopher R. Hill, *Horse Power: The Politics of the Turf* (1988), p. 13.

Chapter 2 — Hot

1. *The People*, February 3, January 27, 1935.
2. *New York Daily News*, December 3, 1932; Toney Betts, *Across The Board* (1956), p. 92; *The New York Times*, July 30, August 19, 1933.
3. *The People*, January 27, February 3, 1935; *The New York Times*, March 24, 1926; *The Morning Telegraph*, October 23, 1925.
4. *The People*, January 27, 1935; *The New York Times*, June 30, 1933. Marks is not mentioned in a recent work on the gang, Paul R. Kavieff, *The Purple Gang* (2000).
5. *The Morning Telegraph*, October 23, 1925; *The New York Times*, October 25, 1925, March 24, 1926.
6. *The People*, February 10, 1935.
7. Betts, op.cit., p. 136.
8. *New York Daily News*, November 25, 1932; *The People*, February 10, 1935.
9. *The Morning Telegraph*, December 10-14, 1932; *The People*, March 31, April 7, June 23, 1935. In Barrie's version of the story, Infante appears as Lima.
10. Alan Hynd, *The Pinkerton Case Book* (1948), pp. 79-83. The chronology, however, is suspect.

11. *New York Daily News*, August 17, 1934.
12. Untitled newspaper cutting, January 1932, Pinkerton, container 151, "Racehorse ringers. Newspaper and magazine articles. 1932."
13. Edward Hotaling, *They're Off. Horse Racing at Saratoga* (1995), p. 218; Joe Hirsch, *The First Century* (1996), pp. 78-9.
14. Julius Debott to William Baird, September 29, 1931, Pinkerton, container 150.
15. *The People*, February 17, 1935.
16. Ibid., January 20, 1935; *New York Daily News*, November 21, 1932.
17. *The Morning Telegraph*, October 4, 6, 9, 1931.
18. *The People*, February 24, 1935. For Coll's vicious career, see Breandan Delap, *Mad Dog Coll* (1999).
19. *New York Daily News*, November 21, 1932.
20. Note from Hialeah, February 24, 1932, Pinkerton, container 151, "Racehorse ringers. Essays and Notes."
21. Maryland Racing Commission ruling, undated (November 18, 1931), Pinkerton, container 150.
22. *The People*, March 3, 1935.
23. A. Hynd, op.cit., p. 95.
24. Ibid., March 10, 17, 1935. Wallace died on February 10, 1932, shortly after his return to Hollywood. Donoghue helped with the funeral arrangements.
25. *The Blood-Horse*, March 5, 1932.
26. A. Hynd, op.cit., p. 97.
27. *The New York Press*, March 16, 1932; *New York Daily News*, August 19, 1934; *The People*, March 31, 1935; undated cutting from *Daily Racing Form*, late 1931 or early 1932.
28. *The People*, January 20, 1935.
29. Ibid., May 12, 1935.
30. Ibid., May 26, 1935.
31. Betts, op.cit., pp. 258-9; *New York World-Telegram*, October 26, 1932.
32. *The Saratogian*, August 15, 1934; *The Morning Telegraph*, December 14, 1932.
33. *New York Herald Tribune*, October 11, 1933.
34. Alan Hynd, "The Pinkertons Smash the Race-Track Ringers," *True Detective Mysteries*, December 1941.
35. *The Blood-Horse*, August 18, 1934; David Alexander, "So Many Interesting People, Part II," *Turf & Sport Digest*, April 1941.
36. Quoted in A. Hynd, "The Pinkertons Smash the Race-Track Ringers," *True Detective Mysteries*, December 1941; Hotaling, op.cit, p. 241; *The People*, June 9, 1935.

Chapter 3 — Simmering Down

1. *The People*, January 20, June 9, 1935.
2. Ibid., January 27, 1935.
3. David Alexander, op.cit.; JCR. Circular issued by P.C. Barrie dated March 12, 1940.
4. *The People*, January 7, 28, 1951.
5. W. Bebbington, *Rogues Go Racing* (n.d. 1947), pp. 81-85. William Bebbington was Senior Jockey Club Supervisor of Racecourse Detective Personnel.
6. *The Sporting Life*, July 10, 1935; *The People*, January 28, 1951; Undated circular issued by P.C. Barrie (1939), reproduced in W.Bebbington, op.cit., pp. 92-3.
7. JCR. Statement by Clarence Bailey, April 12, 1938; James McBeath to Major G.P. Wymer, January 17, 1938; A.C. Watts to Weatherby & Sons, n.d.; *The People*, January 28, 1951.

8. JCR. James McBeath to Major G.P. Wymer, January 7, 17, 1938; T.R. Patterson to Weatherby & Sons, January 2, 1938; Statement by Clarence Bailey, April 12, 1938.
9. Ibid., James McBeath to Major G.P. Wymer, January 30, February 1, 1938; R. Dickens to Weatherby & Sons, January 31, 1938; R. Dickens to G. Jackson, January 31, 1938; R. Dickens to Captain P.C. Wilson, February 2, 1938; J. Marr to A.C. Watts, December 1, 1937.
10. Ibid., James McBeath to Weatherby & Sons, February 19, 1939.
11. Ibid., Statement by Mrs. Dolores Hunter, n.d. (June 1939); A.B.Tully to Weatherby & Sons, June 18, 1939; Cartmel stewards to Weatherby & Sons, May 29, 1939; Addis, Edwards & Co. to Cartmel racecourse, June 9, 1939.
12. Ibid., James McBeath to Weatherby & Sons, November 23, 1938; Circular issued by P.C. Barrie dated March 12, 1940; Robert Gore to Weatherby & Sons, March 15, 1940.
13. W. Bebbington, op.cit, p. 93.
14. Pinkerton, container 152. "Racehorse ringers. Reports," note dated September 30, 1937; ibid., anon. to Post Office Inspector, New York, November 29, 1939.
15. *Racing Calendar*. 1950, October 25 meeting; JCR. Material relating to stewards' review of doping, n.d. 1951; *The Sporting Life*, December 9, 1949, November 28, 1950.
16. The series of weekly articles in *The People* ran from January 7 to February 25, 1951.
17. *The People*, February 4, March 4, 1951.
18. *The Times*, December 7, 18, 20, 21, 29, 1951; *The Sporting Life*, April 5, June 11, December 2, 5, 1952; *Racing Calendar*. 1961, May 10, October 13, December 11 meetings.
19. Kent Hollingsworth, "What's Going On Here," *The Blood-Horse*, June 5, 1972, p. 1870; National Archives of Australia, World War I Service Records, Series B2455, No. 384.

Part Two

Chapter 4 — Possums

1. *The Sydney Morning Herald*, January 28, February 3, 1932.
2. *The Argus*, June 9-10, July 4, 1931.
3. *The Sydney Morning Herald*, June 23, 1931.
4. Ibid., July 22, August 16, 1932; *The Argus*, January 29, 1932.
5. *The Argus*, November 10, 1934; *The Sydney Morning Herald*, October 19, 1934.
6. *The Sun*, March 22, 1954; *The Sydney Morning Herald*, August 17, 1934.
7. *The Argus*, August 16, 1934; *The Sun*, March 22, 1954.
8. *The Herald*, July 30, 1934.
9. *The Argus*, August 11, 1934; *The Herald*, August 13, 1934.
10. *The Sydney Morning Herald*, September 14, 1934.
11. Ibid., October 19, 1934; *The Argus*, November 20, 1934.
12. *The Sun*, March 22, 1954.

Chapter 5 — The Frantic Forties

1. *The People*, January 27, 1935; *Daily Racing Form*, January 29, 1992.
2. *The Blood-Horse*, March 23, 1946.
3. Ibid., May 18, 1946; *The New York Times*, August 1, 1946.
4. *The New York Times*, December 7, 1950; ibid., February 24, 1947.
5. *The Sporting Life*, January 18, February 1, March 7, 1949.
6. *The Times*, December 19, 1950.
7. *The Sporting Life*, June 15, October 25, 1951.

8. Ibid., October 24, 1951.
9. Interview with author, June 10, 2002.
10. *The Sporting Life*, August 23, 1949, June 30, 1951.
11. Ibid., October 26, 1951.
12. Ibid., October 27, 1951.
13. Ibid., June 29, 30, October 31, 1951.
14. Ibid., June 27, 1950.
15. Ibid., March 8, 1950.
16. Ibid.
17. Ibid., December 1, 1949.
18. Ibid., June 27, 1950; *Irish Independent*, November 25, 1950.
19. *The Sporting Life*, June 27, 1950; Tommy Weston, *My Racing Life* (1952), pp. 88-9.
20. *The Sporting Life*, May 11, 25, 1951; JCR. F.E. Birch to Weatherby & Sons, May 5, 1952; Weatherby & Sons to F.E. Birch, August 26, 1952; F.E. Birch to Major R. Macdonald-Buchanan, November 3, 1952.

Chapter 6 — The Unrequired Ringer

1. *The Sporting Life*, March 4, 1954.
2. Marriage certificate, August 6, 1939.
3. *The Sporting Life*, January 27, 1954.
4. JCR. Statement by Henry Amos Twite, August 4, 1953.
5. Ibid., *The Sporting Life*, January 23, 1954.
6. *The Sporting Life*, January 13, 1954.
7. JCR. Weatherby & Sons to Maurice Williams, May 26, 1953.
8. *The Sporting Life*, January 13, 1954.
9. Ibid., January 15, 1954.
10. *Bath and Wiltshire Chronicle and Herald*, October 9, 1953.
11. *The Sporting Life*, July 17, 1953.
12. JCR. Stewards' enquiry, Ascot, July 18, 1953; *Bath and Wiltshire Chronicle and Herald*, March 18, 1954.
13. *The Sporting Life*, January 13, 1954.
14. JCR. Dennis Bushby to Weatherby & Sons, July 22, 1953.
15. *The Sporting Life*, July 22, 1953.
16. Ibid., August 7, September 19, 1953; *Bath and Wiltshire Chronicle and Herald*, September 19, 1953.
17. Interview with author, February 11, 2002.
18. *Bath and Wiltshire Chronicle and Herald*, October 23, 1953.
19. *The Sporting Life*, January 21, 1954; *Maidenhead Advertiser*, February 5, 1954.
20. *The Sporting Life*, February 3, 1954.
21. Ibid., February 19, March 18, 1954; *Maidenhead Advertiser*, March 19, 1954.
22. *The Times*, January 11, 1967; *South Wales Echo*, January 10, February 9, 1967; JCR. Michael and Peter Charles to Weatherby & Sons, February 12, 1963.

Chapter 7 — A Used Car Salesman

1. *The Age*, June 12, 1973.
2. Ibid., May 31, 1972, June 15, 1973.
3. Ibid., July 26-27, 1972; P. Opas, *The Great Ring-In* (1982), p. 95.
4. *The Age*, June 21, 1973.
5. Ibid., May 17, 1972.
6. Ibid., May 25, 30, 1972.
7. Ibid., May 31, 1972.
8. Ibid.

9. Ibid., June 1, 5, 6, 8, 1972.
10. Ibid. June 20, 24, 1972.
11. Ibid., June 23, July 1, 1972; P. Opas, op.cit., pp. 120-1.
12. *The Age*, July 28, 1972.
13. P. Opas, op.cit., p. 44.
14. *The Age*, June 12, 1973; P. Opas, op.cit., pp. 79, 134-5, 155.
15. *The Age*, June 22, July 3, 1973; P. Opas, op.cit., pp. 71-72, 143.
16. *The Age*, June 14, July 9, 1973; P. Opas, op.cit., p. 43.
17. *Barrier Daily Truth*, October 17, 1984.
18. Ibid., October 12, 1984.
19. Ibid., September 30, 1983.
20. Ibid., October 27, 1984.
21. *Central Western Daily*, January 11, 1982.
22. *The Sunday Age*, August 16, 1998.

Chapter 8 — The Return of the Ringers

1. House Select Committee on Crime. 92nd Congress Hearings, pp. 806-7, Statement submitted by Spencer J. Drayton, November 1972.
2. *Daily Racing Form*, June 1, 1972.
3. For Berube's testimony, given on May 25, 1972, see House Select Committee on Crime. 92nd Congress Hearings, pp. 772-805.
4. *Daily Racing Form*, January 10, May 26-27, June 1, 12, 1972.
5. Ibid., September 10, 26, 1977; Kent Hollingsworth, "Cinzano Case," *The Blood-Horse*, November 13, 1978, p. 5461.
6. William Leggett, "Is This Horse That Horse?" *Sports Illustrated*, November 14, 1977, p. 31.
7. *Daily News*, November 4, 1977.
8. *Daily Racing Form*, September 14, 1978.
9. Rita Ciolli, "Mark & Alice & F. Lee & Lebon," *The Horsemen's Journal*, November 1978, p. 33-32; Hollingsworth, op.cit., p. 5459.
10. Ciolli, op.cit., pp. 33-32.
11. Hollingsworth, op.cit., p. 5459; "Belmont Ringer Defendant Loses Appeal," *Sports Law Reporter*, July 1980; *Daily News*, June 19, 1980.
12. John McEvoy, *Great Horse Racing Mysteries* (2000), p. 135.
13. *Chicago Tribune*, December 14, 29, 1978.
14. McEvoy, op.cit., p. 142.

Chapter 9 — Sewing and Reaping

1. Interview with author, September 25, 2001.
2. *The Sporting Life*, June 23, 1976.
3. *The Western Morning News*, March 5, 1980.
4. Interview with author, September 25, 2001; *The Western Morning News*, March 5, 12, 1980.
5. Telephone interview with author, November 5, 2001; *The Sporting Life*, March 5, 1980.
6. *The Sporting Life*, March 11-12, 1980, June 14, 1978; Interview with author, September 25, 2001.
7. *The Sporting Life*, June 15, 1978, March 5, 1980.
8. Telephone interview with author, September 30, 2001.
9. *The Sporting Life*, March 7, 1980; *The Western Morning News*, March 11, 1980; JCR. Chief Inspector (unidentified) to P. Smiles, September 9, 1978.
10. *The Sporting Life*, September 9, 1978.

11. Ibid.; Brian Radford, *Taken for a Ride* (1981), pp. 146, 150.
12. *The Western Morning News*, March 5, 1980; *The Sporting Life*, March 5-6, 1980; Radford, op.cit, p. 140.
13. Interview with author, September 25, 2001; *The Western Morning News*, March 12, 1980.
14. *The Sporting Life*, October 14, 1978; Radford, op.cit., pp.165-6.
15. *The Western Morning News*, March 14-15, 18, 1980.
16. *The Sporting Life*, January 13, 1998.

Chapter 10 — A Detective Story
1. Trial transcript, May 21, 1984.
2. Ibid., May 4, 1984.
3. Ibid., May 31, 1984.
4. *The Sporting Life*, May 16, 1984; Trial transcript, May 21, 1984; Interview with author, February 20, 1996.
5. Trial transcript, May 31, 1984; *The Sporting Life*, May 25, 1984.
6. *The Sporting Life*, May 25, 1984.
7. Julia Foster and Ivy Cook, interviews with author, April 15-16, 1996; Derek Gardiner, interview with author, April 15, 1996.
8. Trial transcript, May 31, 1984.
9. Petition to Home Secretary, Kenneth Baker, 1991.
10. *The Sporting Life*, December 6, 12, 1996.
11. Interview with author, April 16, 1996.
12. Telephone conversation with author, May 7, 1996.
13. Colin Tinkler, *A Furlong to Go* (2001), p. 286.

Chapter 11 — Fine Cotton
1. Kevin Perkins, *The Gambling Man* (1990). My account of the Fine Cotton case draws extensively on Perkins' invaluable work.
2. Perkins, op.cit., p. 403.
3. Ibid., pp. 405-6.
4. Kevin Perkins, *Against All Odds* (1996), p. 128.
5. Perkins, *The Gambling Man*, p. 422.
6. Telephone interview with author, November 20, 2001.
7. Perkins, *Against All Odds*, p. 171.
8. Ibid., pp. 217-8, 225.
9. Telephone interview with author, November 20, 2001.
10. *The Australian*, July 21-22, 2001.
11. Telephone interview with author, November 20, 2001.
12. *The Bulletin*, February 7, 2002.
13. *The Daily Telegraph*, February 22, 2002.
14. NSWTRB. Stewards' Panel Reasons for Decision in the matter of Robert W. Waterhouse, April 15, 2002; *The Daily Telegraph*, April 20, 2002.
15. NSWTRB. Announcements, August 2, 16-17, September 6, 2002; *The Sydney Morning Herald*, September 9, 2002.

Chapter 12 — Au Revoir
1. *The Sporting Life*, August 11, 1995.
2. Ibid.
3. Ibid, August 12, 1995.
4. *Daily Racing Form*, May 17, 2002.
5. *South Florida Sun-Sentinel*, July 24, 2002.

Sources

For a sport with such a rich history of skulduggery, surprisingly little work has been devoted to the subject. The history of Turf fraud lies hidden in scattered fragments, and research is made more difficult by some authors' unhelpful habit of neglecting to identify their sources.

Here, constraints of time, resource, and knowledge mean that, for some cases, some significant sources may have been missed, but we have to start somewhere.

Part One

Peter Barrie's early life in Scotland and Australia remains largely a mystery. He first becomes a solid figure in the National Archives of Australia in Canberra, in the World War I Service Records, Series B2455, No. 384.

The two main sources for Barrie's first wave of ringers are newspaper reports of his 1920 trial — *The Times* and *The Sporting Life* provided ample coverage — and his own confessions, published in *John Bull* between February 17 and June 9, 1923. The confessions are essential reading but must be treated with caution, a proviso that applies to everything Barrie wrote and said.

The articles are reproduced verbatim in John Welcome's (ed.) *Winning Colours: Selected Racing Writings of Edgar Wallace* (1991). Welcome provides a sound account of the Coat of Mail and Silver Badge cases in *Infamous Occasions* (1980), pp. 177-201, and there's a slighter version in Richard Onslow's (ed.) *Great Racing Gambles & Frauds*, Vol. 3 (1993), pp. 123-129.

There is some useful material in the Jockey Club's records, which are in need of an archivist. The *Racing Calendar* and *Ruff's Guide to the Turf* are inevitable reference works.

Edgar Wallace's racing interests and association with Barrie are discussed in Welcome's introduction to *Winning Colours*. They can also be traced in Margaret Lane's *Edgar Wallace: The Biography of a Phenomenon* (n.d. 1938).

Wallace was friendly with several jockeys and journalists and crops up briefly in Jack Leach's *Sods I Have Cut On The Turf* (1961); Meyrick Good's *The Lure of the Turf* (1957); Steve Donoghue's *Donoghue Up!* (1938); and even in Sidney H. White's *I Gotta Horse: The Autobiography of Ras Prince Monolulu* (n.d.).

For Horatio Bottomley, I have relied largely on Julian Symons's *Horatio Bottomley* (1955, 2nd ed. 2001), now old but still engaging, and Jack Waterman's "England's Superman Alights on the Turf," in Richard Onslow's (ed.) *Great Racing Gambles & Frauds*, Vol. 4 (1994), pp. 89-99.

Having pursued Barrie around North America, I know how Pinkerton's detectives must have felt. Barrie's own substantial account, serialized in *The People* between January 25 and June 9, 1935, although needing to be treated with a fine comb, is a vital source.

So are contemporary newspapers, including the *New York Daily News*, which, between November 21 and December 3, 1932, serialized a more limited set of confessions. In addition, I have resorted particularly to *The Morning Telegraph*, *Daily Racing Form*, *The Blood-Horse*, *The New York Times*, and *The Havana Post*.

Newspaper cuttings make up a significant part of containers 150 to 152, the relevant section of Pinkerton's National Detective Agency Records in the Manuscript Division of the Library of Congress, Washington, D.C., but there are also useful notes, correspondence, and reports by operatives.

Alan Hynd was allowed access to Pinkerton's records when writing "The Pinkertons Smash the Race-Track Ringers," *True Detective Mysteries*, December 1941. There is a section on Barrie, not all of it accurate, in Hynd's *The Pinkerton Case Book* (1948), pp. 65-102. Part of this was reproduced in Roger M. Williams's (ed.) *The Super Crooks* (1973), pp. 116-133. There is also a brief section on Barrie in Fred J. Cook's *The Pinkertons* (1974), pp. 167-171.

Some of the gangsters Barrie claimed to have known were either fictitious or presented under false names, but others were real. There is a vast literature on the Prohibition era, the fringe of which includes Paul R. Kavieff's *The Purple Gang* (2000) and Breandan Delap's *Mad Dog Coll* (1999). I have also found the Internet a useful source of information.

Barrie's American escapades have occasionally been revisited, as in Bob Moore's "The 'Old Master Horse Painter,'" *Turf & Sport Digest*, February 1970; Kent Hollingsworth's "What's Going On Here," *The Blood-Horse*, June 5, 1972; Horace Wade's "A Horse of Another Color," *The Backstretch*, April 1989; and John McEvoy's *Through the Pages of Daily Racing Form* (1995).

At a more general level, I have been grateful for Toney Betts's *Across The Board* (1956); William H.P. Robertson's *The History of Thoroughbred Racing in America* (1964); and Joe Hirsch's *The First Century* (1996).

Keeping track of Barrie after his enforced return to Britain becomes progressively more difficult. The Jockey Club's records, although incomplete, are important. So, too, is a slender volume by one of their employees, W. Bebbington, *Rogues Go Racing* (n.d. 1947).

Barrie's own final (as far as I know) confession, published in *The People* between January 7 and February 25, 1951, is the least substantial, largely because he had less to confess, but is still illuminating.

Part Two

Possums

Jack Pollard's *Australian Horse Racing* (1988) contains useful references, and there are brief sections on ring-ins in Neville Penton's *A Racing Heart* (1987) and Bert Lillye's *Backstage of Racing* (1985). The subject receives more coverage in Cecil Cripps's *Racetrack Ring-ins and Rorts* (1989), a book marred by factual errors.

I have relied heavily on contemporary newspaper coverage, notably Melbourne's *The Argus*, *The Sun*, and *The Herald*, and *The Sydney Morning Herald*.

The Frantic Forties

It is unfortunate that the Thoroughbred Racing Protective Bureau's records, even those dating back to the 1940s, are not accessible to researchers, particularly since their investigations tended to span several states. Periodic public statements by TRPB officers are an important, if incomplete, source of information.

I am not aware of any published work on cases from the 1940s, beyond a brief account of the Peaceful William affair in Brian Radford's *Taken for a Ride* (1981), pp. 109-110. Edgar Britt, who twice, unwittingly, rode the ringer, makes brief reference to it in his autobiography, *Post Haste* (1967), pp. 163-4.

Harry Sprague, who rode the ringer in a pre-race gallop, and Cynthia Sheerman, the former wife of jump jockey Tommy Cross and a neighbor of Edward Hill, provided useful information.

The bulk of the material on Peaceful William, Liffey Valley, and Carmeen is drawn from contemporary newspaper reports in *The Sporting Life*, *The Times*, and the *Irish Independent*.

The Unrequired Ringer

There are short accounts of the Francasal case in R. Rodrigo's *The Racing Game* (1958), pp. 148-50; Radford, op.cit., pp. 110-116, and Jack Millan's "The Francasal Fiasco," in Richard Onslow's (ed.) *Great Racing Gambles & Frauds*, Vol. 3 (1993), pp. 153-159.

The main source is *The Sporting Life*'s extensive coverage of the investigation and court proceedings, supplemented by reports in the *Bath and Wiltshire Chronicle and Herald* and *Maidenhead Advertiser* (two of the defendants, Harry Kateley and William Rook, lived in the Maidenhead area).

There is also some useful material in the Jockey Club's records.

May Phillips, the widow of Leonard Phillips, unlocked the mystery of Phillips' accomplice.

A Used Car Salesman

The bulk of this chapter is based on the extensive coverage provided by *The Age*, and on P. Opas's *The Great Ring-In* (1982), an idiosyncratic but charming account of the Royal School case written by Rick Renzella's barrister, Philip Opas QC.

Stephen Wood's later exploits can be followed in the *Barrier Daily Truth* and *Central Western Daily*, local papers covering Broken Hill and Orange, respectively. Cripps, op.cit., pp. 81-88, is also useful.

The Return of the Ringers

The testimony of Paul Berube and statement by Spencer Drayton to the House Select Committee on Crime, 92nd Congress Hearings, Second Session, 1972, provide a useful introduction to the new outbreak of ringers.

For the high profile Lebon case, in addition to coverage in the *Daily Racing Form*, and cuttings from the *New York Post* and *Daily News*, I have benefited from William Leggett's "Is This Horse That Horse?", *Sports Illustrated*, November 14, 1977; Kent Hollingsworth's "Cinzano Case," *The Blood-Horse*, November 13, 1978; Rita Ciolli's "Mark & Alice & F. Lee & Lebon," *The Horsemen's Journal*, November 1978; and Phil Maggitti's "A Horse Without A Course," *Spur*, November/December 1984.

For the later cases, associated with Charlie Wonder and employing counterfeit foal certificates, I have found useful material in the *Chicago Tribune* and made limited use of the *Daily Racing Form* and *The New York Times*, but have leant heavily on "Hot at Hawthorne" in John McEvoy's *Great Horse Racing Mysteries* (2000).

Sewing and Reaping

The prime sources for the case of In the Money are newspaper reports of episodes involving John Bowles and "Taffy" Salaman during the years preceding the ring-in and beyond. I have drawn, in particular, on *The Western Morning News* and *The Sporting Life*, with additional material from the *Western Mail* and *Racing Post.*

Brian Radford, who attended the trial, quotes extensively from courtroom exchanges in a very useful piece in *Taken for a Ride* (1981), pp. 130-175.

The Jockey Club's records contain some helpful information, with more supplied by Salaman, Anthony Mildmay-White, and Wilfred Sherman.

The case was the subject of an unpublished article by the late Bob Anderson, Racecourse Security Services' chief investigator, but I have not had access to this.

A Detective Story

My account draws on an extensive range of interviews with many of the individuals connected with the case, but as so often in Turf frauds, the most valuable material stems from the trial.

Much of the account is based on a transcript of part of the evidence, supplemented by coverage in *The Sporting Life*, with additional material from the *Hull Daily Mail.*

The Jockey Club's records contain some worthwhile information, and there is a slim piece by John Morgan, "A Northern Ringer in 1982," in Richard Onslow's (ed.) *Great Racing Gambles & Frauds*, Vol. 1 (1991). The case is also referred to in Colin Tinkler's *A Furlong to Go* (2001), pp. 285-300.

Fine Cotton

Kevin Perkins's *The Gambling Man* (1990), although not a neutral account, is an extraordinary one, and essential reading. Perkins' later biography of Gai Waterhouse, *Against All Odds* (1996), updates the Fine Cotton saga, which rumbles on.

The ring-in and its aftermath have been the subject of extensive press coverage, and additional material was drawn from a wide range of newspaper and Internet reports and statements by the New South Wales Thoroughbred Racing Board, with further information from interviews with Robbie Waterhouse, John Mort Green, and Alan Brown, brother of George Brown.

There is a useful article on Brown's murder in *The Sunday Age*, September 27, 1997. For his brother's continued pursuit of justice, see the *Racing Post*, February 16, 2002.

Au Revoir

The case of Pretty Average is covered in articles researched by the author, which appeared in *The Sporting Life* in August 1995.

My account of the case of Forty Two is based largely on contemporary press coverage, particularly in the *Daily Racing Form* and *South Florida Sun-Sentinel*, and on press releases issued by the FBI's Miami Field Office and U.S. Department of Justice.

Thank yous

It is a reward to be able to thank the many people who have helped me with this book, in particular all those who, with varying degrees of enthusiasm, apprehension, or reluctance, agreed to tell me what they knew, in interviews spread over ten years.

Alan Byrne, former editor of the *Racing Post*, gave typically enthusiastic encouragement, coinciding with a series of articles published early in 2002.

I have benefited from the previous efforts and advice of other workers in the field, including John Brennan (a ringer for John Welcome), Richard Onslow, and Brian Radford. From the United States, John McEvoy kindly supplied copies of articles about Peter Barrie, while Joe Hirsch, not only a fine journalist but also a generous and brave man, supplied copies of articles about the Lebon case and other useful guidance.

Paul Berube, president of the Thoroughbred Racing Protective Bureau, pointed me in helpful directions.

Evan Hammonds arranged access to past copies of *The Blood-Horse*, housed at the magazine's offices in Lexington, while Cathy Schenck and Phyllis Rogers at Keeneland Library supplied useful references despite being submerged in the demands of moving to a new site.

Patrick Kerwin, Manuscript Reference Librarian at the Library of Congress, Washington, D.C., introduced me to the Pinkerton's National Detective Agency Records, and I am grateful to other members of the staff for their help with newspaper archives and other material.

I became a regular visitor to the British Newspaper Library at Colindale, North London. Its collection extends far beyond the domestic press, and I am grateful to the staff who serviced my numerous needs.

Staff at the British Library and at public libraries in Newmarket, Cardiff, and Maidenhead have also been helpful. Thanks also to the *Bath Chronicle* for access to their collections.

The Family Records Centre in London and General Register Office for Scotland in Edinburgh were valuable sources of information about births, marriages, deaths, and the census.

Charlie Toller introduced me to the case of Carmeen, and John Mort Green to the long-running saga of Fine Cotton.

The Australian Racing Museum and staff at various libraries in Australia, including Vicky Prestwidge at the Orange City Library and David Pearce, editor of the *Barrier Daily Truth*, provided useful help.

Thanks also to Elizabeth Lally at the Victoria Racing Club and John Digby at the Australian Jockey Club, who pointed me toward some useful sources, as well as explaining the evolution of identification methods.

Paul Greeves, Weatherbys' knowledgeable racing director, performed a similar role for the UK.

At the Jockey Club, I am particularly grateful to John Maxse and Owen Byrne for help in accessing archived records. Thanks also to the Irish Turf Club.

A wide range of institutions and individuals have helped with my search for illustrations, with a particular thank you to Manjit Sandhu at MGN's picture library in Watford.

Jon Winter, the *Racing Post*'s talented picture editor, has provided enthusiastic help and designed an excellent cover.

Thank you to Julian Brown at Highdown for his management of the book's publication, and to my agent, John Pawsey, a reliable source of sound advice, some of which I have the sense to take.

Lesley Ashforth eliminated some stylistic flaws and breaches of the rules of punctuation, a process taken further by proofreader Richard Lowther. The remaining shortcomings are all my own.

Index

About the Author

DAVID ASHFORTH is a senior reporter and columnist with the *Racing Post* in Great Britain. After pursuing an academic career, he joined *The Sporting Life* in 1990 and in 1998, moved to the *Racing Post*. For much of the 1990s, he also contributed a regular column to the *Racing Times* and *Daily Racing Form*. In 1996 he was voted Horserace Writer of the Year.

Ashforth, 54, has written a number of books on social history, education, and horse racing, including the 1996 volume, *Hitting the Turf*, about his racing and betting experiences.